Evolutionary Art
and Computers

Dedicated to Ken Latham

Evolutionary Art
and Computers

Stephen Todd and William Latham
IBM UK Scientific Centre,
St. Clement Street,
Winchester, UK.

ACADEMIC PRESS
Harcourt Brace Jovanovich, Publishers
London   San Diego   New York
Boston   Sydney   Tokyo   Toronto

ACADEMIC PRESS LIMITED
24–28 Oval Road
London NW1 7DX

US edition published by
ACADEMIC PRESS INC
San Diego, CA 92101

ISBN 0–12–437185–X

Typeset by Chapterhouse, The Cloisters, Formby L37 3PX
Printed and bound in Great Britain by Butler and Tanner Ltd., Frome, Somerset.

Contents

The colour plate sections are located between Chapters 2 and 3 and Chapters 6 and 7.

Acknowledgements

We thank our families, Kitty, Helen and Peter Todd and Belinda Channer for their help, artistic criticism and encouragement, and for putting up without us so much during the writing of this book.

We thank the staff at the IBM UK Scientific Centre. Peter Quarendon first encouraged William to come to the centre. Peter Alderson, Roger Hake, Tom Heywood, Geoff Robinson, David Steventon, Andy Walter, and John Woodwark all gave us continued support and encouragement. Especially David Bowdler and Brian Duffin gave us the support and facilities required for the writing of this book, and the students Richard Wilkes, Mark Owen, Peter Hughes, Lo Chi, Ramin Sen, and Andrew Lomas did so much of the programming and production work for our animations.

Thank you also for the feedback on our work and on this book from Kazuo Amano (O Art Museum, Tokyo), Barry Barker (Heywood Gallery, London). Anthony Brown (Connaught Brown Gallery), Andrew Carrick and Sutapas Bhattacharya (Academic Press), Alan Craig (designer), Masaki Fujihata (Frogs Inc, Tokyo), Paul Huxely (Royal College of Art), Mike King (City of London Polytechnic), John Lansdown (Middlesex Polytechnic), Chris Osland (Rutherford Laboratories), John Patterson (University of Glasgow), John Vince (Rediffusion) and Richard Voss (IBM Research Yorktown Heights).

About the authors

William Latham studied Fine Art at Christ Church, Oxford from 1979–1982 in The Ruskin School of Drawing and Fine Art, receiving a B.A. (Oxon, Hons first class) and M.A. He then went as a Henry Moore scholar to The Royal College of Art where he studied printmaking and received an M.A. in 1985. He worked as a part-time lecturer at Middlesex Polytechnic, St. Martins School of Art and Central School of Art before gaining the position of Artist (Research Fellow) at IBM UK Scientific Centre in Winchester in 1987.

Latham has had many major exhibitions including 'The Conquest of Form' Exhibition organised by The Arnolfini Gallery, Bristol which toured the UK going to ten UK galleries including the Natural History Museum, London, this show then toured Germany going to four museums including The Deutches Museum in Munich.

In 1990 Latham presented a one person exhibition at The 'O' Art Museum, Tokyo called 'The Empire of Form'. His 'Evolution of Form' exhibition toured Australia during 1990.

As well as showing his work in the world of art, his animated films have been shown in the computer world at SIGGRAPH Film and Video show, Arts Electronica, NICCOGRAPH and many other conferences. He has won many prizes including First Prize in Animation Research at Imagina 90, First Prize in Art Animation at The International Computer Film Festival of Montreal, Canada 90.

His work has received wide international press and TV coverage, often focusing on the evolutionary aspect to his work. Interestingly his work is covered in wide variety of areas due to it's broad multi-disciplinary nature. He has published a number of papers with the mathematician Stephen Todd on the evolutionary techniques used in the work.

The artist is represented by The Connaught Brown Gallery, Albemarle Street, London W1.

Stephen Todd studied Mathematics at Christ Church, Oxford from 1965–1971, where he received a B.A. (Oxon, Hons first class), M.A. and Diploma of Advanced Mathematics. He also took an active part in the musical life of the University. In 1971 he joined the IBM United Kingdom Scientific Centre in Peterlee, Co. Durham. His main research there involved the Peterlee Relational Test Vehicle, the first relational database system to handle significant volumes of data. He was also involved in research in image processing.

He spent 1979 to 1981 at the IBM Research Laboratory in San Jose, where he worked in text processing and coding theory. He rejoined the Scientific Centre (by then in Winchester) to work on graphics applications. He has researched a number of graphics and visualisation areas, including picture generation from databases, languages to create solid models for a variety of applications, and realistic rendering of these solid models.

He has published many papers and holds several patents in the areas of database, coding theory and graphics.

He is a visiting professor at the Universities of Glasgow and Keele, and spent the academic year 1989–1990 at Glasgow. Some of the work described in this book, including the first implementation of Mutator, was done at Glasgow University.

He has been working with William Latham since 1987.

Chapter 1
Why use computers to make art?

What made William Latham† decide to use computers to make art? Any artist is subjected to a wide range of influences (Figure 1.2), but we focus on three main formative influences: constructive systems for generating art seemed to link naturally to computer systems; Latham was fascinated by the interaction between man and machine, as seen in computer games and science fiction; and finally, computer rendering is a new medium in which pictures without paint of objects that do not exist are created: in effect ghosts of sculptures.

Figure 1.1. Latham and Todd in Computer Studio.

---

†This book is a personal account of our work on computer art and so is mostly written using the first person plural ('we' and 'us'). When we need to emphasize the role of the artist we refer to Latham by name.

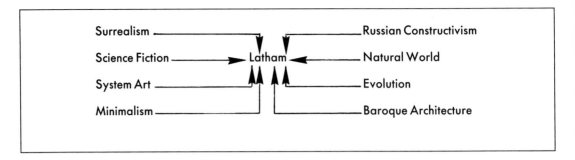

Figure 1.2. Factors affecting Latham's work.

Systems of art Latham was inspired by natural systems, and how they often relied on the repetition of very simple steps, such as crystal growth, or the creation of stalagmites by water dripping in underground caverns. Even biological processes are related to simple geometries, as shown by D'Arcy Thompson (1961), and the repeated small changes in mutation and natural selection give rise to a huge variation of interesting biological forms.

These natural systems have a huge potential for creating artistic forms. Latham wanted to exploit these to go beyond art systems such as Russian Constructivism and Kenneth Martin's creation of drawings based on random dice throws (Martin 1985), and to create a new system for producing synthetic organic forms. He had already observed that he was using some kind of system when applying techniques such as lithography to gradually change an image as he repeatedly printed it, and he set out to produce his own experimental system for making art.

Latham's first experimental system for art generation, FormSynth (Latham 1989), was a system for drawing on paper, and not a computer system. The rules, sphere, cone, bulge, scoop, and so on, were typed out, and Latham applied them by hand (Figure 1.3). Repeated application of the rules created an evolutionary tree of increasingly complex forms, some like spiders, some like strange African pots, some with an architectural quality. Latham used a photocopier to scale down some areas and simplify the drawing of visually complex images. He selected some of the more aesthetic forms to sculpt out of wood or plastic (Figure 1.4). Simple as the rules of FormSynth were, they seemed to have a creative power of their own. Even though Latham created and applied the rules, they produced imaginative forms he had not expected. As the drawings grew larger – up to 10 metres long (Figures 1.5, 1.6) – he realized that the FormSynth system defined an infinite world of predetermined forms, which the artist explored to reveal only a selected few.

Figure 1.3. Small hand-drawn FormSynth tree.

Figure 1.4. FormSynth sculpture.

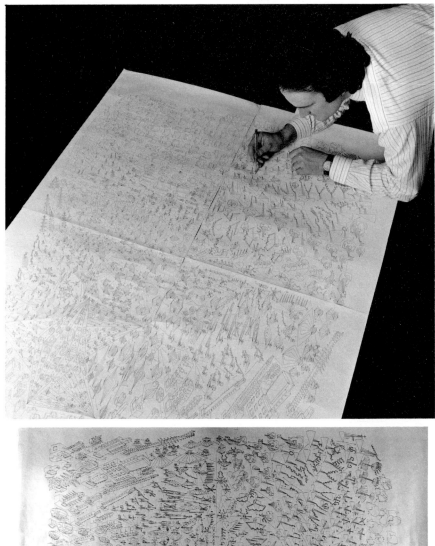

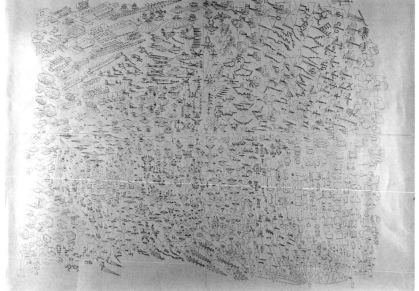

Figure 1.5. Latham drawing a FormSynth evolutionary tree, and completed drawing.

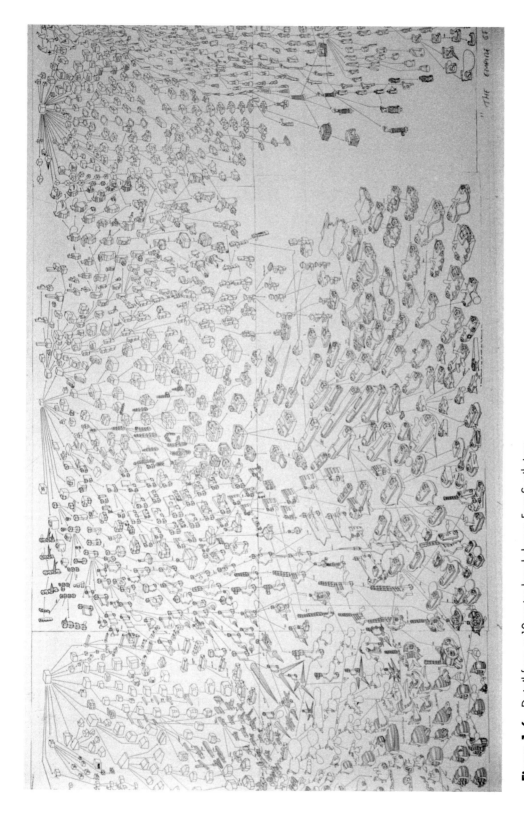

Figure 1.6. Detail from a 10 metre hand-drawn FormSynth tree.

Systems can assist an artist to create imaginative forms, and computers are good at applying systems, and very fast at drawing. It seems natural to apply the power and speed of computers to realize the potential of artistic systems and extend the creative power of the artist. Many of the artist's ideas are captured in setting up the system, which he or she then uses again and again to create characteristic but individual works of art. Our systems involve interaction with the artist; the computer does not blindly follow the rules, but uses them to give suggestions, and leaves the artist to make the final aesthetic selections.

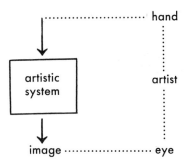

Man and machine   Much of science fiction is based on the interaction between people and machines. Latham's ideas were influenced by films and television programs such as *Star Trek*, *Stepford Wives*, *Dr Who* and the half-man half-machine Dalek, and finally by the interaction between HAL and the astronaut in *2001: A Space Odyssey*. Could machines really interact with an artist to help him make art? When Latham was a student the computer game *Space Invaders*, in which humans destroy spider-like aliens, was addictively popular. Could the destructive power released by such games be harnessed creatively for the generative production of art?

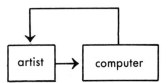

Computers, an art   Once interested in computer graphics, Latham became aware of three
medium   dimensional rendering techniques in which the computer holds a 'model' of an object, and behaves like a 'camera obscura' or Durer's drawing device (Figure 1.7) opening a window onto a virtual stage. It applies rules of perspective (Figures 1.8–1.10) as used by Ucello and Renaissance artists (Figure 1.11), understands the physics of lighting (Figure 1.12) and colouring (see Plates), and can carve sculptures from textured blocks such as marble (Figure 1.13). Computer graphics is a new art medium. It has some attributes

of painting, but with no paint, and some of sculpture, but with no clay. It is used to create photographs and animations of sculptures that do not exist, an attractive thought in its own right, especially as it saves the artist work at the same time.

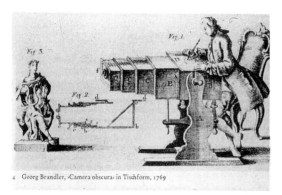 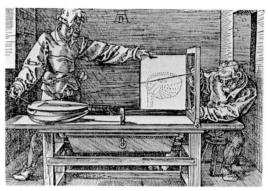

Figure 1.7. Mechanical devices used to assist an artist with precise perspective drawing. (a) Camera Obscura; (b) Durer's drawing device.

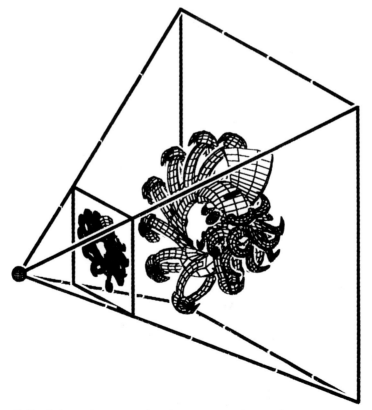

Figure 1.8. Spherical computer 'eye' viewing a sculpture. The lines indicate the volume that the computer sees, and a two dimensional image of the sculpture is seen projected onto the viewing plane.

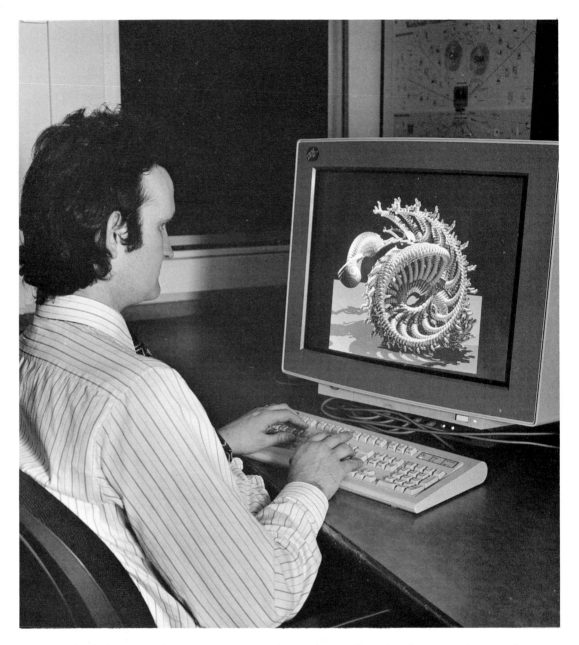

Figure 1.9. Latham sits at the computer screen and views the two dimensional computer drawing of a virtual sculpture.

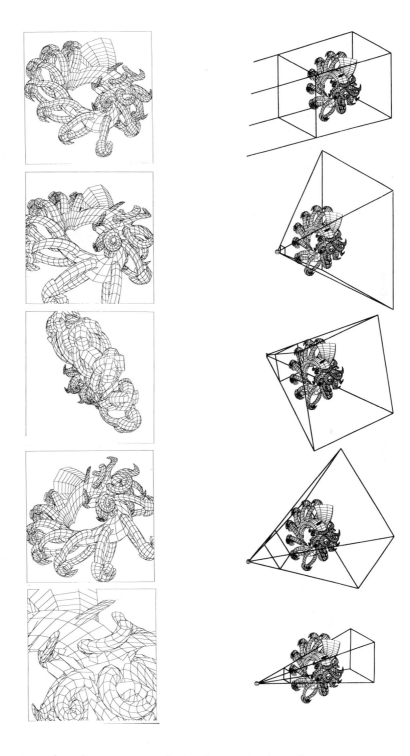

Figure 1.10. This demonstrates how the computer can look at the virtual sculpture from any viewing position. The viewing position is shown above, and the resulting computer image below.

Figure 1.11. Painting showing perspective ('Rout of St Romano', Uccello, National Gallery, London). Reproduced with permission.

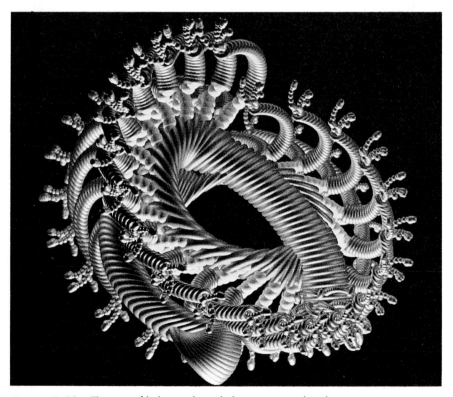

Figure 1.12. The use of lights and spotlights on a virtual sculpture.

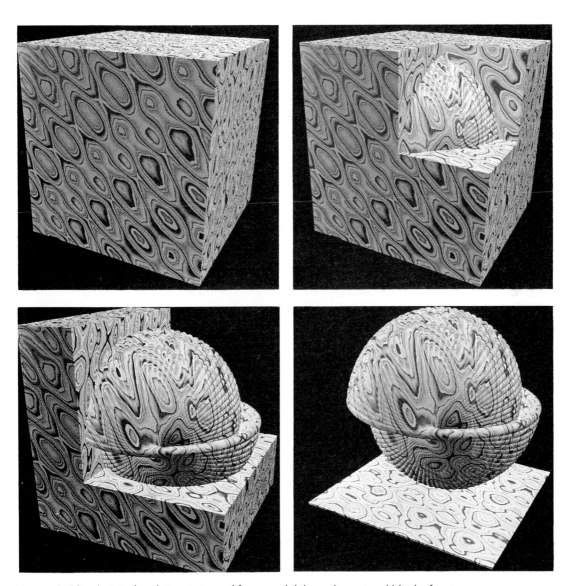

Figure 1.13. A virtual sculpture is carved from a solid three dimensional block of texture.

Artificial life   Art has periodically toyed with the idea of investing life into inanimate materials using mechanical devices, as with the singing nightingale, Fabergé eggs, and the whole world of puppetry. Following in this tradition, the systems we have developed are based on biological processes, so called 'artificial life'. These systems animate the actors on our virtual stage without strings or clockwork mechanisms; the actors on this stage are manipulated by computer programs.

In this book we describe three complementary artistic systems based on artificial life: *Form Grow* generates lifelike forms using geometric rules;

Mutator is a system based on mutation and natural selection which helps the artist explore the world of these forms; and *Life Cycle* animates these forms by rules of birth, growth and death. Latham is a computer puppeteer choreographing an evolution of imaginary forms. These systems give artificial life to virtual sculptures, and provide a double mystery: life is invested into inanimate objects which, though seen, have no material reality.

Art created using these systems has a distinctive philosophy, and generates unique results with a distinct artistic style which we call *evolutionism*:

$$\text{Art Style} = \begin{matrix} \text{IMPRESSIONISM} \\ \text{CUBISM} \\ \text{REALISM} \\ \text{SURREALISM} \\ \text{POP ART} \\ \downarrow \\ \text{EVOLUTIONISM} \end{matrix}$$

Artist as creative gardener   Latham was attracted by the idea of creative human computer interaction (HCI), exploiting the potential of artistic systems, and was finally led by the power of three dimensional computer graphics into an artificial virtual world. The artistic process takes place in two stages: creation and gardening. The artist first creates the systems of the virtual world, applying whichever physical and biological rules he chooses: light, colour, gravity, growth and evolution, and other rules of his own invention. The artist then becomes a gardener within this world he has created; he selects and breeds sculptural forms as a plant breeder produces flowers, and records the evolutionary process in animations which show skeletal forms unfolding and surreal lobsters breeding:

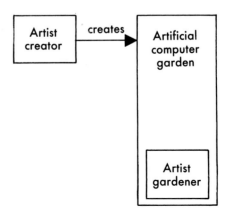

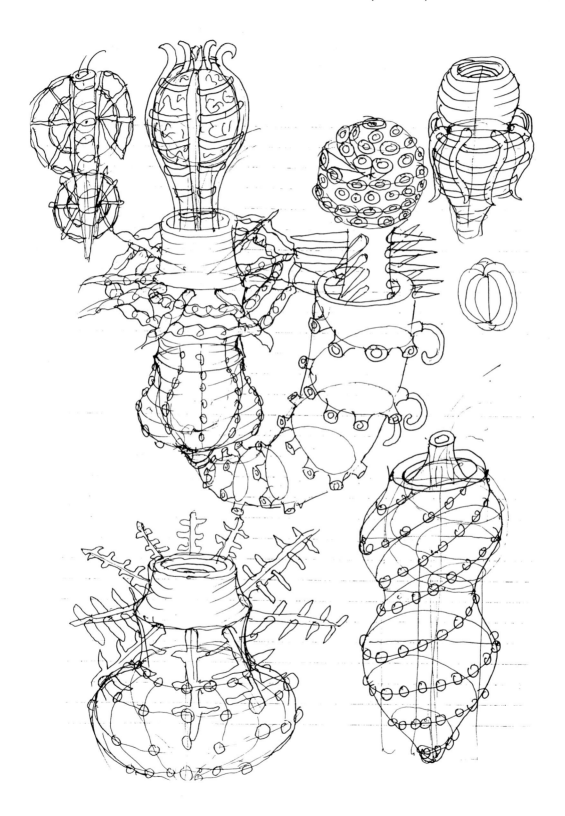

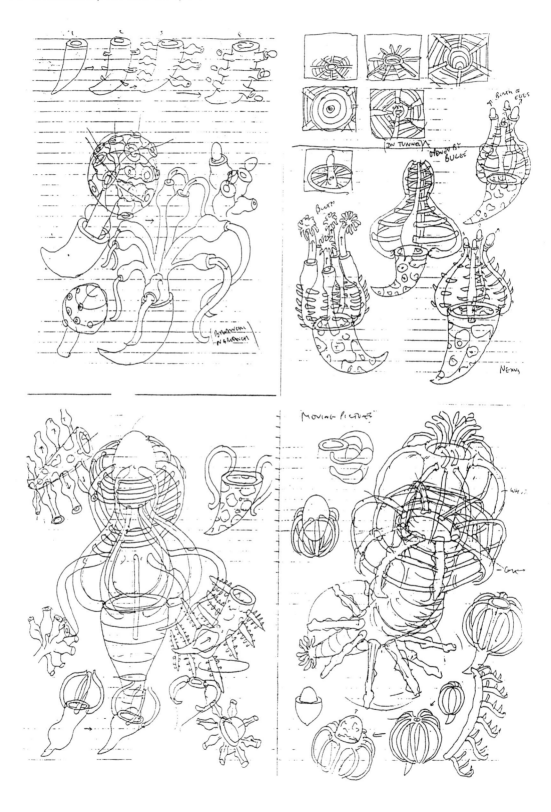

Chapter 2

Creating computer sculptures and animations

This chapter explains how we design and use computer systems to make animations and artworks for the gallery. It shows the main steps, from first ideas to recording the final videotape. The making of one animation is never quite the same as the making of another, and preparing a group of works for display in a gallery raises its own problems. The chapter is based on the making of the film *Mutations* (Plate 31e.f.g), with a few general digressions, and should give the reader a flavour of what is involved when we use these systems to create computer artworks. It serves as an introduction to the rest of the book, putting into context the steps that are required, and which are detailed in the following chapters.

When making an animation, we first decide on the overall theme of the film. The stories of our last two films, metamorphosis and mutation, are both connected to the theme of evolution. We then think about how we will create the computer form 'actors' that are to appear in the film, and define programs that generate families of forms – for example, skeletal forms with twisty tails. Details such as the number of ribs or the length of the horn are decided at the next stage, in which the artist selects aesthetic individual forms from the family, using *Mutator* running on the computer to act as a creative partner. The artist uses the same system for many artworks, but each individual form is usually used only once.

Now that the actors' forms are prepared we have to set up their animation, how the form of the actor changes, and how the actor moves in space. Again, this takes place in two stages: we program the systems of movement to be used into the computer, and then select exact timings and choreography. We now see a preview of the animation on the screen. Several iterations of the timings are needed, with several preview versions, but when we are satisfied we go into the final preparation stages. We set up detailed colouring and lighting, and instruct the computer to save the precise definition of every frame and render it to produce a high quality image. These images are recorded, again one frame at a time, with 25 frames per second, onto the film or tape:

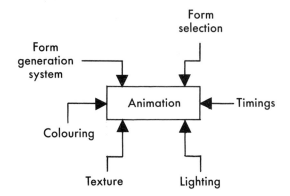

The preparation of artworks for a gallery follows much the same steps in form preparation, colouring and lighting. It is particularly important to select a good viewpoint where the viewer is only going to see a single static image, and images for gallery presentation are rendered to a very high resolution. The rendered image is then saved onto film, printed, and framed.

All our work is produced by a team, usually three people. William Latham makes artistic decisions; Stephen Todd decides how Latham's ideas can be mathematically realized on a computer; and the third member of the team is a student, who does much of the programming and production work involved in creating an animation. We have had several students over the years – Richard Wilkes, Mark Owen, Peter Hughes, Lo Chi, Ramen Sen and Andrew Lomas. There is no precise demarcation between the tasks – ideas come from everyone in the team, and from others outside the team as well. Todd has done much of the programming: Latham has even done some of the programming, and cannot escape from much of the production work.

Other computer artists use different techniques such as paint systems, image processing and artificial intelligence (for example, the Cohen show at the Tate Gallery, London (Cohen, 1983)). Three dimensional computer graphics is being increasingly used (Fujihata 1989; Kawaguchi 1982) as lower hardware prices and better interfaces make it more accessible. What is unique about Latham's work is the evolutionary system he uses with its highly stylized results.

Concept of the film 'Mutations'

The making of a film begins with an idea: let's make an art film that illustrates life and natural selection. This idea is refined over quite a time. The computer is hardly used at all at first, except perhaps to try out a few experiments to check whether particular ideas will work. The main communication between the team is discussion, with a huge number of hand-drawn sketches. Figures 2.1 and 2.2 show sketches for the pterodactyl-cum-lobster forms used in *Mutations* (Figure 2.1) and the way birth was to be represented (Figure 2.2).

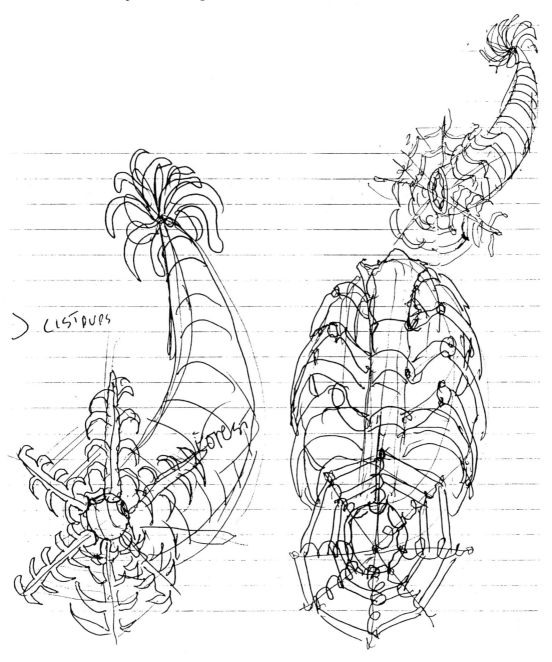

Figure 2.1. Hand-drawn sketch of a lobster form drawn by Latham while working out concepts for the film *Mutations*.

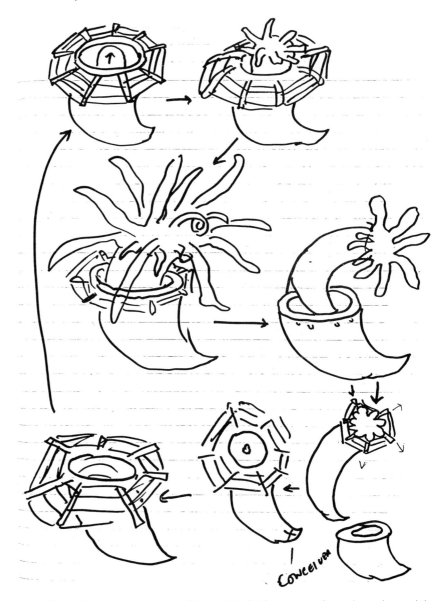

Figure 2.2. Hand-drawn sketch of the artistic 'birth' process drawn by Latham while working out concepts for the film *Mutations*.

Decisions on style

Before we discuss the next step in the making of *Mutations*, we digress to consider what makes a Latham sculpture the way it is, and what gives it its characteristic style? The style and form of a sculpture are determined by decisions at four levels (Figure 2.3).

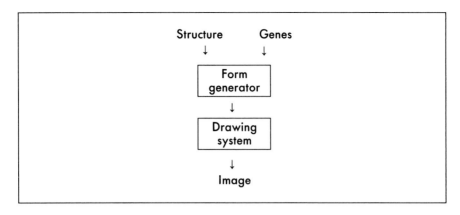

Figure 2.3. Overall process of creating a computer image of a virtual sculpture. The style of the image may be changed by making alterations at any point in the process.

Medium   What is the computer medium to be used? Objects are created out of simple primitive objects such as spheres and tori (see Chapter 7), with certain techniques of colouring and texturing (see Chapter 11) and rendered by Winsom (see Chapter 9) using photo-realistic techniques. In the same way that a choice of marble or bronze imposes the first constraints on the style of a sculptor, so the low level graphic techniques constrain the style of computer art works.

Form generation system   How is the medium to be applied? The low level techniques we use are also used in computer aided design (CAD) and in the visualization of scientific data (Figure 2.4). What makes Latham's sculptures different is the use of the form generation system *Form Grow* (see Chapters 3 and 8) which lays out primitives to make computer forms according to artistic rules. The rules hidden inside *Form Grow* determine a second level of style. *Form Grow* itself is written in the geometric programming language ESME (see Chapter 7).

Figure 2.4. Application of constructive solid geometry modelling to engineering, molecular graphics and art.

Family   What kind of objects are to be represented? *Form Grow* can produce not just horns, but pumpkins, shells, mathematical shapes and many other shapes as yet unseen and unnamed. A decision is made to restrict the *Form Grow* system to a subsystem which creates a related family of forms and artworks, each with its family style (see Chapter 4), defined in a file called the *structure* (Figure 2.5). The choice of families defines the virtual world of the animation.

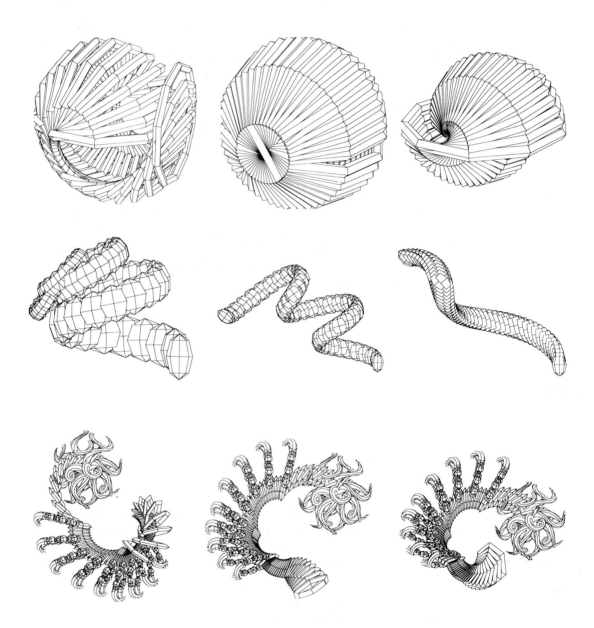

Figure 2.5. Three members each from the pumpkin, Oryx horn and lobster families.

Selection   What will appear in the artwork? Even when *Form Grow* has been set up to produce, for example, lobster-like forms, there are many forms in the lobster family to choose from. They all have curved backs, but how curved? They all have tails, but how long? These characteristics are controlled by the 'genes' of the structure. The selection by the gardener artist of an individual lobster generated by its own particular set of genes, probably using *Mutator* (see Chapter 5) provides the final level of style (Figure 2.10).

As we go from the lower level to the higher level of style, the choices depend less and less on detailed programming, and more and more on subjective decisions. At the level of the medium, the Winsom renderer implements the shapes of the primitives and the photo-realistic techniques, and is programmed in Pascal. The *Form Grow* system that lays these out is implemented using higher level programming techniques (see Chapter 7), but it is still very much a program. The structure file that directs *Form Grow* to create the lobster family is again a form of program, but now at such a high level that we do not usually think of it as such. Finally, the selection of members of the lobster family is made completely subjectively by the artist.

Biological parallel   There is a biological parallel to family and selection. The genes for an individual form are the *genotype*, the form itself is the *phenotype*, and the process of generation by the system and family structure file is the *expression*. As we will see, *Mutator* extends this parallel, borrowing concepts of mutation and sexual reproduction, but with 'survival of the fittest' replaced by 'survival of the most aesthetic'.

Actors for 'Mutations'

For *Mutations* we made an implicit decision that the medium should be the Winsom renderer, as we were already set up to use it, and we were left making the higher level decisions.

Form Grow system and Ribcage   At the concept stage we decided on the general shape of forms we wanted to use; for example, the surreal lobster. This must now be described to the computer, which involves the system and family design levels. In the case of *Mutations*, the main spiralling linear body of the lobster was easily described using the *Form Grow* system (Figure 2.6), which was already written. However, the symmetric protruding ribcage structure was not easily generated, but required a *Ribcage* extension (Figures 2.7, 2.8) to be written for the skeletal part of the forms.

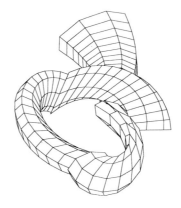

Figure 2.6. Horn form used as the body for lobster forms. This was created by the *Form Grow* artistic system using features already designed before the film *Mutations* was made.

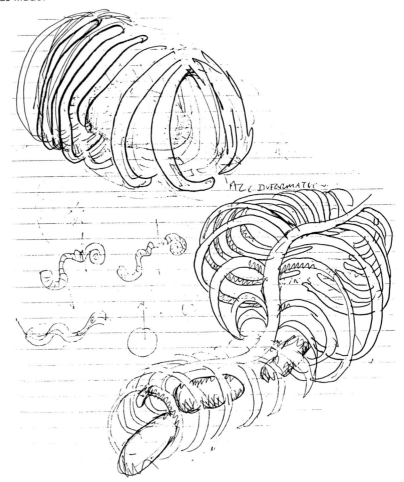

Figure 2.7. Hand-drawn sketch for a ribcage structure drawn by Latham while working on the concepts for the film *Mutations*.

Figure 2.8. Ribcage generated by the *Ribcage* feature of the *Form Grow* artistic system. The *Ribcage* feature was implemented to match the artist's concepts for the film *Mutations*.

Lobster family   William Latham then designed the structure file for the lobster family using *Form Grow* and *Ribcage* (Figure 2.9). Members of the family have long curved spines with symmetric ribs, and look somewhat like lobsters, though they were inspired by animal skeletons at the Natural History Museum in London.

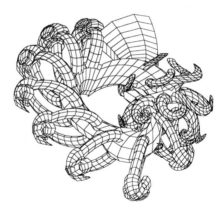

Figure 2.9. Complete lobster form prepared using *Form Grow* for the film *Mutations*.

Mutator selects   Once the computer understands the family of forms to be used, the artist
aesthetic lobsters   uses *Mutator* (see Chapter 5) to breed and select aesthetic members of the family to appear in the animation and related artworks (Figure 2.11). *Mutator* operates by generating gene values and displaying to the artist the associated forms (Figure 2.10): the artist then makes subjective decisions such as 'good' or 'bad' on these forms (Figure 2.12). *Mutator* keeps these forms in a gene bank and operates on the genes for selected forms using techniques similar to biological mutation and breeding in order to make further suggestions to the

artist. Thus, with *Mutator* making suggestions steered by the preferences of the artist, we create a bank of forms for use in the animation.

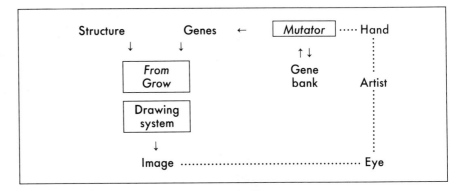

Figure 2.10. *Mutator* helps the artist to select aesthetic forms. Notice the feedback here: the artist sees the forms, makes judgements which he communicates to *Mutator*, and *Mutator* then uses this feedback to produce new forms.

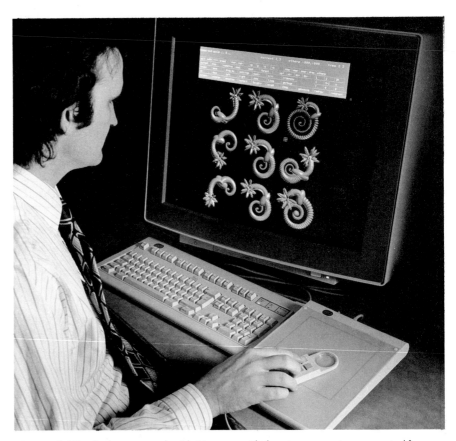

Figure 2.11. Latham at work with *Mutator*, with the nine computer generated forms and selection menu on the computer screen controlled by the mouse held in Latham's hand.

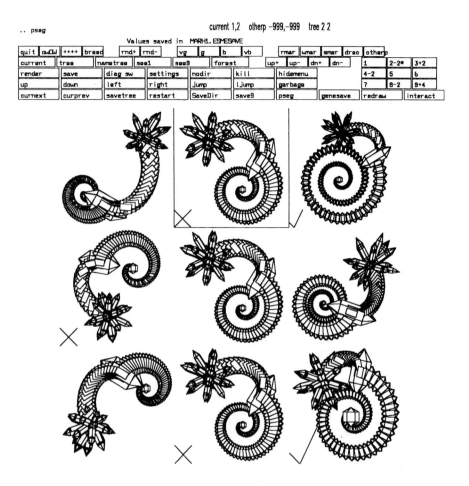

Figure 2.12. Nine forms generated by *Mutator*. The ticks and crosses indicate judgements the artist has made on the forms.

Animation

To create a computer animation we must tell the computer what actors are going to appear, what they look like, what they do, and when they will do it. The animation definition is written into a file which is interpreted by the *Life Cycle* system (see Chapter 6 and Figure 2.13). *Life Cycle* includes rules of life for how long the actor lives, for the metamorphosis of an actor from conception to birth to death (Figures 2.14 and 6.12), for how the actor moves (Figure 2.15). The artist takes forms for the actors from the *Mutator* session, with each actor having a different form for each key stage of metamorphosis. The family tree for the animation is taken from *Mutator* and the animation is then ready to execute.

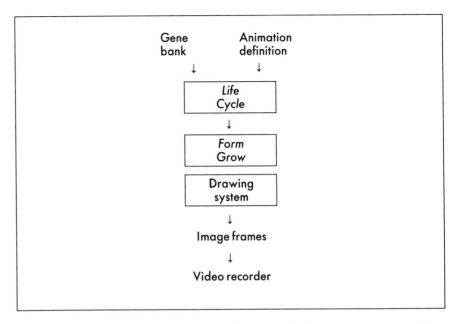

Figure 2.13. Overview of an animation. The gene bank for an animation is taken from a *Mutator* session. The animation definition is written by the artist.

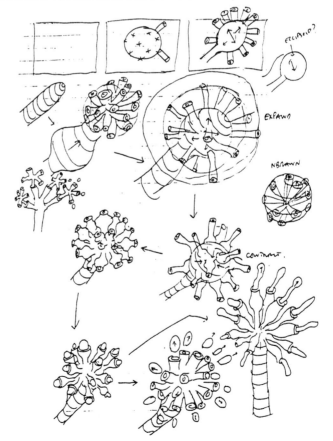

Figure 2.14. Metamorphosis of an actor during various stages of its life.

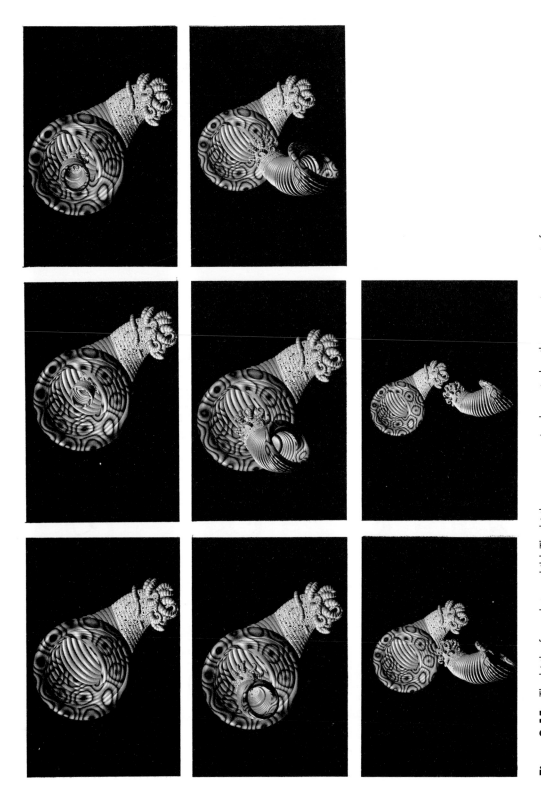

Figure 2.15. The birth of a sculpture child. The birth process was implemented on the computer as part of the *Life Cycle* software to match Latham's conceptions for the film *Mutations*.

Executing the animation involves *Life Cycle* applying its rules and setting up a detailed storyboard, which is then read by the lower level *Director* animation control program (see Chapter 10 and Figure 2.16). *Director* has many options to allow for the generation of a quick preview of an animation, looking at individual frames, and so on. The artist makes several experiments at this stage to get the precise timing and flow of the scene as he requires it, modifying *Life Cycle* definition and timing parameters as necessary. Eventually the scene is as the artist wants, and *Director* writes to disk Winsom files for all the frames to be rendered.

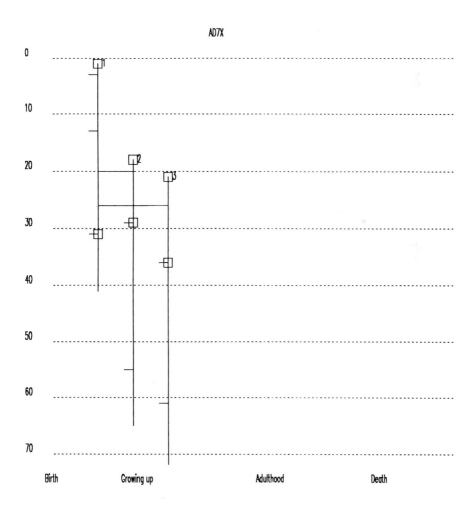

Figure 2.16. Detailed timings for an animation. Each vertical line depicts the life of an actor, with time running down the chart. The horizontal lines show where one actor gives birth to another.

Choice of viewpoint

We control viewpoints in two ways. In animations the camera control may be part of the overall system (see Chapter 10), and the three dimensional nature of the objects is in any case clear from the movement. With gallery prints the viewer sees a virtual sculpture from just one viewpoint, and so this must be very carefully selected to make the most of the sculpture's three dimensional aesthetic qualities.

The viewpoint is selected by interactively moving the virtual sculpture on-screen (see Chapter 9 and Figure 2.17). This interaction involves the computer redrawing new views of the object many times a second (in real-time) to give the impression of a continuously rotating form. It helps the artist fully to understand the three dimensional form, and may make him decide to modify it.

Unfortunately, real-time interaction must be performed on wireframe images or crudely rendered approximations as our hardware is not powerful enough to draw fully rendered images of a virtual sculpture in real-time. We can also adjust the relative positions of a group of forms in real-time, but can only manipulate the shape of a very simple form.

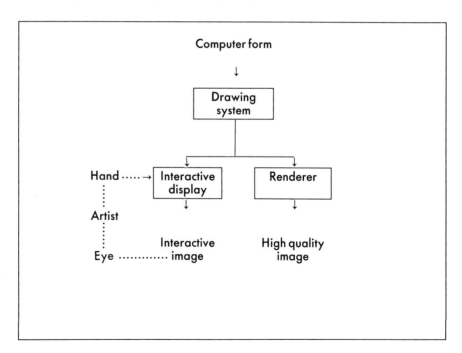

Figure 2.17. The drawing system. This shows the distinction between the interactive drawing and high quality rendering. The drawing is first displayed interactively, and the artist chooses a view by real-time interaction. When a good view is found, the view and form are passed to the renderer to generate a high quality image.

Once the artist is satisfied with both the form and the viewpoint, he directs the computer to save them and then to invoke the renderer.

Colour, texture and lighting

Colour, texture and lighting are an important part of the visual impact of Latham's art works, giving an impression of reality to the forms depicted both in animations and gallery prints, as illustrated in the colour plates. With powerful hardware we can now effectively mutate colour and lighting, and so in future we will include these within our artificial life systems. A new version of Winsom is more tightly coupled to ESME, which also gives us the opportunity to control texture from within our systems.

Final production

The final production of an art work is very time consuming, and requires special hardware. A still computer image is sent to a high quality computer camera, and is then printed, signed and framed for hanging in a gallery (Figure 2.18). We are currently experimenting with techniques such as lenticular three dimensional printing. An animation must be recorded one frame at a time on to a single frame video or film recorder (see Chapter 10). However complex or intricate the techniques, the real test is how the people respond to the artistic content when the work is shown in the gallery or cinema.

Figure 2.18. Latham's work in 'O' Art Museum, Tokyo, Japan in 1991.

"SHRINKAGE ON DEATH"

(1) Pod 1. Latham 1987. Computer/Cibachrome. 56×56 cm. (Frame from animation "Conquest of Form").

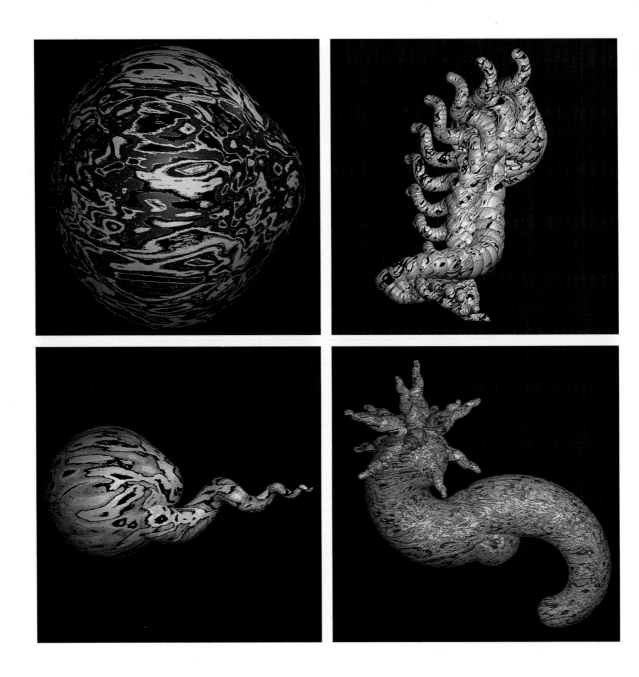

(2a) Yellow Egg. Latham 1988. Computer/Cibachrome.

(2b) Complex A (Horn of Horns) Latham 1987.
Computer/Cibachrome. 56×56 cm.

(2c) Egg with Horn. Latham 1988.
Computer/Cibachrome. 56×56 cm.

(2d) Sprouting. Latham 1988. Computer/Cibachrome.
56 cm×56 cm.

(3) Twist 4. Latham 1987. Computer/Cibachrome. 56 cm×56 cm.

(4a) Sub-textured Globe. Látham 1991. Computer/Cibachrome. 30×30 cm.

(4b) Pumpkin Ball. Latham 1988. Computer/Cibachrome. 40cm×30 cm.

(4c) Blue Globe Form 1. Latham 1987. Computer/Cibachrome. 56×56 cm.

(4d) Drilled Globe. Latham 1988. Computer/Cibachrome. 56×56 cm.

(5) Globe and Eggs 5. Latham 1989. Computer/Cibachrome. 137×122 cm.

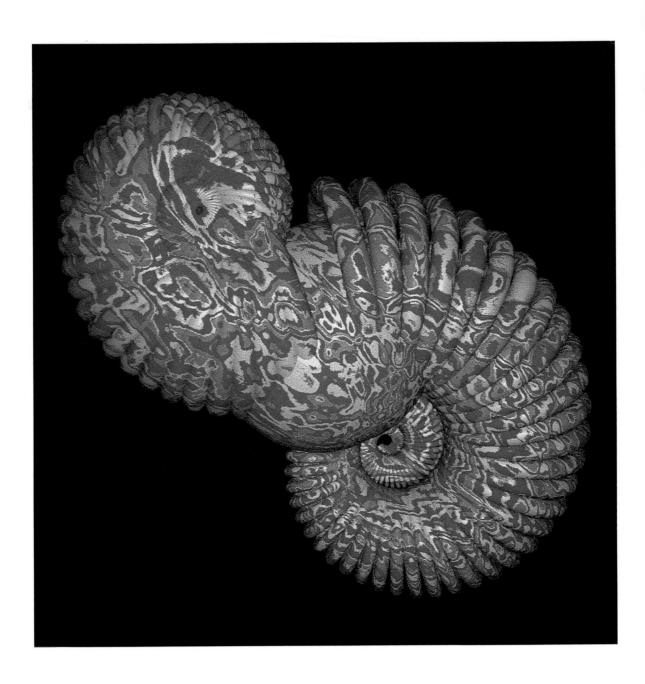

(6) Double Ammonite. Latham 1989. Computer/Cibachrome. 56 cm × 56 cm.

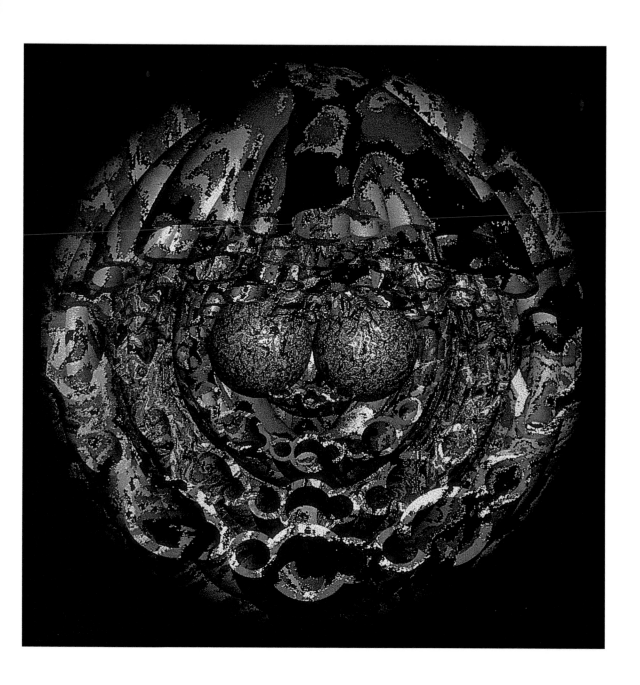

(7) Artww. Latham 1988. Computer/Cibachrome. 56×56 cm.

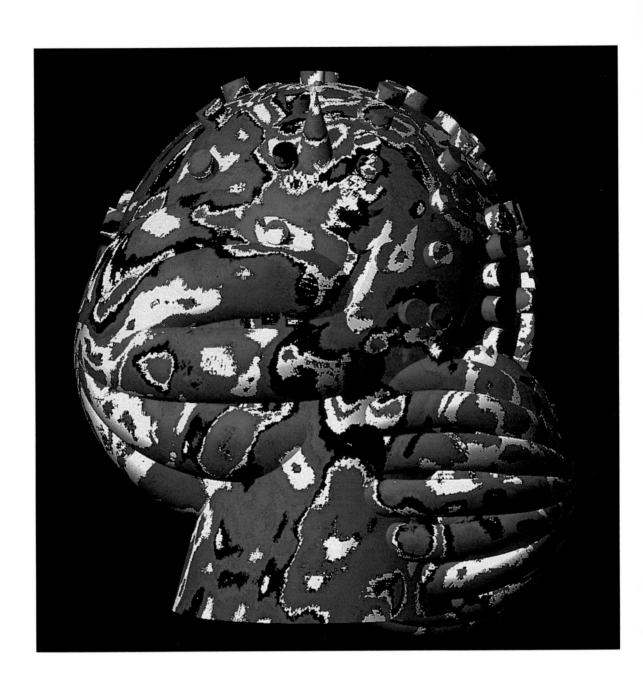

(8) Twister 1. Latham 1988. Computer/Cibachrome. 103×103 cm.

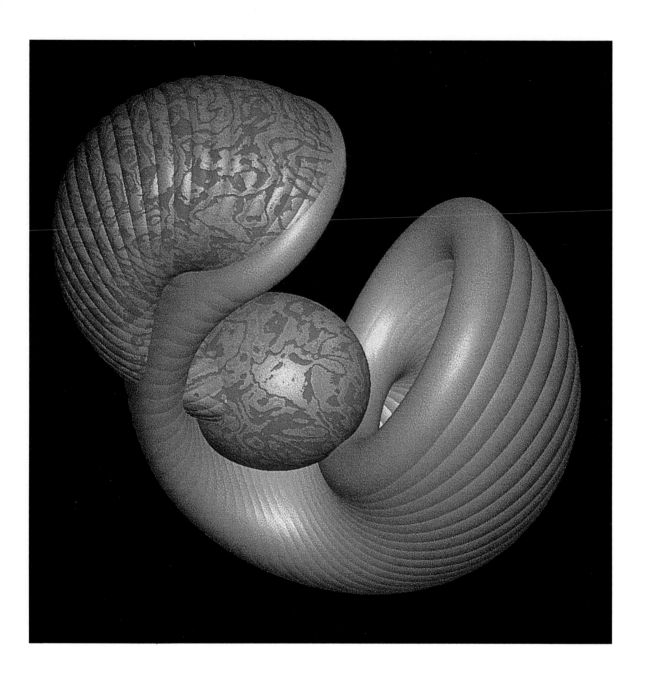

(9) Tube Horn with Egg. Latham 1988. Computer/Cibachrome. 103 × 103 cm.

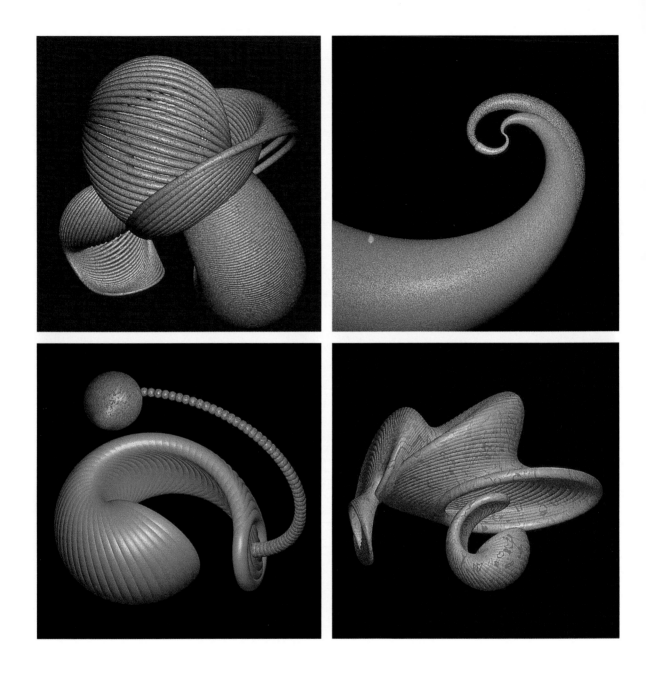

(10a) Folded Red Form. Latham 1988.
Computer/Cibachrome. 56×40 cm.

(10b) Unexpected Form. Latham 1989. Computer Image.

(10c) Horn Egg. Latham 1988. Computer/Cibachrome.
56×56 cm.

(10d) Show 35. Latham 1988. Computer/Cibachrome.
152×152 cm.

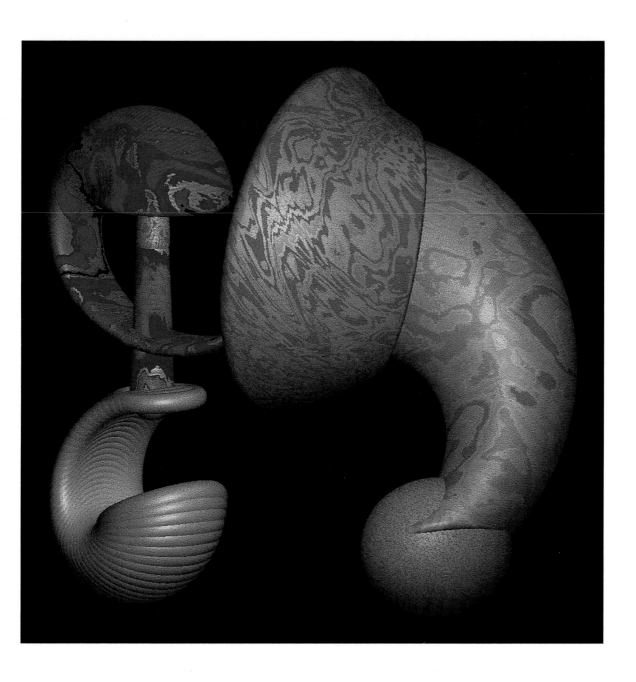

(11) **Standing Horns.** Latham 1989. Computer/'C' Type. 152×152 cm.

(12) Inside the Form 1. Latham 1989. Computer Image. (Still from "The Conquest of Form").

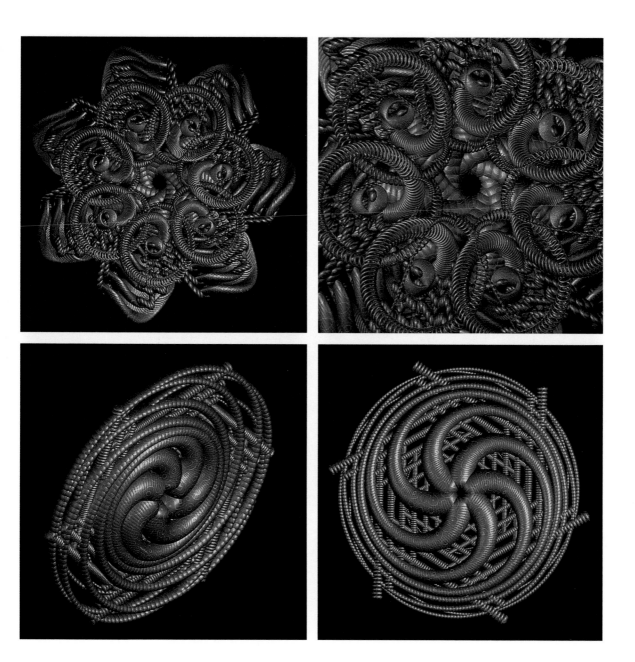

(13a) Celtic 4. Latham 1989. Computer/Cibachrome. 137×122 cm.

(13b) Celtic 4. Latham 1989. Computer/Cibachrome. 137×122 cm. (Detail).

(13c) Frame from Animation "A Sequence from The Evolution of Form". Latham 1991.

(13d) Flash I. Latham 1989. Computer/Cibachrome. 137×122 cm.

(14) Plant Form. Latham 1989. Computer/Cibachrome. 103×103 cm.

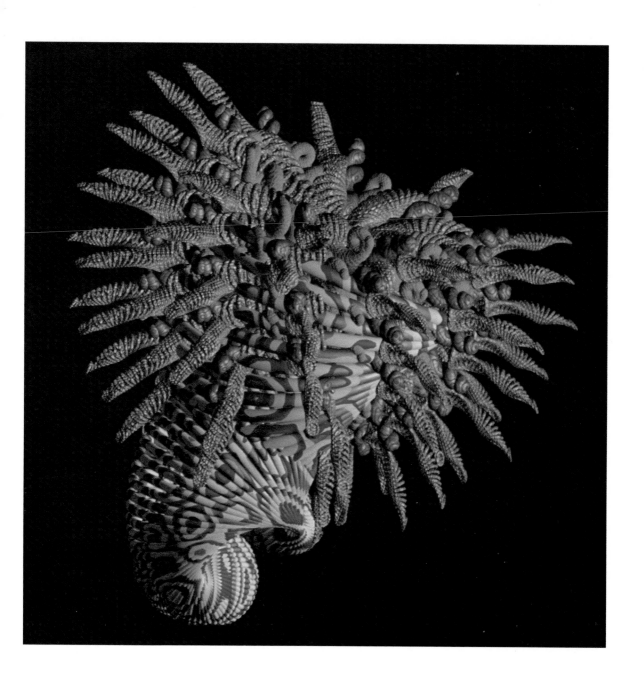

(15) Grown Form. Latham 1989. Computer/Cibachrome. 152×122 cm.

(16a) Bumped Stems. Latham 1989.
Computer/Cibachrome. 13×13 cm.

(16b) Bumped Coiling Stems. Latham 1989.
Computer/Cibachrome. 13×13 cm.

(16c) New Growth Shoots. Latham 1989.
Computer/Cibachrome. 13×13 cm.

(16d) Flower Form. Latham 1989.
Computer/Cibachrome. 103×103 cm.

Chapter 3
Evolution of form generation systems

This chapter shows the transition from hand-drawn systems to computer systems for form generation. We follow a historical approach to show that our systems themselves are the result of a process of evolution from the hand-drawn *Form Synth*, and how artistic ideas derived from biological themes are translated into geometric functions. More technical details of the systems are given in Chapter 8. All the systems we describe generate three dimensional computer forms, though these forms often manifest themselves only as two dimensional images.

Interactive generation

The first computer forms generated by Latham used an interactive editor, *Form Build*, built on ESME and incorporating variants of the rules used by the *Form Synth* hand-drawn form evolution system.

Form Synth (Figure 3.1) is based on a simple set of rules for constructing objects: add, bulge, beak and scoop. *Form Build* is a simple experimental system based on features of *Form Synth* selected for ease of implementation. *Form Build* does not include bulge and scoop, for example, because these do not easily fit the primitives of the lower level systems in which *Form Build* is implemented.

Figure 3.1. Transformations allowed by the *Form Synth* hand-drawn system.

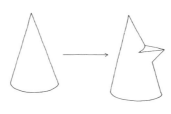

BEAK

Figure 3.1. continued.

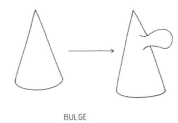

BULGE

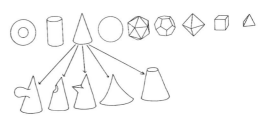

Primitives   *Form Build* uses cubes, spheres, cylinders and cones. These are all of a set size and shape, and following on from *Form Synth* are provided with fixed points, called *location points*, at which attachments are permitted (Figure 3.2). The only function provided is addition. The user places the first object on the screen by a command, and starts the editor. He selects the primitive to be added, a cube for example, from a menu and then the location point on it to use – for example, a corner. He then selects *add*, points at the location point to which the addition is to be made, and the computer makes the addition (Figure 3.3). The pointing method finds the front primitive pointed at by the mouse, and searches for the nearest location point on that primitive.

This sequence is repeated at will. The user can view the computer form from any angle by using the real-time interaction features (see Chapter 9) to rotate the form. With the form rotated, the user can also select location points that were previously at the back of the form (Figure 3.4). The forms generated by this system tend to look somewhat molecular rather than artistic, perhaps because of the relationship of the location points to regular polyhedra and thus to crystal structures (Stiny, 1980).

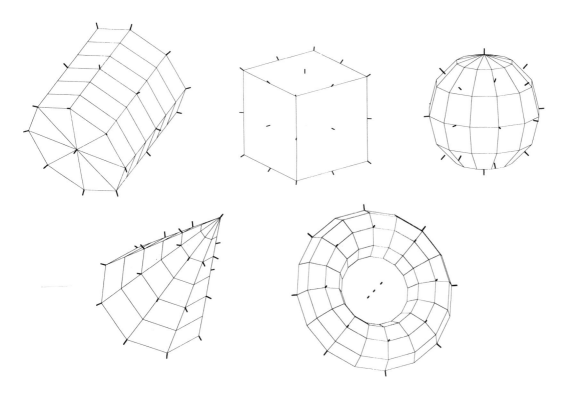

Figure 3.2.   Primitive forms of *Form Build* and their location points. Forms may only be attached with a location point of one form aligned with a location point of another.

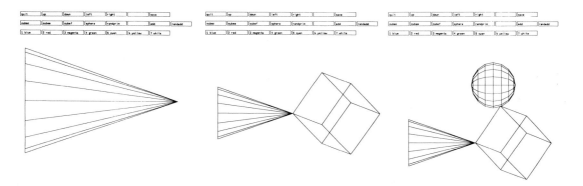

Figure 3.3.   Two steps of addition to a form in *Form Build*. The artist selects the new primitive form and location point to be added. He then selects the form and location point on the existing form at which the addition is to be made.

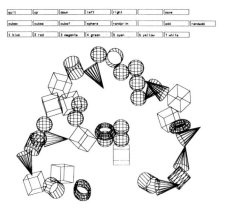

Figure 3.4. The form after the artist has made many manual additions.

Random generation   *Form Build* provides two kinds of random generation. In one the primitive to be added is selected at random. In the other, the location point is chosen at random. These may be used together to add a random primitive to a random point, or independently to add, for example, a sphere to a random point, or a random primitive to a selected point.

The random selection of a point simulates a human selection: the form is given a random orientation, and then a random mouse position is used (Figure 3.5). This produces a form that grows evenly from the centre. In earlier experiments the computer randomly selected an individual primitive from the large computer form and a location point on that primitive, but this often gave location points internal to the form, with over clustered ingrown results.

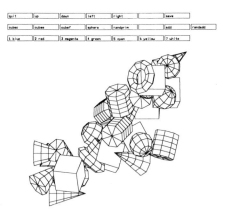

Figure 3.5. The form after the computer has made several 'random' additions. For each addition a random selection is made of the new form and location point. The position at which the addition is to be made to the form under construction is chosen by the computer making an arbitrary rotation of the form and firing a ray to find the first primitive hit. The nearest location point on the primitive to the ray intersection point is selected for addition.

Substitution   Our final experiment with *Form Build* involves the substitution of primitives. The user builds a form, perhaps using randomness, or perhaps with deterministic choices. He then substitutes all occurrences of one primitive with another, say all spheres by tori (Figure 3.6). The results are surprising, and sometimes aesthetic.

Substitution requires that all primitives have the same number of location points. When the primitives are substituted, the location points on the old form must correspond uniquely to the location points on the new one. This is a departure from the rules of *Form Synth*.

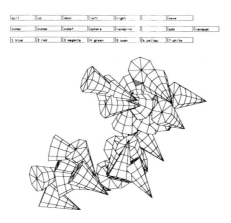

Figure 3.6.   All the primitives in the form shown in Figure 3.5 have been replaced by cones. Substitution requires that all primitives have the same number of location points.

Tree walk   *Form Build* includes options to walk up and down the evolutionary tree, to visit past forms, and to find alternative evolutions from them.

Repetitive work

Latham realized that much of the work used in generating a regular computer form was highly repetitive, as was already clear for some of the hand-drawn forms generated in *Form Synth* (Figure 3.7). He implemented a small set of special functions such as *Fan* and *Stack* to create repetitive forms. Repetitive work in *Form Synth* involved repetitive drawing: with *Form Build* the computer undertook the drawing, but the artist still had, for example, to manually select the *add* menu items 50 times to perform 50 additions. With *Fan* and *Stack* the repetition was captured in the iterative 'do loop' of the program, and the artist merely identified the function to apply and the number of times to apply it.

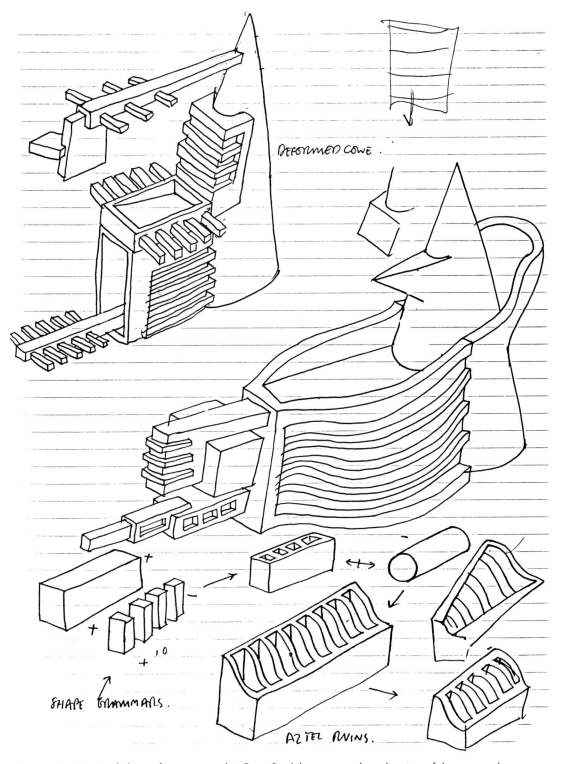

Figure 3.7. Hand-drawn forms created in *Form Synth* by repeated application of the same rule.

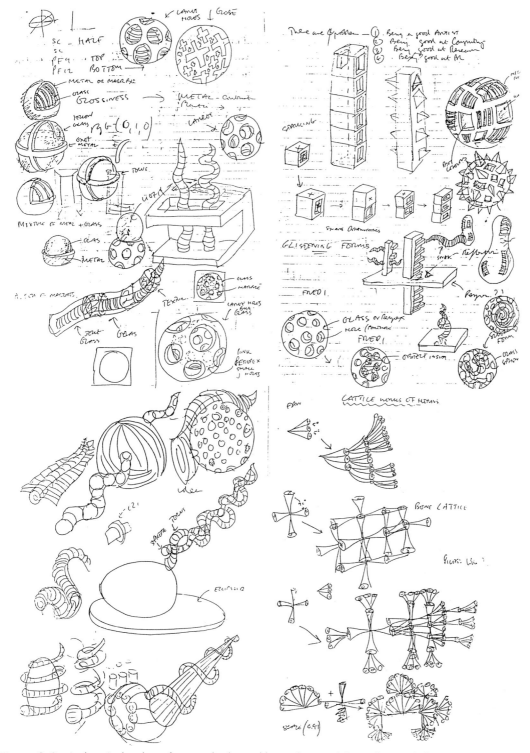

Figure 3.8. Latham's sketches of various biological forms drawn while working with the concepts for our iterative artistic system.

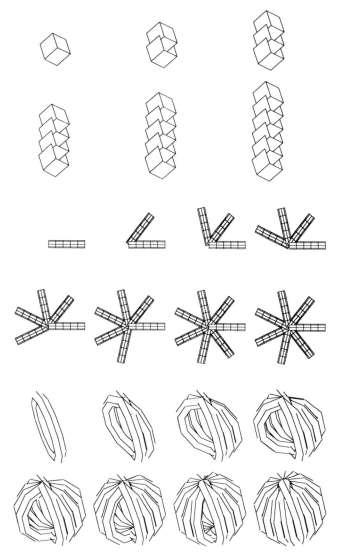

Figure 3.9. Simple repetitive forms generated by separate programs *Fan* and *Stack*.

Natural geometry   The original idea was to program the geometry of the natural world, such as branching and spirals (Figure 3.8) and to exploit it to produce natural-looking computer forms such as fans and pumpkins (Figure 3.9).

L-systems   This is similar to work in biology on L-systems (Prusinkiewicz and Lindenmayer), but with a very different background. L-systems are scientific tools that model the geometry of plants to explain their biology, often producing attractive forms on the way. Our systems are partly inspired by biological forms, but their purpose is to produce aesthetically interesting forms which often bear no relation to biological reality.

Generalization of functions

All these repetitive functions are similar, in that they repeatedly apply some transformation to a basic input form. The next step was to write a general function, *Tentac*, in which the transformation was also a parameter. The name *Tentac* arose because the function was first used to produce tentacle forms. *Tentac* could also be used within a single loop to apply transformations that combined operations such as stacking and the twisting operation used in *Fan* (Figures 3.10, 3.11).

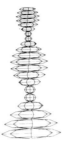

Figure 3.10. A form generated by *Tentac* in which each primitive is placed by stacking it above the previous one and also twisting it.

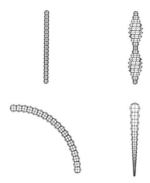

Figure 3.11. Four horns, using simple stacking and growing, all generated by the form generation program *Tentac*.

Branching

Surface is a complementary function to *Tentac*. Examples are shown in Figure 3.12. *Surface* radiates a branching structure around a central point. The branches are by default approximately equally spaced. Branching may be controlled to radiate around a particular direction, or to follow a spiral pattern.

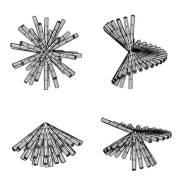

Figure 3.12. Examples of the branching function. A simple branch is shown on the top left-hand side. The right-hand side pictures show a 'texture' parameter applied to cause the branches to be placed in a more regular pattern. The lower pictures show partial branching.

More complex forms

The artist wished to generate more complicated forms using a variety of horns, horns of horns, and branching horn forms (Figures 3.13, 3.14). An additional *tail* parameter to *Tentac* permits horns to be strung together end to end, creating segmented forms. Horns of horns are made by creating the subhorn and using it as the input form to the main horn; this was a new way to use *Tentac*, but did not involve changing the *Tentac* function itself. Finally, we integrated the code from *Surface* into *Tentac* to permit branching horns (Figure 3.15).

Figure 3.13. Hand-drawn artist's sketches for compound horns, made up using several simpler horns.

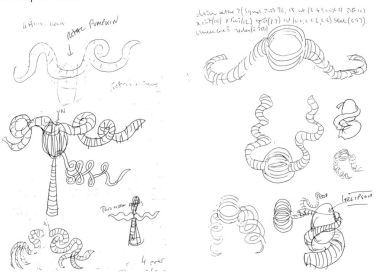

Figure 3.13. Continued

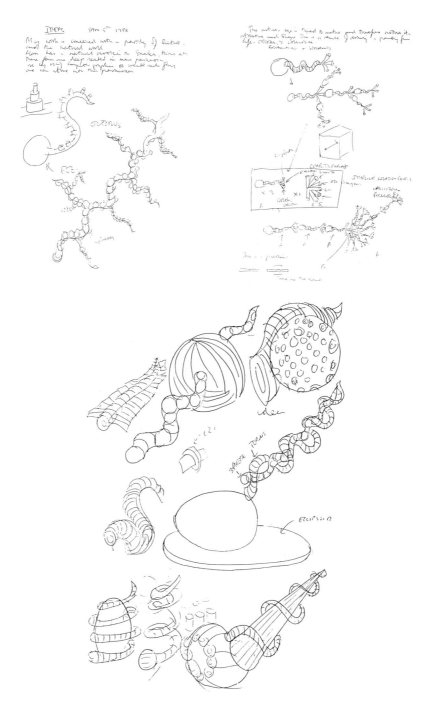

Figure 3.14. Hand-drawn artist's sketches for compound horns, made up using several simpler horns.

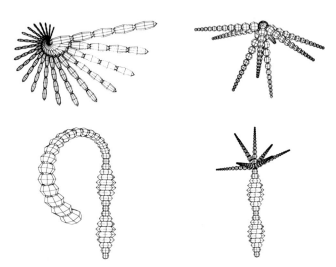

Figure 3.15. These examples show the combination of various functions. Top left: a horn of horns; top right: a branch of horns; bottom left: a horn at the tail of another; bottom right: a simple horn with a form of branching horns at its tail.

Better terminology

Names for transforms

Tentac gives the artist a lot of flexibility in generating forms by specifying a variety of transforms. However, it is not easy to see what the effect of a particular transform is going to be, and even more difficult to decide what transform will achieve a required effect.

This is largely solved by creating functions with indicative names such as *Bend, Stack,*[1] *Twist* and *Grow*, some of which relate to the original rules of *Form Synth*. The functions are little more than synonyms for the original transform functions such as *XROT*, but they make the specification of forms much more reliable as they permit the sculptor to think in his own concrete terms rather than worrying about the Cartesian frame of reference of the form.

Naming parameters

As more options became available to the user, such as an optional tail, the less appropriate became the conventional function calling syntax with positional parameters and no defaults. The next version thus collects all the parameters into a single *horn definition*. Access functions query, set and reset its various fields, and a single *Csg* function takes a horn definition and performs the *Tentac* task of creating a computer form as a constructive solid

---

[1] The two uses of the function name *Stack* do not get confused because they occur in different contexts. ESME uses the programming concept called *overloading* to decide which one is appropriate based on the parameters given.

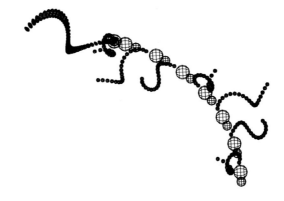

```
hh1: =   horn ribs (20)            /*  make a horn with 20 ribs */
         sphere (0.4)              /*  out of spheres */
         stack (12) twist (400,2) bend (60); /* deformed thus */


hhorn: =  (horn ribs (20)          /*  another horn */
           sphere (1)              /*  uses three input forms */
           sphere (1.5)            /*  two sphere of different size */
           (csg (hh1) xrot (90))   /*  and the old horn */
           stack (40) twist (400) bend (40))
    ¢                              /*  This makes a list of horns */
          (horn ribs (40)          /*  that joins this one */
           ellipsoid (1, 0.5, 0.3) /*  to the tail of the other. */
           stack (20) twist (400,4) bend (40))
```

Figure 3.16. This shows the syntax currently used to define horns. The example was prepared by Stephen Todd, not William Latham: it demonstrates that it requires a sculptor and not just the artistic system to create interesting forms.

geometry model understood by the rest of ESME (Figure 3.16). The *Form Grow* system is the complete package of programs that operates on the horn definition.

Object oriented programming

The horn definition was originally made purely to give us a mechanism for named parameters with defaults. It also proved to simplify many other programming tasks. We realized later that it was a typical example of the object-oriented approach to programming.

One task simplified by the use of horn objects is the 'in-betweening' of two horns, used for animation and experimentation in horn design. Another is the generation of approximate representations of a horn (see Chapter 8) for fast interactive display.

Complex twists and bends

It is easy to use *Tentac* to produce, for example, twisted or bent forms, and to use combinations of operations such as stack and twist. The construction rule of *Tentac* composes operations such as twist and bend into a single operation, which it then applies repetitively. Thus when applied to make three copies of an object it produces:

- object twist bend
- object twist bend twist bend
- object twist bend twist bend twist bend.

The twists effectively act on the bends, so the bends do not all operate together, but cancel each other out (Figure 3.17).

Early versions of *Form Grow* permitted a second transform operation. The *i*th rib of the result is generated by applying *i* copies of the first transform to the input form, followed by *i* copies of the second transform. Applying twist and bend three times to an object now produces:

- object twist bend
- object twist twist bend bend
- object twist twist twist bend bend bend.

The extra flexibility is demonstrated in Figure 3.17.

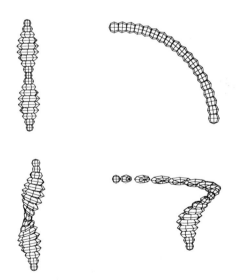

Figure 3.17. The need to separate the twisting forms. The top two forms show simple twisting and bending. When the bend and twist are combined and then applied many times, as in the third form, the bends almost cancel each other out as the twists force them to bend in different directions. When the bend and twist are used independently, the object is first bent and then the bent object is twisted.

There are some pairs of operations (such as stack and twist) that may be applied in any order and the result is still the same: mathematically we say that the operations commute:

$$stack\ twist\ stack\ twist = stack\ stack\ twist\ twist$$
$$= twist\ twist\ stack\ stack$$

That it why *Tentac* is able to combine some operations. Figure 3.18 shows various operations applied in different orders.

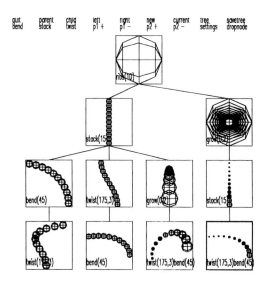

Figure 3.18. Tree showing operations applied in different orders. Each form of the tree is derived from the form above by adding an extra transform.

Lists of transform rules   Simpler specification leads to attempts to do more complicated things. Thus the two transformation rules soon became inadequate, and were replaced by a single *list* of transform rules. The list can be of an arbitrary length, so the sculptor is able to think in terms like 'make this horn, pull it out, twist it, now bend it, give it a second twist', and so on.

Applying texture

Colouring and texture are applied to the forms using the *texture* function to make them more realistic and interesting (see Chapter 11). Pure colour can be applied to a form at any time, and however much the form is bent and stretched the colour remains unchanged. This is not true with texturing. When a form is textured, any bending or twisting applied to the form is also applied to the texture. Thus it is important at which stage texture is applied to a horn during its construction by bending, stretching and twisting. For example, if a horn is growing along its length, do we want the scale of the texture to be uniform over the horn, or do we want the scale of the texture on each rib to match the scale of that rib?

Form Grow uses two lists of transforms, one to be applied before texturing, and the other after. When a transform is applied to an untextured horn definition, it is added to the first list, and when a transform is applied to a textured horn definition, it is added to the second list. Thus when the artist creates a horn:

horn object twist texture bend

the result includes:

- object twist texture bend
- object twist twist texture bend bend
- object twist twist twist texture bend bend bend

(see Figure 3.19).

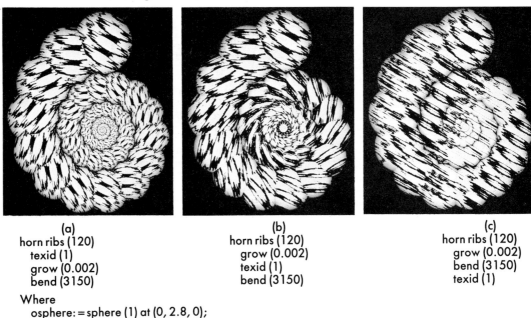

<table>
<tr><td align="center">(a)
horn ribs (120)
texid (1)
grow (0.002)
bend (3150)</td><td align="center">(b)
horn ribs (120)
grow (0.002)
texid (1)
bend (3150)</td><td align="center">(c)
horn ribs (120)
grow (0.002)
bend (3150)
texid (1)</td></tr>
</table>

Where
osphere: = sphere (1) at (0, 2.8, 0);

Figure 3.19. Different applications of texture to a horn. The form is made by growing an offset sphere and bending it. In the left hand picture the texture is applied to the sphere before any transformations are applied, and so follows the scale and direction of the form. In the centre picture it is applied after the scale, and so follows the direction of the form but does not reduce in scale towards the centre. In the right hand picture the texture is applied after all the transformations, and so a single texture overlays and camouflages the entire form.

Camouflage   Texture applied independently to each primitive emphasizes the geometric construction of the horn. Texture that is applied to the entire horn emphasizes the shape of the horn, and camouflages the individual primitives. The ribbing caused by individual primitives causes a texturing effect, and the interaction between this and the texture itself can be very confusing, especially where many primitives are used and the scale of the texture is larger than the scale of geometric ribbing.

Mixed horns

Originally, all the ribs of a horn had to be identical, except for their size. Use of a list of input forms permits different ribs to have different forms (Figure 3.20).

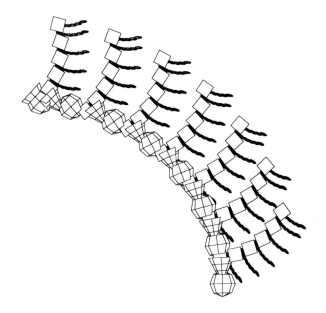

Figure 3.20.   The main horn has three different input forms: a sphere, cone and another horn. This horn has two input forms: a cube and a horn of ellipsoids.

Web forms

The features of *Form Grow* described so far create a simple list of horns, though the use of particular twists and of horns of horns often gives a more visually complex feel to the result. Latham wished to create weblike forms (Figure 3.21) for an animated film *A Sequence from the Evolution of Form* (Plate 13c). The *Hornweb* feature of *Form Grow* generates a web-like mesh of horns radiating from a central point, with one horn form making the spokes of the form, and another the cross-parts (Figure 3.22).

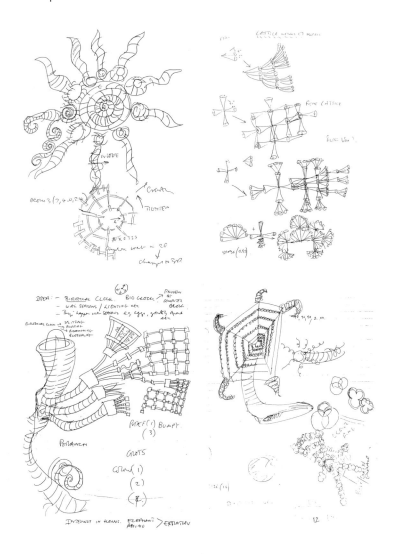

Figure 3.21. Hand-drawn artist's sketches drawn during design of the *Hornweb* feature of *Form Grow* used in the film *Evolution of Form*.

Figure 3.22. Example of the use of the *Hornweb* feature of *Form Grow*.

We are working on a generalization that will permit any two dimensional mesh form to be produced, in the same manner that *Tentac* generalized *Fan*, *Stack*, and so on. This will probably be extended to three (or even higher) dimensions, though we suspect that the resulting forms will be too complex to make sense to a viewer.

Fractal horns

We have already described how the objects that make up a horn may be smaller 'subhorns'. The subhorn of a horn may be a smaller copy of the horn itself, with subhorn itself made of yet smaller copies, and so on, creating a recursive or fractal horn (Figure 3.23, Plate 20).

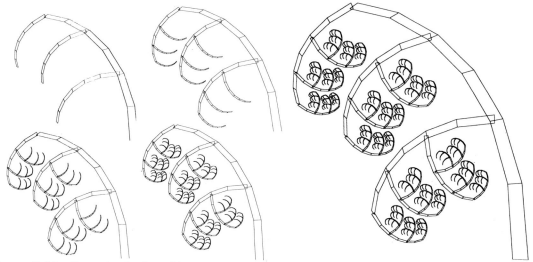

Figure 3.23. Example of a fractal horn with different levels of fractal detail.

Ribcage

Ribcage produces a symmetric structure of horns each side of a main 'former'. It was designed for the film *Mutations* (Figures 3.24, 3.25).

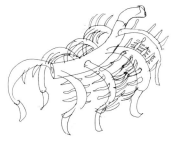

Figure 3.24. Hand-drawn artist's sketch made during design of the *Ribcage* feature of *Form Grow* for the film *Mutations*.

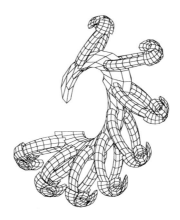

Figure 3.25. Computer form generated using *Ribcage*.

Conclusion

We have shown how iteration, recursion and the geometry of nature combine into an artistic system for form generation, and how this system evolved through use. The system produces forms with a complexity that goes beyond the drawing capabilities of even the most obsessive human artist.

Choice and human computer interface The disadvantages of this systematic approach are that it takes away from the artist the opportunity of applying aesthetic choice at each stage of the iterative process, and that it forces him into a hostile computer programming environment. We use techniques such as menus and visual programming to reduce the hostility of the environment, but it remains a programming environment. The following chapters show how the *Mutator* interface retains the advantages of iterative form generation, but gives back the opportunity to apply subjective aesthetic choice to the artist.

Chapter 4
Using form generation systems

In this chapter we show how the artist exploits form generation systems to make complex forms. We first show the use of visual programming to make it easier to read the definition of a form, and analyse an example of complex definition.

This analysis does not necessarily correspond to the way in which the artist creates the definition. He does not build a complex definition from nothing, but has a concept towards which he is working, and builds a simple definition which he gradually expands and combines with others. He often reuses large parts of previous definitions in building a new one. The ability of the computer to reconstruct and redraw quickly from an edited definition permits the artist to refine his concept and his implementation of it very much more easily than is possible with physical sculpture.

One way in which to simplify editing is to identify some parts of the form definition as a fixed structure, and the rest as genes which can be changed. This leads to the notion of a family of related forms with different genes but with the same structure, which is important for selecting and animating forms.

Making a complex form

Visual language

The artists cannot easily understand definitions written in the textual definition language. A mathematician uses a mathematical language of equations, and a programmer uses a programming language. In general, the artists likes form definitions to be expressed with a visual language. Each of the important structural elements is shown pictorially as an icon, a bend as a spiral, a twist as a helix, and so on (Figure 4.1). Transform rules in a list are shown horizontally, and the segments of a segmented horn are shown vertically (Figure 4.2).

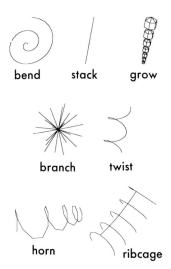

Figure 4.1. Elements of a visual definition. The top group shows the icons for the transform rules and the bottom group shows the icons for horn and ribcage.

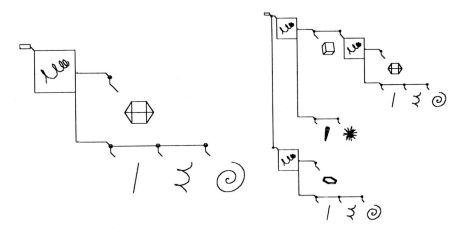

Figure 4.2. Example visual definition. The left example shows a horn of spheres with a transform rule list of stack, twist and bend (drawn horizontally). The right example shows a list of two horns drawn vertically. The first horn has two input forms (drawn horizontally), a cube and a copy of the horn of the left hand example. The second horn is made of tori stacked, twisted and bent.

We can only use our visual language to display definitions already created; to edit them we resort to the text editor. In future we intend to build a mouse-driven interactive visual definition editor. The visual definition does not attempt to show numeric details such as the degree of twist, but we are experimenting with icons which change their characteristics to represent this.

Dissection of the lobster definition

We show how complex definitions work by analysing the steps taken in building a computer lobster. These steps show the way in which the computer analyses and executes the complex definition, rather than the evolutionary changes made by the artist in the original creation of the definition.

The first step is to build the five horn segments that make up the central backbone (Figure 4.3). The construction of each of the different segments is similar. The five segments are then connected to create the backbone (Figure 4.4). This is only a test of the overall shape: the parts must not be glued at this stage as they have to be separated again so as to apply the detailing.

We now prepare ribs for the ribcage. Each rib is a horn made up out of two segments (Figure 4.5). Many copies of the ribs are made and collected into the ribcage (Figure 4.6). At first the ribcage is a collection of ribs with nothing on which to hang, but the ribcage takes shape when it is applied to the torso.

To apply the ribcage to a double horn segment, we must first connect the two segments and then apply the ribcage:

torso: = (tors1 with tors2) cage;

The brackets illustrate the problems an artist has with a textual form definition language. They are necessary to make sure that the construction is in this order. Without the brackets the cage is applied to *tors2*, and then the caged *tors2* attached after *tors1*. We could also force the correct order by using an extra step.

baretorso: = tors1 with tors2;
torso: = baretorso cage;

We now construct the Gorgon head (Figure 4.7). Each snake is made of a twisty horn, and then the snakes are collected in a branching form to create the Gorgon head. When we place the head on the neck (Figure 4.8) we find that parts of the Gorgon are obscured, therefore we have to leave out the first few primitives of the neck.

The components are now all ready, and we assemble them to make the lobster (Figure 4.9).

Complete definition We have shown the step-by-step assembly of the lobster. This is written out in a single definition file, usually in fragments in much the same way as we have shown the lobster's construction (Figure 4.10).

```
neck:=horn                tors1:=horn               tors2:=horn
   ribs (12)                 ribs (15)                 ribs (18)
   torus (1.8, 0.5)          torus (1.7, 0.4)          torus (2.1, 0.4)
   twist (10, 1.3)           twist (10, 1)             twist (40, 1)
   stack (9.0)               stack (9.5)               stack (8.0)
   bend (40)                 bend (60)                 bend (80)
   grow (0.9)                grow (0.92)               grow (0.9)
   texid (15);               texid (1);             texid (12);


tail1:=horn               tail 2:=horn
   ribs (15)                 ribs (9)
   torus (1.65, 0.26)        torus (1.65, 0.26)
   stack (3.3)               stack (2.7)
   bend (55)                 twist (30, 1)
   grow (1.3)                bend (55)
   texid (12);               grow (1.8)
                             texid (13);
```

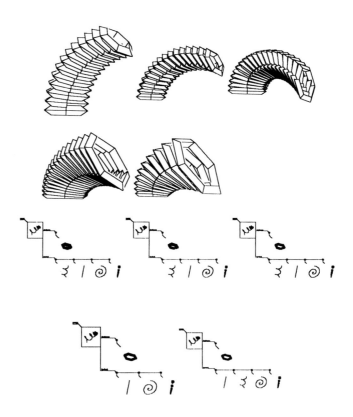

Figure 4.3.   First stage of creating the lobster form: five simple horns are prepared for the backbone.

back1: = neck;

back2: = back1;
with tors1;

back3: = back2;
with tors2;

back4: = back3
with tail1;

backbone: = back4
with tail2;

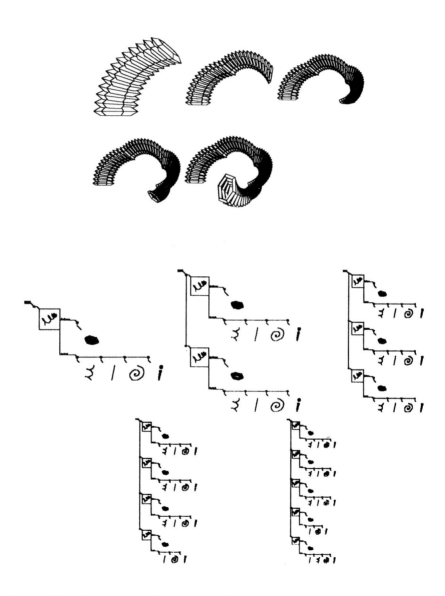

Figure 4.4. Testing the backbone shape. The simple segments are concatenated to form the backbone. This is only a test of the backbone shape: detail must be added to the simple horns before final assembly.

```
ribs1:=horn              ribs2:=horn              rib:=rib1
  sphere (0.4)             ribs (8)                 with rib2;
  sphere (0.8)             torus (0.6, 0.1)
  sphere (0.7)             twist (40, 1.0)
  ribs (12)                stack (4.0)
  twist (40, 1.0)          bend (80)
  stack (7.5)            grow (0.89)
  bend (70)             texid (10);
  grow (0.87)
  texid (8);
```

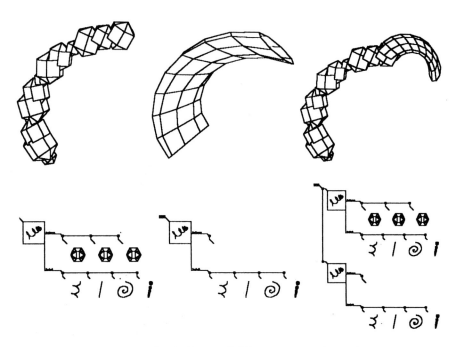

Figure 4.5.   Preparation of a rib. The two left forms are contributing horns and the right form is a complete rib.

```
cage: = ribcage
    ribs (9)
    flap (90)
```

```
torso: = (tors 1
    with tors2
    )cage;
```

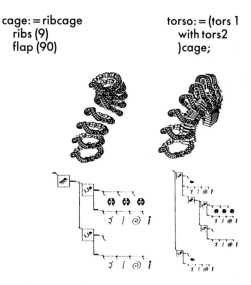

Figure 4.6. Making and applying the ribcage. On the left the ribcage has been defined, but no backbone on which to hang it has yet been defined; it is therefore shown hung on a 'typical' backbone. On the right the ribcage is attached to a part of the main body of the lobster.

```
tentacle: = horn
    ribs (15)
    sphere (0.75)
    twist (400, 1.5)
    stack (14.5)
    twist (10, 1)
    bend (0.001)
    grow (0.46)
    texid (6);
```

```
shaper: = horn
    longcyl
    ribs (21)
branch (360)
    grow (0.83);
```

```
gorgon: = shaper
    inform (tentacle);
```

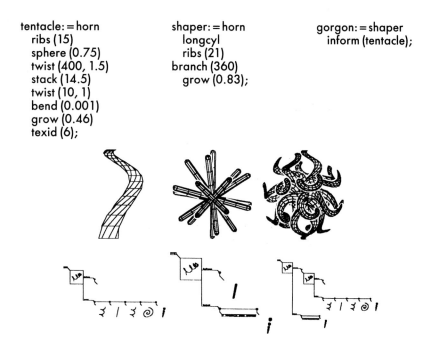

Figure 4.7. On the left is a single tentacle horn. In the centre is the horn used to shape the branching of tentacles which are fitted to it to create a complete head on the right. The shaper is for illustration only. In practice, the shaper is not created as a separate object, but the Gorgon head is created directly.

headparta: = neck
head (gorgon);

headpart: = neck
head (gorgon)
start (3);

headpartb: = neck
head (gorgon)
start (6);

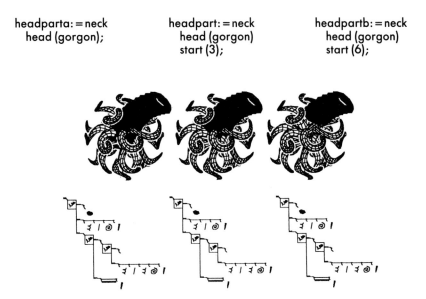

Figure 4.8. In the first attempt to fit the headpart (left) the neck obscures some of the interesting parts of the Gorgon. We remove the first few primitives of the neck to reveal more of the Gorgon (centre). On the right, too much is revealed, and the neck is starting to separate from the head.

lobster: = headpart
   with torso
   with tail1
   with tail2;

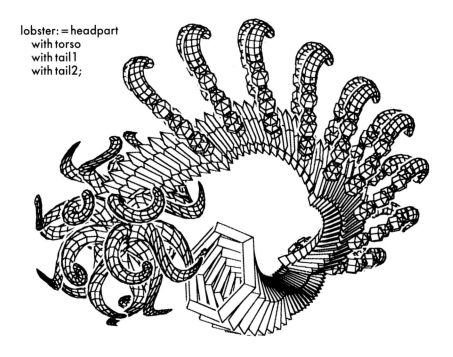

Figure 4.9. The final lobster is created by assembling the main parts.

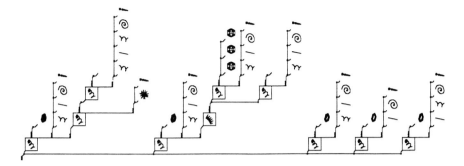

Figure 4.10. The complete lobster definition brings together all the fragments of the preceding examples (shown rotated).

Changing a form

We have seen how a form can be built from a complex form definition, but in practice the artists builds up definitions from previous ones by splicing and merging and making a sequence of evolutionary changes (Figure 4.11). Suppose the artist has created a form from definitions, and he does not like the image he sees. How should he change it?

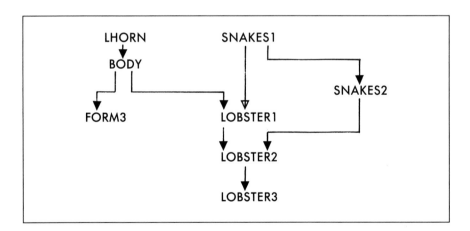

Figure 4.11. Evolution of form definitions. The artist has the concept of a lobster form. This shows how the lobster definition may have been derived. The artist already has definitions LHORN for a long horn and SNAKES1 for a snaky head. He develops a new version BODY of LHORN suitable for the main lobster backbone, and attaches SNAKES1 as a head to get LOBSTER1. He sees that SNAKES1 does not create a suitable head, so he evolves it to create SNAKES2. When he is satisfied with SNAKES2, he grafts it into LOBSTER1 to create LOBSTER2, which undergoes further modifications to produce the final LOBSTER structure.

There are many stages in the production of the final image from the definition, and the user may make the change at any stage of the process (Figures 4.11, 4.12). If the image is printed, he may paint over the print, or make another print using photographic editing techniques.[2] If the image is on the display, he can change it using display knobs for brightness and contrast, or he may edit the computer image using an image processing or a paint box system, or with the computer form using an appropriate form editor. He can edit or recreate the definition. Finally, he can complain to someone else and get the form generation system or even the drawing system reprogrammed. However, this vast choice of options can make it difficult to decide when a work of art is finished.

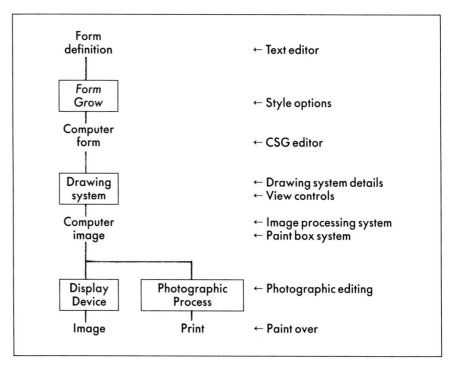

Figure 4.12. Levels at which to change an image. This shows the process of generating an image, and how the process can be intercepted at each stage to change the final image.

Changing the definition   We concentrate here on change at the definition level (Figure 4.13) for two reasons. One is that it is in keeping with the concept of a system for art, and the other is that it avoids laborious detailed work for the artist. Avoiding detailed hand work is especially important for an animation, where it must be repeated on every frame with a risk of inconsistencies between frames. However, all the other kinds of change are reasonable under appropriate circumstances: no system of rules can possibly be followed without breaking

[2]He can paint over an image on a computer display or even take a hammer and chisel to it, but that might not be popular.

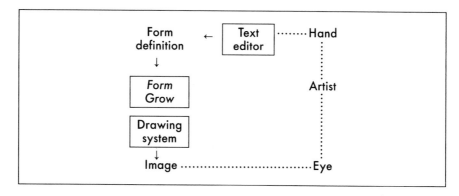

Figure 4.13. Changing a form: the definition editing loop. This shows the editing loop used when the artist edits the form definition. At each iteration the computer generates a form from the definition. The artist looks at the form and decides on modifications. He modifies the definition using a text editor. The interaction continues as the computer generates the new form.

some, and the artist often wants detailed control to achieve the desired aesthetic results.

Visual feedback and interaction are an important part of definition editing, as they are of most art processes. The artist sees the image and knows what is wrong. He decides how it might be corrected by changing the definition, and makes the change; the computer redraws the image, and the artist looks at the result. Usually it is still not correct, and so the artist makes another change, creates another image, and takes another look, and so the form evolves until the artist is satisfied. There are two kinds of change to the definition (Figure 4.14): one changes the way in which the definition is put together; the other leaves the underlying structure of the definition intact – for example, the visual program is unchanged – but alters the numeric

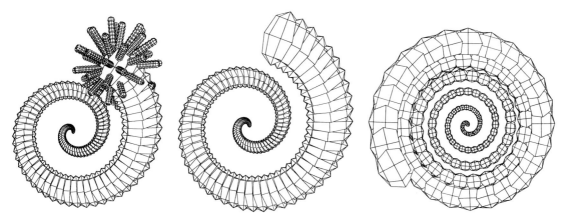

Figure 4.14. Changing structure and numbers. This shows three computer forms. The two outer forms are derived from the central one. The left form is derived by changing the structure of the form definition. The right form is derived by changing numbers in the definition.

details. Changing the underlying structure usually has a more dramatic visual effect, but not always. As the artist gets close to finding a satisfactory form he is usually experimenting with the numbers only, and the structure remains fixed.

Structure and genes

We make this division between the overall structure and numeric detail precise by tagging in the definition the numbers that the artist is changing. We tag them with the string 'eg', indicating that the values in the definition are an example only, and are not fixed. To create a precise definition we plug in a particular set of numbers (Figure 4.15). We call the set of numbers the *genes*, and we call the definition into which the genes are plugged the *structure*. Anyone with a knowledge of programming will see that a structure is a parameterized function which takes numbers (the genes) as input and produces a form definition as output.

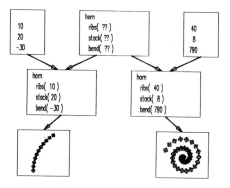

Figure 4.15. A single structure is combined with two different sets of genes to produce two form definitions. *Form Grow* uses these two definitions to generate two forms.

Keys The visual program representation of a structure looks like a key. We think of a structure as a key which unlocks the potential of the genes to create the computer forms.

Family Each set of genes combined with its structure produces some definition, and thus some form,[3] and so an effectively unlimited number of forms can be produced from a single structure. We call the complete set of all such forms a *family* (Figure 4.16).

---

[3]Unless it stirs up a problem such as division by zero.

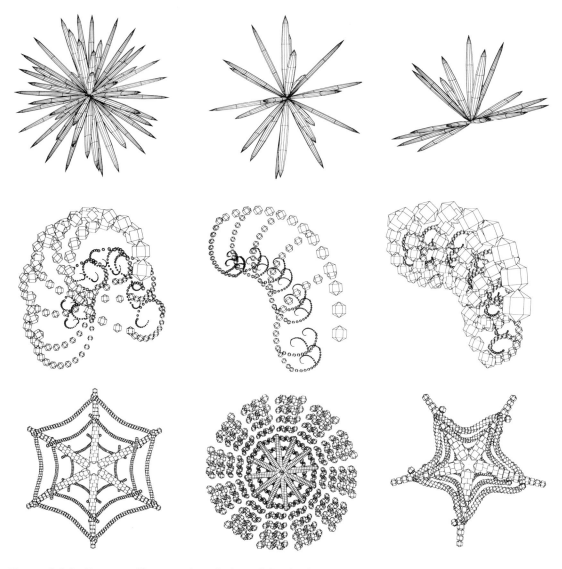

Figure 4.16.   Top row of forms are from the branch family, the second row are from the fractal family, and the third row are from the Hornweb family.

Advantages and disadvantages of families   We have described how we define families of forms by splitting the form definition into structure and numeric genes. This makes a flexible system that is easily understood both by people and by computers, and which we exploit both with *Mutator* in searching for forms, and in the animation of forms. There are disadvantages as well. With our definition of family, two similar forms may well lie in different families, and the artist cannot easily move between families.

The distinction between structure and genes is somewhat arbitrary. We see in the technical section on form generation (see Chapter 8) how we may write programs that completely blur the distinction, but for the sake of simplicity we keep the distinction for the next two chapters.

Form space

Lines of forms   As one gene changes, so the three dimensional form changes. If we fix all but one of the genes, we can attach the different forms at points along a line. For each point on the line we use the distance from the start of the line as the value of the varying gene, and find the corresponding form (Figure 4.17). We can use different values for other genes, and make a second line of forms for our chosen gene (Figure 4.18). We can do this for another of the genes (Figure 4.19).

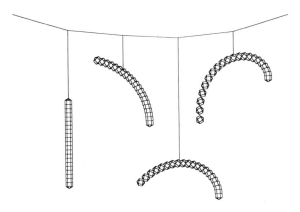

Figure 4.17. Washing line of bent forms. As we move along the line the forms are more and more bendy.

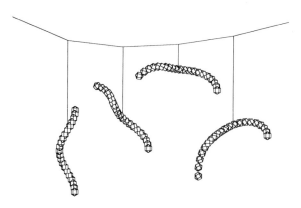

Figure 4.18. Second line of bent forms. As we move along the line the forms are more and more bendy, but all the forms on this line are also twisty.

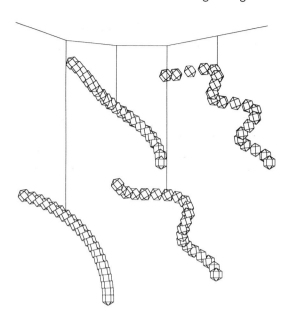

Figure 4.19. Line of twisted forms. As we move along this line the forms are more and more twisty.

Two and three dimensions   We can let both genes vary at the same time, and lay the forms out on a wall, using the distance along the wall for one gene value, and the distance up the wall for the other (Figure 4.20, 4.21). With three genes varying, the forms must be laid out in three dimensional space, so as we come away from the wall the forms have more scaling along their length (Figure 4.22). The space is filled with forms, and every point in the continuous space reveals a different form.

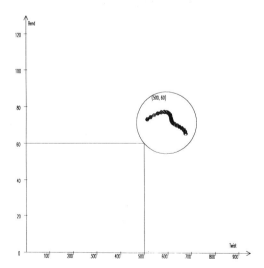

Figure 4.20. Form on a wall. The position of this form on the wall determines how bendy and twisty it is.

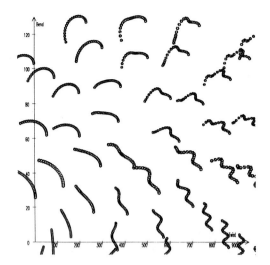

Figure 4.21. Wall of forms. The forms are laid out on a wall. Straight forms are at the bottom left, with twisty ones to the right and bent ones at the top. The forms at the top right are bent and twisty.

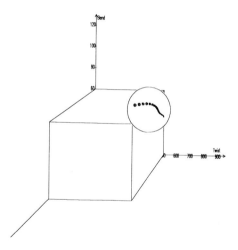

Figure 4.22. Forms in three dimensional space. the bend, twist and grow are all changing here, as indicated by the axes. The growth factor increases as we move forwards away from the wall.

Direction in form space　Starting with our position in two dimensional form space we can move up for more bend, down for less bend, right for more twist, or left for less twist (Figure 4.23). In three dimensional form space we can also move away from the wall for more growth, or towards it for less (Figure 4.24). We do not have to move along in these set directions, so we can move down and left at the same time to reduce the bend and twist together, as in the bottom left form (Figure 4.25). In three dimensional space we have even more freedom (Figure 4.26, 4.27).

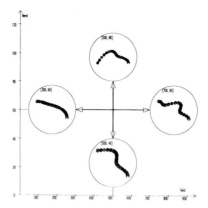

Figure 4.23. Constrained movement in two dimensional form space. We can move up for more bend, down for less bend, right for more twist, or left for less twist.

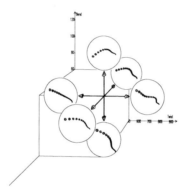

Figure 4.24. Constrained movement in three dimensional form space. We can move up for more bend and down for less, right for more twist and left for less, and away from the wall for more growth and towards it for less.

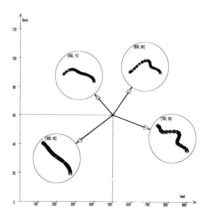

Figure 4.25. Unconstrained movement in two dimensional form space. We can simultaneously move up for more bend and right for more twist, or make any other movement on the face of the wall.

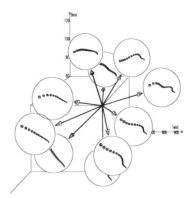

Figure 4.26. Unconstrained movement on three dimensional form space. To reach the forms at the bottom right of the picture we moved away from the wall to increase the growth rate and also down and left to get rid of most of the bend and twist.

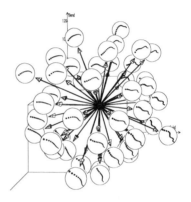

Figure 4.27. Explosion in three dimensional form space. This shows a large number of forms in three dimensional form space radiating around a central point in the space. The directions in three dimensional space were chosen using the *branch* transform rule.

Multidimensional form space

The examples shown above have just two or three genes, but complex structures have tens of genes – for example, the structure used in *Mutations* had 33 genes. We cannot easily show a diagram, but these can be laid out in 33 dimensional space. We call this the 'multidimensional form space'. Suppose each gene could take on 100 distinct values; for example, the integers 1 to 100. That gives 100 to the power of 33 different sets of genes; 1,000,000,000,000,000,000,000,000,000,000,000,000,000,000,000,000,000,000,000,000,000,000 different forms in the family. In practice, each gene can take on not just 100 but an almost limitless number of values, and so the total number of forms is unimaginable. From a gambling point of view, the chance of finding the most aesthetic forms is very small even though they are predetermined.

Structure space

A single structure creates a vast form space. The number of structures is also limitless. Even for structure rules permitting only 10 distinct keywords, and without the use of brackets, there are 1,000,000 structures with just six key-words, and 1,000,000,000,000,000,000,000,000,000,000,000 with 33 key-words. Form space has a regular underlying layout mathematically called a 'vector space'. The connection between structures is more complex, forming a network (Figure 4.28), mathematically a lattice.

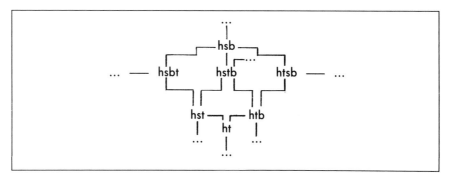

Figure 4.28. Fragment of structure space. We use *hstb* to indicate the structure *horn stack (eg 10) twist (eg 720) bend (eg 60)*, *hsb* to indicate that structure *horn stack (eg 10) bend (eg 60)*, and so on. The lines indicate 'minimal' changes that consist of a single deletion or insertion.

Space of all forms   The space of all possible forms that the form generation system can generate is even larger and mathematically more complex. Each of the vast numbers of structures has an associated vast number of forms, and all these lie in the full space. The space inherits both the vector spaces of genes and the lattice of structure space. Different structures can generate identical forms and introduce extra connections as an added complication:

	horn		horn
	stack(10)	=	stack(10)
			twist(0)
	bend(90)		bend(90)

In mathematical terms, the complete space of generated forms is a simplicial complex.

Searching form space

Let us come back to Earth a little more, and remember that the reason for the distinction between genes and structure was to make our search for aesthetic forms simpler, not more complicated. Restricting ourselves once again to a single fixed structure, how do we find the most aesthetic forms from its huge family (Figure 4.29). The visual effect of changing one parameter is often related to the visual effect of changing another, so if we want to achieve the

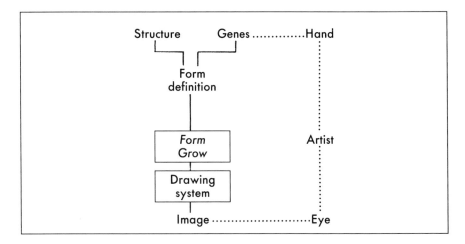

Figure 4.29. Searching the vastness of form space. This shows how the artist searches form space by experimenting with different gene values.

most aesthetic results we cannot even experiment with the genes one at a time. As we experiment with these parameters we are effectively exploring the form space for aesthetic forms: looking for a needle in a multidimensional haystack.

Manual search For about a year, Latham made forms by manually typing in and editing gene values. He changed the numbers in the form definition file, sometimes knowing what effect he was trying to achieve based on analytic thought about the role of the gene in the structure, sometimes almost at random. He then produced a form which he either kept for use as a key frame, or rejected, or used as the basis for further experimentation. He could not anticipate exactly the result even of analytic change to the gene values, so there was always an element of surprise, and some of the most interesting forms were produced as the result of typing errors (Plate 10b).

One way of refining manual searching is to interpolate the genes for two artistic forms. This was the basis of the metamorphosis in the film *Sequence from the Evolution of Form*.

These manual methods for seaching are very laborious. The *Mutator* system discussed in the next chapter is designed to speed up and make more precise the ideas used in the manual search.

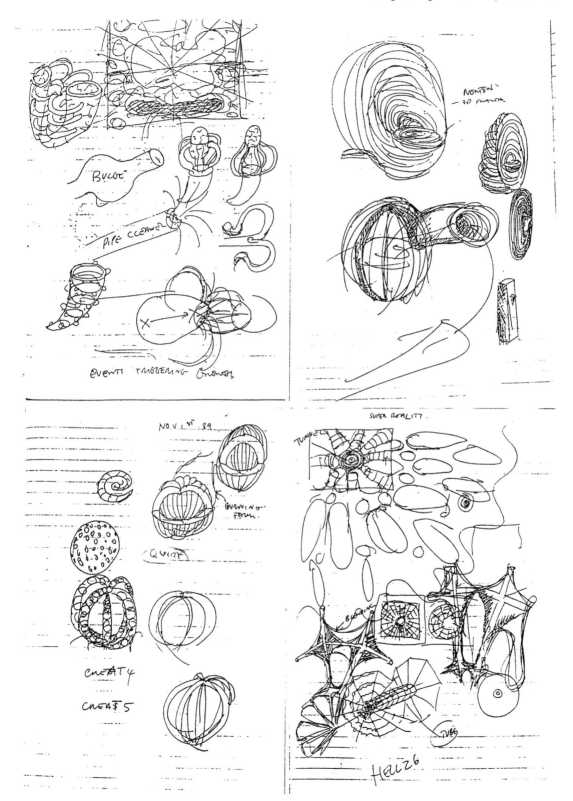

```
        build()
      branch(qq(30,1,1,999))       /* Gives branches */
        torus(0.09,0.04,0,1,0)
        texid(2)
        ribs(qq(24,1,1,999))
        stack(0.03)
        bend(qq(12,1,1,360))
        twist(qq(12,1,1,360))
        grow(qq(0.985,0.01,0.01,999))
        )
        ¢
*/
   (
   horn
    build()
     sphere(0.1)
     ribs( qq(10,1,5,999) )
     grow( qq(0.982,0.1,0.1,999) )
       stack( qq(0.07,0.1,0,999) )
       bend( qq(5.0,5) )
       twist( qq(5,10) )
     fracnum(4¢3¢2¢1)
     orient(bend( qq(45,5) ) ¢ grow( qq(0.98,0.1,0.1,999) ))
    )
 /*
    (
   horn
    build()
     ellipsoid(0.06,0.09,0.05)
     ribs(20)
       stack(0.04)
       bend(5)
     grow(0.97)
     fracnum(4¢3¢2¢1)
     orient( bend(10)¢ grow(0.97))
    )
  */
  /*
        ¢
        (
        horn
        build()
        pic
       texid(3)
        ribs(1)
        stack(0.32)
        bend(5)
        twist(90)
        grow(0.9954)
        )
    */
        ;

 /*autorange(pic);*/
  csg(gazz)
```

Chapter 5
Mutator

The previous chapter shows how the artist designs forms and collects them into families. Each family has countless members laid out in a multidimensional form space, and the artist is now faced with the problem of searching for the most aesthetic forms in this space. Form space may be explored in contrasting ways. In one traditional approach the artist consciously analyses what it is that makes forms the way they are, and acts based on the analysis. 'It think this object needs more bend; I will connect the bend gene to a slider and experiment'.

Subjective search   *Mutator* provides a second way for an artist to explore form space. The artist makes subjective decisions about the quality of forms. Not only does the artist not *need* to think in terms of the structure definition. *Mutator* does not *permit* changes based on such analytic knowledge. This contrasts with almost all other interfaces used in computer art: they make analytic use easier; *Mutator* escapes from it completely.

  Mutator currently implements pure subjective exploration. In practice, it will be part of a hybrid system that also supports traditional techniques, so that the artist uses both *Mutator* and analytic interaction.

  This chapter describes *Mutator*, and how it is used to search for interesting forms and to save their genes in a gene bank (see Figure 2.10). It first describes the basic *Mutator* mechanism, random mutation of the genes by the computer, and selection of forms by the artist (Figure 5.1). The following sections deal with various enhancements: controlling the mutation rate, steering the progress of the *Mutator* session to speed up the search, and marrying forms. It then describes the various control structures to view the evolutionary progress, and to output genes and forms for use by other systems. Finally, we discuss some work in progress and future plans.

FormSynth and   The initial concepts for *Mutator* came from *Form Synth* (Latham 1989)
biomorphs   (Chapter 3) and elements of the two dimensional *Biomorph* system (Dawkins 1986). Biomorph demonstrates, in zoological terms, the power of natural selection. *Mutator* harnesses this power, and extends it with the controls described below to make a fast and effective exploration tool. It is these

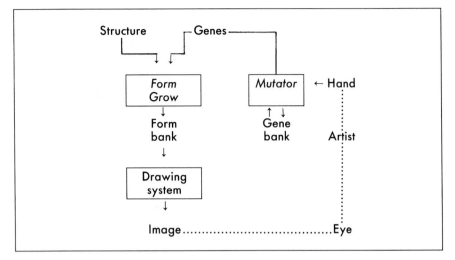

Figure 5.1. *Mutator* keeps a bank of genes and their forms which it displays to the artist. Based on judgements made by the artist, *Mutator* generates and displays new forms, assisting the artist to search for interesting forms and bank the results.

extra features which provide the precision required to make *Mutator* a valuable tool for the artist:

$$
\begin{array}{lcl}
\text{structure} & = & \text{expression} \\
\text{genotype} & = & \text{genes} \\
\text{phenotype} & = & \text{computer form}
\end{array}
$$

Basic method

The basic *Mutator* operates by taking a starting gene vector and placing eight mutated gene vectors into the gene bank. *Form Grow* is used to generate a form from each gene vector, and the nine forms are displayed by the *Mutator* layout component (Figure 5.2). This group of nine forms is called a *Mutator frame* (Figure 5.3).

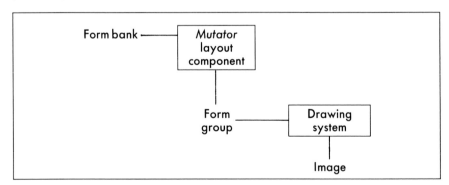

Figure 5.2. The *Mutator* layout component collects forms from the bank and lays them out to create a form group which is displayed.

Figure 5.3. A frame of nine mutations. The parent is in the centre surrounded by offspring.

The artist chooses his favourite displayed form as the current form by selecting it with the mouse. Menu item **breed** (Figure 5.4) uses the current form as the start for a new mutation iteration. The genes of this form are

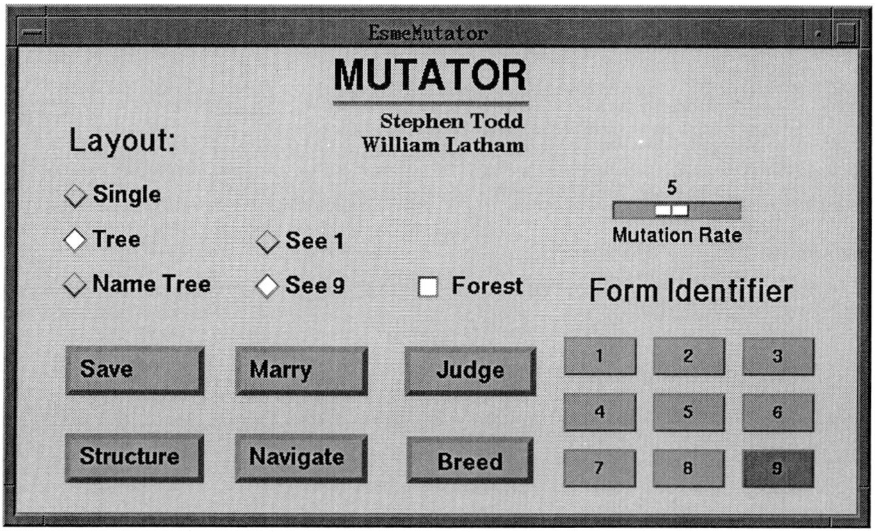

Figure 5.4. Main *Mutator* menu.

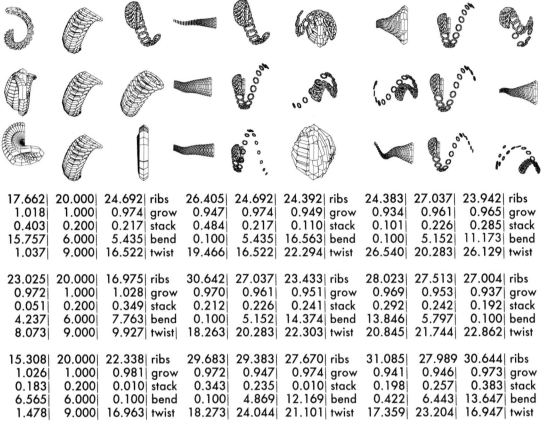

17.662		20.000		24.692	ribs	26.405		24.692		24.392	ribs	24.383		27.037		23.942	ribs
1.018		1.000		0.974	grow	0.947		0.974		0.949	grow	0.934		0.961		0.965	grow
0.403		0.200		0.217	stack	0.484		0.217		0.110	stack	0.101		0.226		0.285	stack
15.757		6.000		5.435	bend	0.100		5.435		16.563	bend	0.100		5.152		11.173	bend
1.037		9.000		16.522	twist	19.466		16.522		22.294	twist	26.540		20.283		26.129	twist
23.025		20.000		16.975	ribs	30.642		27.037		23.433	ribs	28.023		27.513		27.004	ribs
0.972		1.000		1.028	grow	0.970		0.961		0.951	grow	0.969		0.953		0.937	grow
0.051		0.200		0.349	stack	0.212		0.226		0.241	stack	0.292		0.242		0.192	stack
4.237		6.000		7.763	bend	0.100		5.152		14.374	bend	13.846		5.797		0.100	bend
8.073		9.000		9.927	twist		18.263		20.283		22.303	twist	20.845		21.744		22.862	twist
15.308		20.000		22.338	ribs	29.683		29.383		27.670	ribs	31.085		27.989	30.644	ribs
1.026		1.000		0.981	grow	0.972		0.947		0.974	grow	0.941		0.946		0.973	grow
0.183		0.200		0.010	stack	0.343		0.235		0.010	stack	0.198		0.257		0.383	stack
6.565		6.000		0.100	bend	0.100		4.869		12.169	bend	0.422		6.443		13.647	bend
1.478		9.000		16.963	twist	18.273		24.044		21.101	twist	17.359		23.204		16.947	twist

Figure 5.5. Three successive *Mutator* steps with the genes of the forms. The five genes for each form (ribs, grow, stack, bend and twist) are printed vertically.

used as a new state, and a new frame with mutations from this state is created and banked. Iteration of the generation and selection processes continues until the artist is satisfied with one of the forms (Figure 5.5).

Mutator currently displays the form based on the current position in the centre of the frame. The other forms are arranged in pairs, displayed opposite each other. The members of each pair use the same mutation vector with opposite orientations (Figure 5.6). This has some attraction, but reduces the number of independent mutations available. *Mutator* can work with any number of forms per frame, but experience shows that nine forms are generally suitable (Figure 5.7).

s+r1	s	s+r2
s+r3	s	s−r3
s−r2	s	s−r1

Figure 5.6. Layout of forms in a *Mutator* frame. s is the gene vector for the starting form, and r1, r2 and r3 are random mutation vectors. The form for s is repeated for consistency with the layout used with steering.

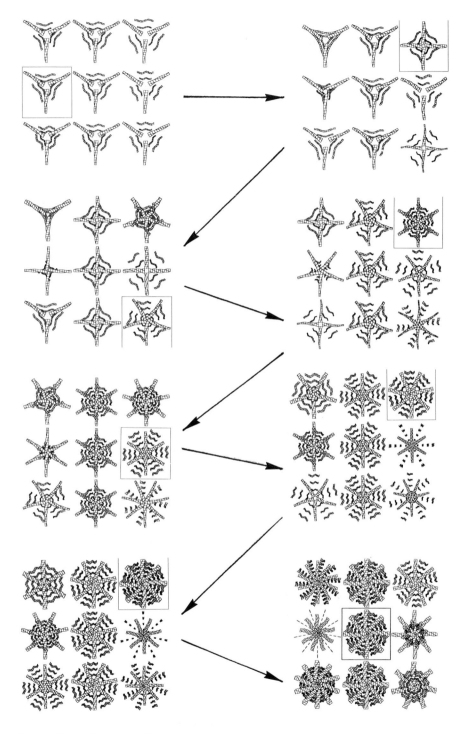

Figure 5.7. The result of eight *Mutator* steps. The forms in the final frame are clearly from the same family as those in the first frame, but there is a large variation over the steps.

Frog graphics   *Mutator* can be thought of as *frog* graphics (Figure 5.12a). The frog jumps to a new point, and where the frog lands it reveals the predetermined form. *Mutator* currently uses six frogs at each **breed** selection.

Evolutionary fruit   Another way of thinking of *Mutator* is as an evolutionary fruit machine.
machine   *Mutator* spins the gene values: the user takes the interesting positions, and pushes the nudge button in the hope that small *Mutator* moves will hit the jackpot form.

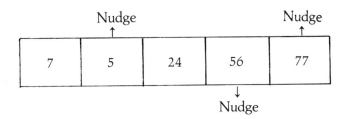

Scale of computer forms

The scale of forms generated by *Form Grow* from the same structure varies a huge amount as the parameters change: a single family can easily include both sculptural whales and insects. This is inconvenient when viewed on the *Mutator* screen, and also for animation. *Mutator* and the animation software automatically scale all computer forms to fit into a standard size box, and the artist has no idea how big the forms are prior to this scaling.

Control of gene space

Distance in gene   Different genes naturally have different scales. For example, a typical horn
space   has sphere radius around 0.5 to 2 acus†, whereas twist is measured in hundreds of degrees. *Mutator* naturally adapts itself where these differences are not too great, a factor of two for example, but it does not behave well with large factors. *Mutator* uses a vector *vdiff* that sets a reasonable value for random changes to each gene: thus a sphere radius may reasonably change by 0.1 in a single mutation, but a twist value of 720° may change by 50° (Figure 5.8).[4]

---

†acu: artist's creative unit

---

[4]*vdiff* effectively defines a transformation between gene space and a Cartesian space. The Cartesian metric corresponds roughly to the perceptual difference between forms. Extending *vdiff* to a matrix permits the designer to indicate that genes are not independent. For example, increasing the stack height and decreasing the sphere size have similar visual effects, so these genes are not independent. The use of *vdiff* as a matrix was suggested by the mathematical uncleanliness of distributing * over a vector.

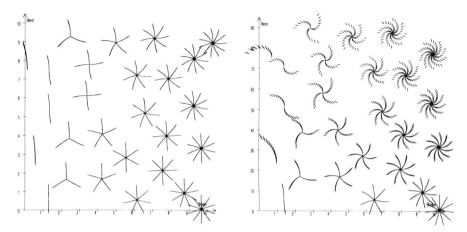

Figure 5.8. Distance in gene space. There are two genes for these forms: the numbers of blades increasing to the right, and the bend of each blade increasing vertically. The group on the left uses the same scaling for each gene giving very little visual change for the bend. The group on the right uses a much greater range for bend genes than for blade genes to give a more even visual change.

Boundary of gene space

Some genes may not validly take on certain values; for example, a growth value may not be negative. There may be other values that the artist does not wish to use (for example, horns with too many ribs), or deep fractal recursion may be too expensive to process. Vectors *vmin* and *vmax* define limits in gene space to which *Mutator* confines itself.

These limits should only be used to mark off no go areas that are in some way dangerous to explore. It is not worth setting limits to impose soft constraints such as 'I do not think that I want to explore this part of space', because the artist's directions will naturally make *Mutator* avoid them.

The function *eg* provides a convenient way in which to set up a starting default value for a gene, and if required its rate of change and minimum and maximum permissible values (Figure 5.9). The change rate defaults to 10 % of the initial value, and minimum and maximum values default to the largest negative and positive real numbers.

```
horn                             /*  define a horn                            */
    sphere (3)                   /*  made of spheres of radius 3              */
    ribs (eg (20, 2, 10))        /*  number of items                         */
    grow (eg (1.4, 0.1, 0.5))    /*  shrinkage or expansion of elements  */
    stack (eg (20))              /*  raise elements up to for stack          */
    bend (eg (90))               /*  bend it                                  */
    twist (eg (720), eg (1))     /*  and twist, amount and radius            */
```

Figure 5.9. Using 'eg' to define a structure and control *Mutator*. The structure designer has specified that the horn will be made up of spheres. Initially, there will be 20 spheres, and never fewer than 10. The designer considers that adding two spheres will make a similar amount of visual difference as changing the growth factor by 0.1, or twisting by an extra 72°.

Implementation *Mutator* uses five global vectors: *vstate* for the vector of the 'main' form from which others have been mutated, *vinit* for for the initial state using the default gene values, *vdiff* to control the rate of change for each slot, and *vmin* and *vmax* for the minimum and maximum allowable values. To create each mutated vector *vmut*, *Mutator* makes a vector (*vrand*) of the appropriate width with each slot a random number in the range [-1..1], and applies:

$$vmut := vstate + randrate * vdiff * vrand;$$
$$vmut := (vmut \max vmin) \min vmax;$$

randrate is a global scalar to control overall mutation rate (see below), and +, *, *min* and *max* are infix operators that distribute over vectors.

Instability of gene space Gene space is not as regular as we have implied. A highly stacked form is very sensitive to changes in bend, whereas a squat form is not so sensitive. Depending on how the structure is set up, there may be unstable volumes of space in which tiny changes to the genes make a huge change to the computer form (Figure 5.10). We have not had any problems for the structures we use, but it is possible that *Mutator* could become very awkward in unstable parts of gene space.

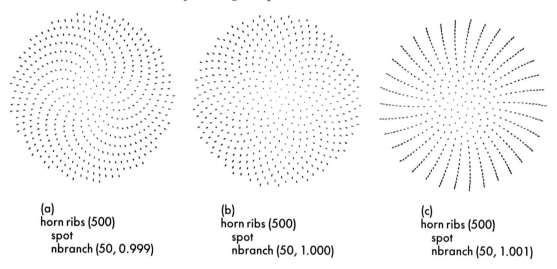

(a)
horn ribs (500)
spot
nbranch (50, 0.999)

(b)
horn ribs (500)
spot
nbranch (50, 1.000)

(c)
horn ribs (500)
spot
nbranch (50, 1.001)

Figure 5.10. Instability of gene space. The only difference between the three examples is the change of a gene from 0.999 to 1.000 to 1.001.

Small irregularities of gene space do not affect the operation of *Mutator*, and the artist can make use of them to get unexpected results, a creative use of chaos.

Mutation rate

The global variable *randrate* controls the overall degree of mutation; that is, how far the frogs jump. A high value gives widely differing mutations, and

Figure 5.11. The artist uses a high mutation rate at the start of the session to quickly search the form space. As he nears an acceptable form he moves to lower mutation rates to 'hone' the details of the form.

is suitable at the start of a *Mutator* session to travel across a wide volume of search space. As mutation continues and approaches a 'good' form, lower mutation rates give more sensitive control (Figure 5.11).

Menu options give the artist a means by which to alter the mutation rate as required. In early experiments, the rate was automatically lowered as the session continued. No formula was found that performed this automatic lowering of rate in a convenient way, and so *Mutator* reverted to the manual method.

Good forms, bad forms, and steering

When the artist is presented with several mutations, just to choose the best one is in some sense a waste of the other mutations. *Mutator* presents the artist with the opportunity to make subjective judgements on all mutations before moving to the next iteration. From the artist's point of view this captures the idea of judgement, and from the system point of view it considerably speeds up the search of form space as it allows the artist to steer the navigation and reduces the number of jumps to reach a target. We do not have millions of years to spare selecting from completely random mutations (Figure 5.12), so these techniques for accelerated evolution are important.

Judgement is made by selecting a mutation, and then making the menu choice **very good, good, bad** or **very bad**. Feedback is provided by a tick or cross against each form, scaled to indicate goodness or badness. When the artist selects **breed**, the next mutation step occurs, based on the mutation chosen as best during judgement.

Implementation of steering

The implementation of this judgement is based on a global state direction vector *vdir* that indicates the general direction the artist is steering in state space, and tells the frog which way to jump. Selections of **good** and **bad** on a mutation with vector *vmut* invoke, respectively:

$$vdir := beta * vdir + alpha * (vmut - vstate)$$
$$vdir := beta * vdir - alpha * (vmut - vstate)$$

When the next mutation step occurs, it establishes the new state *vstate* from the vector *vbest* for the best mutation using:

$$vstate := vbest + vdir$$

Mutations are made from the new *vstate*. Our current values for *alpha* and *betas* are 0.9 and 0.5. As *beta* + *alpha* is greater than 1, this means that as *vdir* is changed its length is likely to increase. *vdir* represents a rate of travel as well as a direction, and this rate increases as a good direction is established. As the artist nears a good form and manually reduces *randrate*, *vdir* is also reduced more quickly to prevent overshooting the form.

The form for vector *vbest* from the old frame is displayed top centre in the new frame to provide a visual link between them. The form for the new state *vstate* is displayed in the centre of the frame, and the form for vector *vstate* + *vdir* is displayed bottom centre. This last form goes twice as far from *vbest* along the steering direction as does *vstate* (Figure 5.13)

Another way to exploit **good** and **bad** decisions is to use particular forms as attractors and repellers in gene space that affect the generation of future mutations.

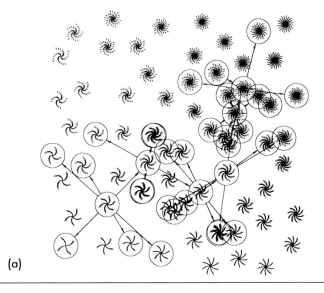

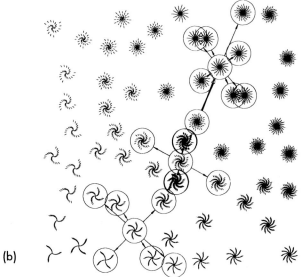

Figure 5.12. Using judgements to steer *Mutator*. (a) This shows an unsteered *Mutator* session moving into a region with many highly bent fan blades. The ringed forms are those visited during the session. The other forms remain undiscovered. The display shows the forms in two dimensional gene space together with arrows indicating mutation. The artist's only option at each step is to select the best form. For example, if one form has many blades and another has very bent blades the artist cannot take advantage of both. Many of the options available move back towards positions already visited, causing some jumble in the picture. (b) This shows the effect of steering. The artist again selects the mutation that gives the most complex form, but he also makes judgements on the other mutations. The heavy arrows indicate the movement made as the result of steering. The form selected by the artist (displayed by *Mutator* at the top of the new frame) is shown at the back of the heavy arrow. The form from which mutations are made (displayed by *Mutator* in the centre of the new frame) is shown at the head of the heavy arrow. The artist moved to the required area of form space in five mutation steps without steering and in two steps with steering.

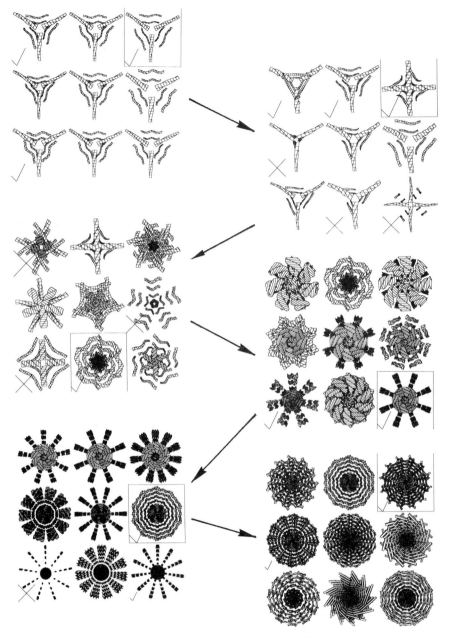

Figure 5.13. The result of six *Mutator* steps with steering. There is more variation in these six steps than in the eight steps without steering (Figure 5.7). The layout of the frames is:

b+d+r1	b	b+d+r2
b+d+r3	b+d	sb+d−r3
b+d−r2	b+2*d	b+d−r1

where *b* is the gene vector for the best form from the previous frame, *d* is the direction vector, and *r1*, *r2* and *r3* are random mutation vectors. The new central state vector is *vstate*=*b*+*d*.

Preferred directions in state space

The use of genes by the structure designer may not correspond to ideas of the user of *Mutator*, though often they are the same person. For example, the structure may define colours using red, green and blue (RGB), whereas the artist operates (subconsciously) in a space closer to hue, saturation and value (HSV). Even though the form of the structure defines a basis for the search space, *Mutator* tries to ignore this; for example, mutation uses a randomly oriented vector in search space, rather than making mutations along randomly selected axes.

The aim is that *Mutator* should gradually 'learn' the artist's thought model. This aim is partially realized by the direction vector, which is generally not aligned with a basis vector. More work is required in this area. One idea is to permit an **arrived** menu option, which indicates that the artist has reached a satisfactory position in the direction of travel *vdir.vdir* is reset, and future mutation is temporarily constrained to be orthogonal to the old direction of travel.

Marriage

A user of *Mutator* arranges a marriage by selecting two parents. The menu choice **other–parent** selects the first parent of a marriage, and the menu choice **marry** make a marriage between this first parent and the current form. Seven children are created by **marry** (all one operation, we do not follow nature here), and the new frame of parents and children is displayed. Inbreeding between two mutations in the same frame is useful for honing or enhancing a particular characteristic of a form. A marriage between distantly related mutations generates interesting new forms which inherit some characteristics from each parent (Figure 5.14).

Child creation shares mixtures of genes from the parents. There are various mixing algorithms (Figure 5.15, 5.16). At present, each mixing algorithm is chosen by its own menu item. This is an undesirable expedient to help experimentation with the algorithms. It imposes an additional analytic decision on the artist: 'What kind of marriage do I want?' (Figure 5.16).

There is no theoretical reason to limit *Mutator* marriages to two parents: a five parent marriage is possible, for example. We are experimenting with multi-parent marriages which look like being a very powerful tool.

Random selection marriage   Random selection generates children by setting each vector slot from the corresponding slot of one of the parents' vectors. The choice of parent is made randomly for each vector slot. Thus vectors $(1,1,1)$ and $(2,2,2)$ might create children $(1,2,1)$, $(1,2,2)$, and so on (Figure 5.17).

inbreeding

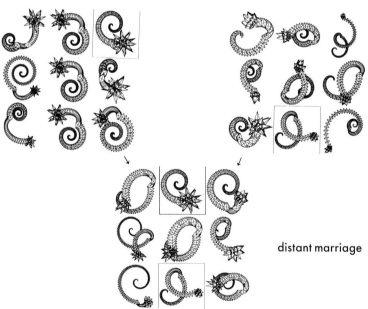

distant marriage

Figure 5.14. Random inbreeding and distant marriage. At the top we see the results of inbreeding. Two similar parent forms are taken from the same *Mutator* frame (above) resulting in a frame (below) of similar inbred forms. Inbreeding is used for fine tuning forms. At the bottom we see the results of marriage of distant cousins, drawn from two different *Mutator* frames (above). The result (below) is a much more varied frame of forms, useful for fast but controlled exploration of form space. Both examples use random gene selection for breeding offspring. The parents are displayed at the top and bottom of the breeding frame and are both highlighted by boxes.

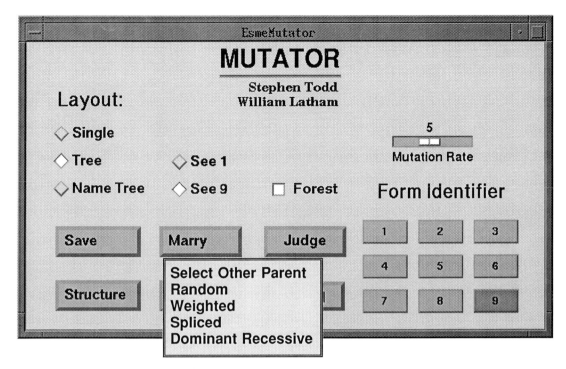

Figure 5.15. *Mutator* marriage submenu.

Random selection is biased towards the axis of the form space imposed by the genes in the structure. This bias is removed by unbiased random selection, which performs random selection in a rotated gene space. It places child vectors on the hypersphere that passes through the two parents, and has its centre halfway between them. Thus parents $(-0.7,-0.7,0)$ and $(0.7,0,0.7)$ can produce children $(0,1,0)$ and $(0,-0.5,0.866)$.

Weighted average marriage In-betweening takes a weighted average of the two parent vectors. Vectors $(1,1,1)$ and $(2,2,2)$ might create children $(1.3,1.3,1.3)$ and $(1.6,1.6,1.6)$. Random weighted average works slot-by-slot, using a different weight in each slot. Thus vectors $(1,1,1)$ and $(2,2,2)$ might create children $(1.3,1.7,1.4)$ and $(1.5,1.2,1.9)$.

Experience shows that averages are not usually good at producing radically different forms, but very useful for fine tuning (Figure 5.18).

spliced

weighted average

Figure 5.16. Spliced (left above), weighted average (left below) and dominant recessive (right). The spliced and weighted average marriages give the frames of the two parents (above) and the breeding frame (below). The dominant recessive breeding rule depends on the judgements used in creating the parent forms. The diagram shows two generations above the marriage with an indication (tick=good, cross=bad) of the judgements made. The 180° mace form has been very favourably judged in deriving the parent on the left. Its genes have therefore become dominant, and all the offspring include a similar mace form. No strong judgements have been made in deriving the right parents, so it does not impose any dominant characteristics on the children. In all three examples the parents are located at the top centre and bottom centre of the lower boxes.

(11,22,13)	(11,12,13)	(11,22,23)
(11,12,23)	(11,12,13)	(21,22,13)
(21,12,13)	(21,22,23)	(21,12,23)

Figure 5.17. Arangements of child forms. When the new frame of forms is displayed, one parent is displayed top centre and the other parent bottom centre. These have genes (11, 12, 13) and (21, 22, 23) in the example. Other children are arranged in opposite pairs, so if a gene is chosen from one parent by one child, it is chosen from the other parent in the opposite child.

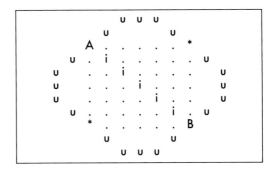

Figure 5.18. Form space accessed by different kinds of marriage. This shows a fragment of two dimensional gene space, and points that may be reached from parents A and B by random selection (*), by unbiased random selection (u), random weighted average (.) and in-betweening (i).

Grouping of genes The genes for a structure are often naturally grouped. For example; when a form consists of many subforms it is reasonable to group the genes of each subform. Grouped gene child generation uses the same random number (for selection or weighting) for all slots in a group.

One grouping *Mutator* supports is splicing, which relies on the ordering of the genes. The first n genes are chosen from one parent, and the remainder from the other. Thus vectors $(1,1,1,1,1)$ and $(2,2,2,2,2)$ might create children $(1,1,1,2,2)$, $(2,1,1,1,1)$ and $(1,1,2,2,2)$.

Splicing has the opposite effect to unbiased random selection. It extracts more information rather than less from the precise way in which the structure is written. The children created derive more obviously recognizable features from their parents.

Dominant and The *Mutator* algorithm picks up the strongest characteristics of each parent. It
recessive genes uses the direction of travel when a form is generated to highlight slot values with which the artist is not fully satisfied. A fast moving gene is assumed to be a gene with which the artist is not happy and so is still experimenting, and so the gene is made *recessive* with a reduced chance of selection. Conversely, a slow moving value is taken to be dominant.

The formula used is shown below. The idea is a powerful, but we are still not happy with the details of the formula, and are experimenting with alternatives.

```
d1: = abs(vvdir1[i]); /* rate of movement of i'th gene for mother */
d2: = abs(vvdir2[i]); /* rate of movement of i'th gene for father */
if (d1 + d2) < 0.01
    break: = 0.5;        /* if both are slow moving, split 50:50 */
else
    break: = d1/(d1 + d2); /* break is high if mother gene recessive */
if random(0,1) < break then /* compare with a random number */
    choice: = 2;
else
    choice: = 1;
```

Suppose the *i*th gene is moving fast in the mother (recessive), and slowly in the father (dominant). Then *d1* is greater than *d2*, and so *break* is greater than 0.5. The *if* clause is likely to be true, and so *choice* is likely to be set to 2, giving the dominant father gene value to the offspring.

Marriage and scale   *Mutator* automatically rescales objects to a standard size, as mentioned above. Not only can whales and insects easily coexist under these circumstances, but they can breed and produce offspring as easily as two forms that would naturally be of the same size.

Evolutionary tree

As the mutation session continues, it creates an evolutionary history of the genes and forms in its bank, which the layout component displays in various ways controlled by its associated submenu (Figure 5.19). The menu item **up** moves to past frames. If **breed** is selected against a frame that already has mutated subframes, the session forms a tree. The artist may navigate the tree with menu items **up, down, left** and **right.**

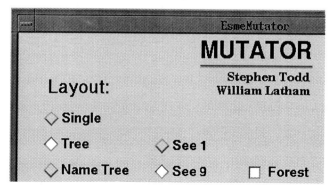

Figure 5.19. *Mutator evolutionary tree submenu.*

Figure 5.20. Evolving tree of forms, parent objects only. The artist has selected **tree** and **see1**. The *Mutator* layout component shows the parent forms for each frame in the evolutionary tree.

Mutator normally shows just one frame. The menu item **tree** displays the entire tree, and **single** reverts to a single frame display. *Mutator* normally shows all forms in each frame. The menu item **see1** displays only the initial form for each frame, and **see9** reverts to display of all forms in each frame (Figures 5.20, 5.21).

The artist may **jump** to any form in the bank either by pointing with the mouse if the form is in the current display, or by entering the gene bank code, which consists of the frame and mutation number: *Jump* helps the artist to move to other forms anywhere in the tree, and to prepare marriages between distantly related forms. When arranging a marriage between distant cousins, the artist jumps around the tree searching for a suitable mate.

Tree display may be simplified by a (temporary) **hide** of the current subtree, or a (permanent) **delete** which is like a lumberjack removing a branch of a tree forever. As trees become large, tree display becomes more important, so we have options to control the number of generations displayed both above and below the current frame (Figure 5.22).

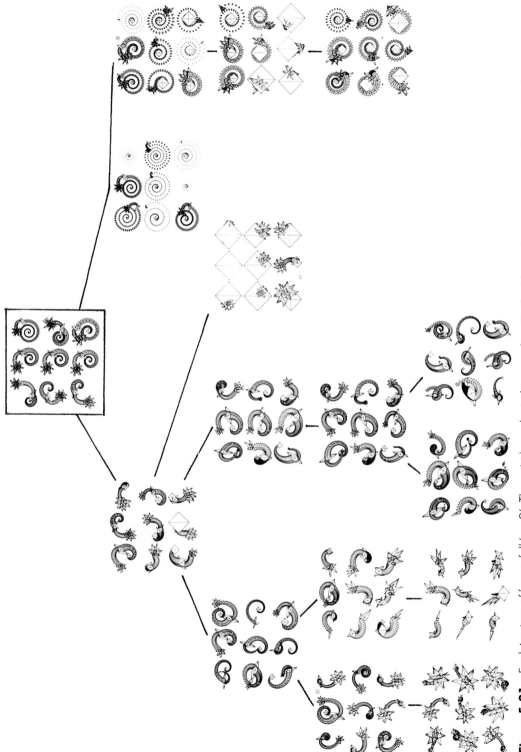

Figure 5.21. Evolving tree of forms, full 'see9'. The artist has selected **tree** and **see9**. The *Mutator* layout component shows in full the frames of the evolutionary tree.

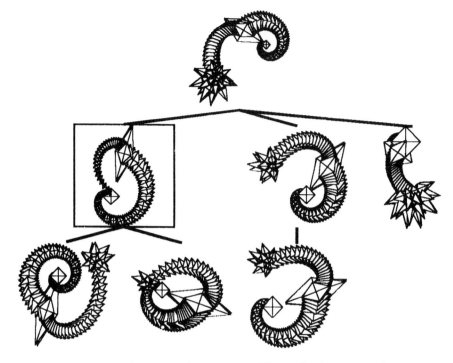

Figure 5.22. Extract from an evolutionary tree. The tree has become too large to display clearly, so the artist has restricted the display to include only frames between one level above and one level below the current frame. Cousin frames are not displayed.

Saving

The results of *Mutator* may be saved in a number of ways (Figure 5.23). The entire session is always logged, and may be restarted later. The current display may be saved as a WINSOM model file at any time for high quality batch rendering, whether the display mode is **single** or **tree**, and **see1** or **see9**. Genes for a favoured form or the entire bank may be dumped into a named gene file for later use as key forms in an animation. Naming conventions prevent the application of a gene vector to an inappropriate structure.

There is the potential to use artificial intelligence techniques such as neutral networks to classify the gene vectors in named gene files. This would try to capture the nature of *gothicness* from the gene file *gothic*. Similar work has already been done, but this sets itself the even more difficult task of analysis at the image level. Work by Voss[5] on the fractal dimension of images may well be a suitable tool for analysis.

---

[5]Private communication.

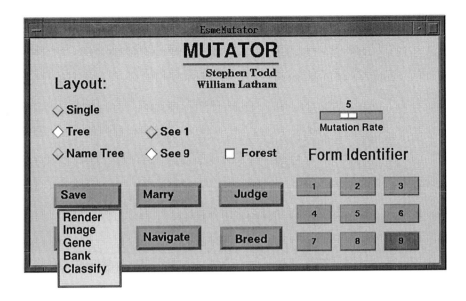

Figure 5.23. *Mutator* save submenu.

Further examples

Examples of *Mutator* being used on other aspects of artistic design are shown in: colour (Plate 31d,e), texture (Figure 5.24) and mathematical equations (Figure 5.25).

Figure 5.24. Mutation of texture. Various parameters of the texture such as thickness and brightness of each band have been used as the genes of the structure.

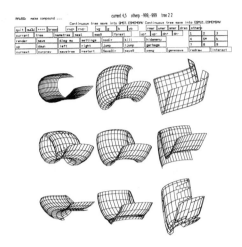

Figure 5.25. Mutation of mathematical equations. The equations are generated by interacting sine and cosine waves, with the genes controlling the 'constants' of the equations.

Nature, mutator and optimization

Nature   *Mutator* was designed to help artists explore form space by means of subjective decisions. The marriage algorithm and other enhancements were suggested as simulations of nature, and implemented to reduce the number of steps needed to find a required form. In nature, new forms of life are created by mutation and marriage. The fittest survive in a process of natural selection. In *Mutator*, the computer generates new forms, and the artist's judgements drive selection. Steering is one of the features that makes *Mutator* effective at searching form space quickly. Steering was implemented to meet the artist's wish to be able to make judgements on forms independently of breeding from them, and was not derived from a biological analog. However, some recent papers in biology suggest that real life mutation is quicker than would be expected for a purely random system, and that there is some mechanism other than natural selection steering intelligent mutation.

From the artist's viewpoint, using *Mutator* is like being a gardener.

$$\text{artist} = \text{gardener}$$

The gardener breeds, weeds out, destroys and selects forms to steer evolution, replacing 'survival of the fittest' by 'survival of the most aesthetic'.

Optimization   Another view of *Mutator* is as an optimization system. Both *Mutator* and optimization systems use the computer to generate alternative solutions, but the cost function in optimization is replaced by the artist's choice in *Mutator*.

The basic random mutation algorithm corresponds to Monte Carlo optimization (Metropolis *et al.*, 1953). The reduction of mutation rate as interaction continues is like the lowering of temperature in simulated annealing (Kirkpatrick, 1983). Making judgements of forms to define a steering direction in form space is analogous to steepest ascent optimization (Dixon *et al.*, 1978), and *Mutator* marriage corresponds to genetic optimization. The problems *Mutator* encounters in irregular parts of gene space are like the instabilities found when optimizing badly behaved functions.

These analogies are not precise, and *Mutator* has not captialized on them. Features of *Mutator* such as steering, inbreeding and the control of mutation rate already permit *Mutator* to be used artistically for honing in on a form. Future work will apply optimization techniques to *Mutator* with the aim of improving its speed, accuracy and stability.

Work in progress

Stucture mutation

Mutator as described so far only changes genes, and not the underlying structure. Many of the principles also apply to structure mutation (Figure 5.26), in particular the method of random mutation.

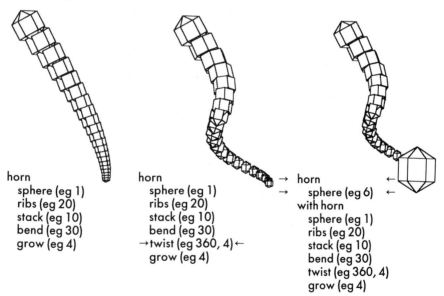

horn	horn	→	horn	←
sphere (eg 1)	sphere (eg 1)		sphere (eg 6)	←
ribs (eg 20)	ribs (eg 20)	→	with horn	
stack (eg 10)	stack (eg 10)		sphere (eg 1)	
bend (eg 30)	bend (eg 30)		ribs (eg 20)	
grow (eg 4)	→twist (eg 360, 4)←		stack (eg 10)	
	grow (eg 4)		bend (eg 30)	
			twist (eg 360, 4)	
			grow (eg 4)	

Figure 5.26. Structure mutation. The left hand structure is mutated to the middle one by adding an extra transform rule, and this is mutated to the right hand structure by the addition of an extra horn segment. Mutation can also shorten structures or interchange elements. In this example the genes are frozen, but it is possible simultaneously to mutate structure and genes.

Steering with mutated structures   Many of the more sophisticated aspects of *Mutator* are an important part of the fine control in its artistic use, and are more difficult to define with structure mutation. For example, steering requires not only the mutation of gene values at a given instant in time, but also the comparison of different sets of gene values. Structure mutation changes the position of genes: in the example shown in Figure 5.27 the 'grow' gene moves from position 5 to position 6. It is thus no longer adequate to keep a simple vector of genes, but the genes must be flagged by some position independent identifier (Figure 5.27).

```
                                                    →horn
                                                     →   sphere (eg rx = 6)
      horn                  horn                   with horn
         sphere (eg r = 1)     sphere (eg r = 1)      sphere (eg r = 1)
         ribs (eg n = 20)      ribs (eg n = 20)       ribs (eg n = 20)
         stack (eg st = 10)    stack (eg st = 10)     stack (eg st = 10)
         bend (eg be = 30)     bend (eg be = 30)      bend (eg be = 30)
                             →twist (eg tw = 360, 4)  twist (eg tw = 360, 4)
         grow (eg gr = 4)      grow (eg gr = 4)       grow (eg gr = 4)
```

Figure 5.27. This indicates how genes are tagged. In practice the tag names are being applied automatically by *Mutator*, and do *not* impose an extra burden on the structure designer.

Marriage and structure matching   Similarly, if breeding two forms with different structures is to have controlled results, the newly bred structure must preserve as much as possible of the parent structures. This requires an algorithm rather like a file compare algorithm to find a best match of the parent structures. Where both parents are descended from some common ancestor and flagged genes are used, then the flags that are common between the parents help guide the structure matching algorithm (Figure 5.28).

Simulated structure mutation   Structure mutation can be simulated by designing a complex structure and using conditional structure programming (see Chapter 8) to make some gene values switch different substructures on and off. The genes for the substructures are always there in a fixed position in the gene vector, but are not always used (Figure 5.29).

Sims (1991) has implemented a system that uses the ideas of *Biomorph* and *Mutator* and permits structure mutation, and has applied it to a wide variety of computer graphics techniques with very interesting results. However, his system does not allow for steering, and the structure matching algorithm used in marriage can give rather wild results. Therefore, we do not consider that this implementation yet gives enough control for artistic applications.

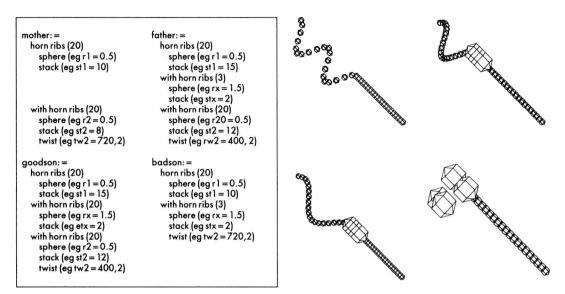

```
mother: =                      father: =
   horn ribs (20)                  horn ribs (20)
      sphere (eg r1 = 0.5)            sphere (eg r1 = 0.5)
      stack (eg st1 = 10)            stack (eg st1 = 15)
                                     with horn ribs (3)
                                        sphere (eg rx = 1.5)
                                        stack (eg stx = 2)
   with horn ribs (20)             with horn ribs (20)
      sphere (eg r2 = 0.5)            sphere (eg r20 = 0.5)
      stack (eg st2 = 8)             stack (eg st2 = 12)
      twist (eg tw2 = 720,2)        twist (eg rw2 = 400, 2)

goodson: =                     badson: =
   horn ribs (20)                  horn ribs (20)
      sphere (eg r1 = 0.5)            sphere (eg r1 = 0.5)
      stack (eg st1 = 15)            stack (eg st1 = 10)
   with horn ribs (20)             with horn ribs (3)
      sphere (eg rx = 1.5)            sphere (eg rx = 1.5)
      stack (eg etx = 2)             stack (eg stx = 2)
   with horn ribs (20)             twist (eg tw2 = 720,2)
      sphere (eg r2 = 0.5)
      stack (eg st2 = 12)
      twist (eg tw2 = 400,2)
```

Figure 5.28. Structure matching and marriage. The father and mother are both derived from the same structure, and so share tags *r1*, *st1*, *r2* and *st2*. The goodson structure respects these tags and produces a controlled result. The badson structure mixes the structures to give a structure not sensibly related to the parents with corrupt mixture of the stubby middle segment and long end segment. In this simple example the structures for both children are the same as the structure for one of the parents. This is not generally true when more complex structures are merged in marriage.

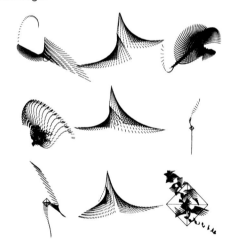

Figure 5.29. A *Mutator* frame in which the structure as well as the genes have been mutated.

Grouped genes

The artist usually uses *Mutator* to change all aspects of a sculpture simultaneously. He may identify certain aspects of a sculpture to work on at a given time: for example, first the basic body shape of the lobster, then the ribcage, and then the head. Work on the ribcage and head may lead the artist back to consider further tuning of the basic body shape, and so on.

Frozen genes   Identification of the different parts of the structure is done by naming groups of genes in the structure file. Sometimes we identify a substructure because we are happy with it, and we wish mutation to continue on the remaining genes with the genes of the identified substructure frozen. Alternatively, we identify a substructure because it is poor, and so mutate genes in the identified group only and freeze the remaining genes.

Grafting   We are currently making *Form Grow* automatically group genes by horn segment, with a segment identified by pointing at it with the mouse. This will also be useful for highly controlled marriages (Figure 5.30), and for interactively constructing new structures from fragments of old ones. The artist gardener is using new splicing tools in his exploration and exploitation of form space. This artistic gene splicing is like a real gardener grafting the stem of a decorative rose on to strong root stock, though with *Mutator* there are no problems with further breeding from the hybrid.

Grafting and the use of a mouse for substructure selection will also help an artist to assemble new structures in a very direct and graphical manner. This is an example of the mixing of subjective mutation with analytic working.

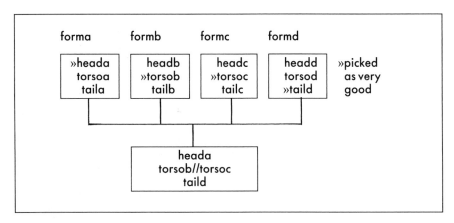

Figure 5.30. Highly controlled marriage. There are four computer forms visible: forma, formb, formc and formd, each with the same head, torso and tail structure. The artist points in turn at heada, torsob, torsoc and taild, indicating that they are good features. The result of the marriage produces forms which all have the head of forma and the tail of formd. The torsos are made by marrying the genes of torsob and torsoc.

Continuous evolution

The current version of *Mutator* works very much in two phases. In the first phase the computer creates and displays the mutations for a new frame, and the artist waits. In the second phase the artist interacts with the frame, and the computer is more or less idle. This is no problem for simple forms, for which a new frame is created and displayed very quickly. Where each form contains several thousand primitives, though, the artist must wait many seconds for the display of a complete frame, which reduces the benefits of *Mutator*.

An alternative is for the computer to continuously prepare new forms, some by mutation and some as children of a marriage. New forms are displayed as they complete. Old forms are allowed to age and die. Mutation continues even without interaction, but interaction directs the exploration as with the implemented system. Such a system should improve the friendliness of *Mutator*, and also its 'natural' feel as an independent evolution of forms from which the user selects. It will also increase its impact as an artwork that could be shown continuously in a gallery being used by the artist.

The continuous version of *Mutator* will not place forms into nine regular boxes, but place them more or less at random on the screen or in three dimensional space (Figure 5.31). Old forms will move to the back, with new ones being created at the front. Alternatively, forms may be laid out according to their position in gene space, with a continuously tumbling multidimensional viewing transform.

Figure 5.31. Forms laid out in a continuous *Mutator* session much as they would be in an animation such as the film *Mutations*.

SAFARI and In the world of virtual reality the process of interaction becomes more like
virtual reality hunting than gardening. We are combining the natural representation of
evolution depicted in our animations with the interactive selection processes
of *Mutator* in a system called *SAFARI* (Selection of Artistic Forms with an
Artificial Reality Interface). We need considerably more computer power
before *SAFARI* becomes effective. *SAFARI* is a virtual reality system in
which the artist hunts in the artificial sculpture garden:

artist = hunter

The rifle fires many kinds of shot that correspond to the items on the *Mutator*
menu: bullets to inject mutation causing drugs, deadly poison, aphrodisiacs,
and so on.

A destructive user hunts to kill, but an artist uses *SAFARI* to hunt for
exciting new forms of life and control an evolving population of sculptures
in an accelerated evolution environment. Another possibility is to let several
hunters loose at once, each with a different idea of what the hunt is about,
and to include predators which automatically kill forms under certain
circumstances, such as when the screen is too full or the horns are too
complex.

Autonomous mutation

One of the purposes of artistic systems is to allow the artist to express
general ideas, and to have the computer undertake much of the hard work.
Autonomous mutation operates by the artist initially identifying features
such as surface area, and the computer measuring these features and
performing selections based on them; for example, randomly breed a family
of forms, select the form with the largest surface area and repeat the breed
and selection process many times. In real life, lung shapes evolve to
maximize surface area and so improve breathing ability and survival, and the
results have very interesting and sometimes artistic shapes. We will
experiment to see whether the simulation of these evolution processes on
the computer will help the artist to derive new and interesting forms.

From the computer science point of view, autonomous mutation replaces
Mutator with a standard system to optimize a stated function. The interesting
task is to combine autonomous mutation with artist controlled mutation. For
example, a jeweller wishes to use as little silver as possible, but not at the
expense of the artistic design. The system may highlight forms that are most
economical, but leave the artistic decision to the jeweller.

Potential applications

This chapter described the application of *Mutator* to form selection. The
implementation is general: *Mutator* supports any process that is driven by a

gene vector. There are two important constraints on the application of *Mutator*. The application domain must be mostly smooth in the sense that small changes to the genes or structure make small changes to the result. The generation of a visual result from the structure and genes must be fast: we would like to use *Mutator* as a tool for controlling animation timings, but animation generation is too slow.

Even people who are used to working analytically will perform certain tasks much better in a subjective way. Potential applications of *Mutator* include the selection of a viewpoint for multidimensional data, setting control parameters in scientific visualization, helping witnesses to prepare Identikit pictures of suspects, education, and even financial modelling. In this application, the structure designer would be an economist, and the user of *Mutator* a manager exploring possible outcomes of parameters such as reinvestment rates.

Summary

Mutator is a general purpose interface that assists exploration of multi-dimensional gene spaces. It relies on the definition of a structure which produces a form or other visible result for any position in gene space. The structure is defined using conventional programming, though *Mutator* is also beginning to help here.

Mutator is driven by subjective user choices such as **good** and **bad**. Different *Mutator* algorithms support random exploration of space, directed steering, and generation of hybrid children of a marriage.

Mutator derives its methods from processes of nature, and was partly inspired by a simulation of natural selection. These methods are related to Monte Carlo, simulated annealing and genetic optimization techniques.

Conclusion

Certain aspects of *Mutator* still need development and tuning: detailed control of the steering and child generation algorithms, menu handling, and the sharing of control between the computer and the artist. Application of optimization techniques will help with tuning, and higher level programming tools with the other aspects.

Mutator has proved itself in some aspects of form design, and is ready to be tested in other applications.

Use of *Mutator* for the design of forms and animations has already produced very promising results. Some artists feel that it provides a genuinely new way of working, and it has certainly led to the creation of forms that would not have been created by other methods (Figure 5.32).

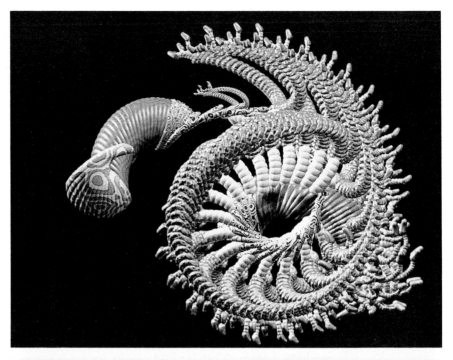

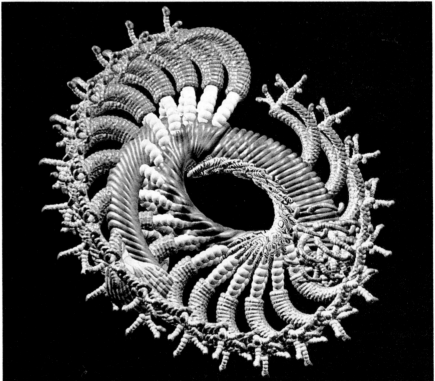

Figure 5.32. Two 'final' evolved forms resuting from the use of a *Mutator* session.

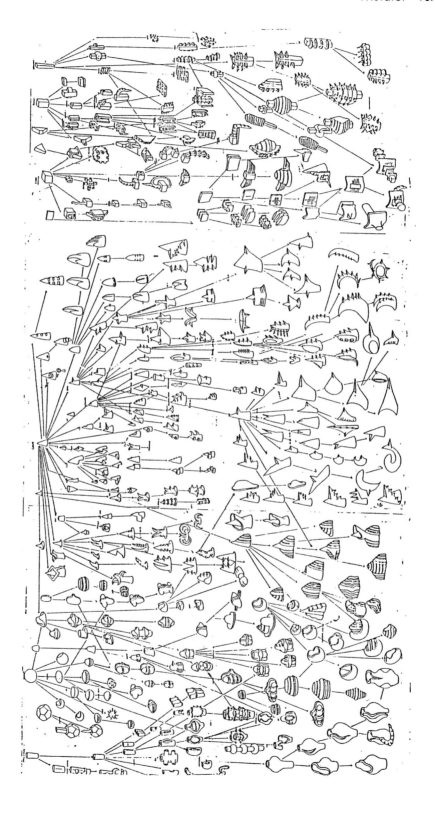

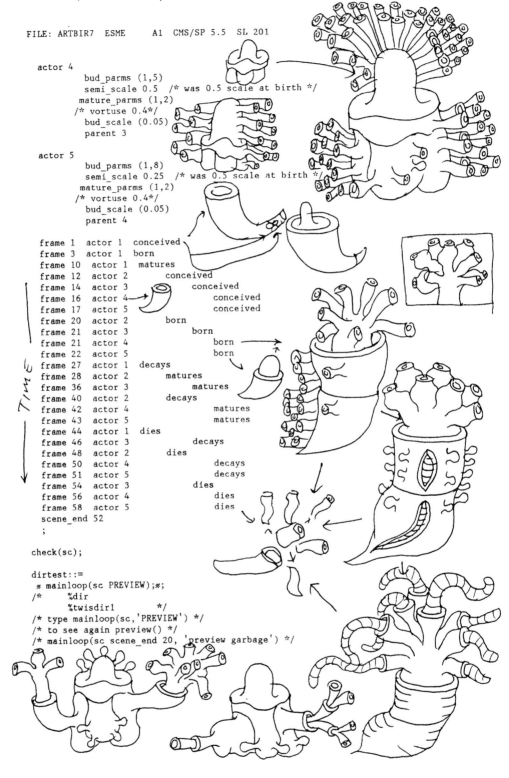

```
FILE: ARTBIR7  ESME     A1  CMS/SP 5.5  SL 201

    actor 4
            bud_parms (1,5)
            semi_scale 0.5   /* was 0.5 scale at birth */
          mature_parms (1,2)
         /* vortuse 0.4*/
            bud_scale (0.05)
            parent 3

    actor 5
            bud_parms (1,8)
            semi_scale 0.25  /* was 0.5 scale at birth */
          mature_parms (1,2)
         /* vortuse 0.4*/
            bud_scale (0.05)
            parent 4

    frame 1    actor 1   conceived
    frame 3    actor 1   born
    frame 10   actor 1   matures
    frame 12   actor 2        conceived
    frame 14   actor 3           conceived
    frame 16   actor 4              conceived
    frame 17   actor 5              conceived
    frame 20   actor 2        born
    frame 21   actor 3           born
    frame 21   actor 4              born
    frame 22   actor 5              born
    frame 27   actor 1   decays
    frame 28   actor 2        matures
    frame 36   actor 3           matures
    frame 40   actor 2        decays
    frame 42   actor 4              matures
    frame 43   actor 5              matures
    frame 44   actor 1   dies
    frame 46   actor 3           decays
    frame 48   actor 2        dies
    frame 50   actor 4              decays
    frame 51   actor 5              decays
    frame 54   actor 3           dies
    frame 56   actor 4              dies
    frame 58   actor 5              dies
    scene_end 52
    ;

  check(sc);

  dirtest::=
   * mainloop(sc PREVIEW);*;
   /*     %dir
          %twisdir1          */
   /* type mainloop(sc,'PREVIEW') */
   /* to see again preview() */
   /* mainloop(sc scene_end 20, 'preview garbage') */
```

Time

Chapter 6

Animating evolution

This chapter describes the systems we use for creating animations. In our earliest animation, *The Conquest of Form*, the view of the rigid forms moved but the forms themselves did not change – so called 'view animation'. Later in *A Sequence from the Evolution of Form* the forms metamorphosed using a technique called *gene interpolation*,[6] but only a single form was visible at any one time. Our latest animation *Mutations* illustrates the process of a surreal evolution, involving breeding and growth, with many forms animating with complex interactions. This uses software to describe the individual processes (*Grow*, *Movedown*), timing software (*Life Cycle*) based on a biological clock, and software (*Director*) to provide overall control.

View animation

Our first animation, *The Conquest of Form*, did not involve forms changing shape; it was only the view of the forms that changed. The purpose was to emphasize that the objects were genuine three dimensional forms, and to give the viewer a chance to comprehend them. In the simplest animation we moved around the object, as if walking around a sculpture in a gallery (Figure 6.1). When the form is displayed in a void with no background reference, it is impossible to distinguish between the viewer walking round a stationary form and a stationary viewer looking at a rotating form.

The computer view is not as constrained as a person or a camera. We took advantage of this to provide views from the inside of hollow objects, and to animate these with a fly-through of a tube form (Plate 12).

Flying through a sculpture makes use of the fact that the form is understood by the computer, so the computer is able to work out the path of the fly-through, and the artist only has to control the speed. Computer generation of the view is not quite as straightforward as it seems, as we have to set up the viewing direction as well as the viewing position. In our first attempt, the view was set up to point along the orientation of the elements within the form, which gave us a skewed view (Figure 6.2). It was as if in

---

[6]This is usually called *parameter interpolation*, but *gene interpolation* fits better with our terminology.

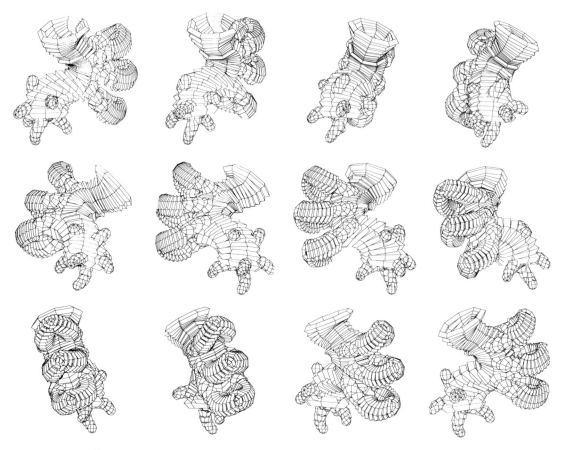

Figure 6.1. Frames from an animation created by rotating a fixed form. As there is no background we cannot tell the difference between rotating the form and walking around the form.

driving a car along the hollow form the computer guided the car to avoid collisions, but did not point the car in the direction it was going. We then programmed the computer to set up the view in the direction of travel. The individual views were then good (Figure 6.3), but with too jerky a movement when going from one segment of the form to the next, as if the driver's head was rigidly fixed to look straight ahead. This was improved by looking ahead to where we expected to be in a few frames time, and thus to a certain extent anticipating corners.

Metamorphosis and gene interpolation

In our second animation, *A Sequence from the Evolution of Form*, the sculpture changed its form in a continuous metamorphosis. All the forms came out of the same family (see Chapter 4) described by a hornweb structure, but with different values for the 17 genes. 'Key' forms were chosen by the artists, and

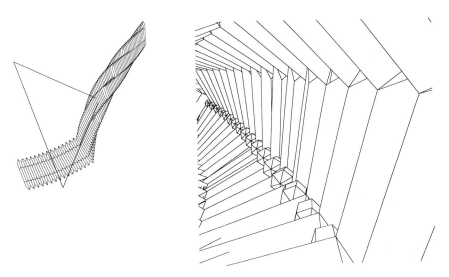

Figure 6.2. Skewed fly-through. The camera is looking in the direction of the y-axis of the torus.

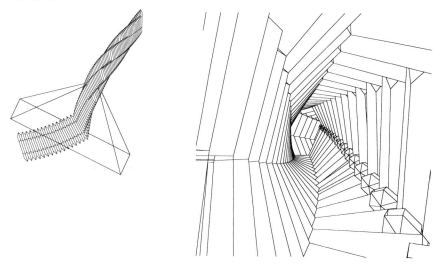

Figure 6.3. Tunnel fly-through. The camera is looking along the centre line of the horn.

the genes for these saved in a gene bank (Figure 6.4).[7] It was partly this experience that led to the design of *Mutator*. In the next stage, the artist made a storyboard which specified the sequence and timings in which these key forms were to be used (Figure 6.5). The computer generated forms for the intermediate frames by working out intermediate gene values using a process called *interpolation*, and re-running the form generation program for each frame using these interpolated genes (Figure 6.6).

---

[7]*Mutator* was not invented when this animation was made, so the genes for the key frames had to be found manually.

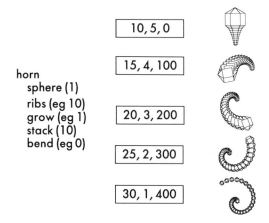

horn
    sphere (1)
    ribs (eg 10)
    grow (eg 1)
    stack (10)
    bend (eg 0)

10, 5, 0	
15, 4, 100	
20, 3, 200	
25, 2, 300	
30, 1, 400	

Figure 6.4.   Gene interpolation. This shows a simple structure with two key forms and several interpolated ones.

time	genes		
1.0	10	5	0
3.4	30	1	400
4.2	20	3	600
6.7	40	4	700
10.0	60	4	900

Figure 6.5.   This simple storyboard shows the three gene values used to create the form at each of five different key frame times.

This gene interpolation is much simpler for a computer than the in-betweening required when key frames are defined as images, as the computer program already 'understands' from the structure what the form and movement are about. The work becomes mainly numeric, with lots of calculation; just what a computer is good at, but totally impractical for a human animator.

Chaos   Gene interpolation gives more varied results than might be expected. We exploited the irregularity of gene space to create chaotic unfolding and imploding forms, with subtle and beautiful choreography generated automatically as the visual effects of the genes changed at different speeds.

Methods of   Gene interpolation can be done in several ways. The obvious method is to
interpolation   use linear interpolation (Figure 6.7), but this causes jerks between the key frames. The most common is a method called *cubic splining*, which looks not just to the previous and next key frames to work out an intermediate value, but also to the key frames before the previous one and after the next one. This gives much smoother motion, but in some circumstances makes the motion unstable. We usually use cosine interpolation (Figure 6.8), which

Figure 6.6.   These frame extracts from *Sequence from the Evolution of Form* demonstrate form metamorphosis by gene interpolation.

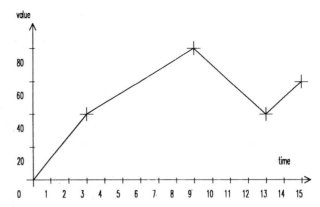

Figure 6.7. Linear interpolation of a single gene value. Time moves to the right, and the gene value is displayed vertically. The key values are marked with crosses. Note the rapid changes at the key frames.

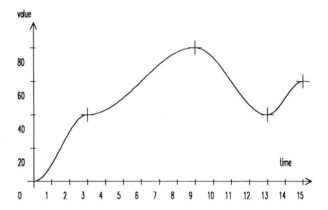

Figure 6.8. Cosine interpolation of a single gene value. Time moves to the right, and the gene value is displayed vertically. The key values are marked with crosses. Note how the gene value always levels off at each key frame, giving a temporary 'still' form.

smoothly stops the motion before each key frame, and smoothly starts it again after the frame. For many applications, this stopping and starting is not appropriate, but with metamorphosing forms the stillness at the key frames gives the viewer a chance to appreciate the key forms before they metamorphose.

Continuity of animation

The use of gene interpolation makes a very important assumption: that as the genes vary smoothly, so do the forms and images generated. With the programs we use this is generally true, but not always. We have encountered two problems with this, one where objects suddenly popped into the picture, another where the form seemed to start vibrating.

Popping occurs where interpolation is used on a value that is meant to be a whole number, such as the number of ribs in a horn. Over a sequence of frames the number may move smoothly from 6.8, 6.9, 7.0, 7.1, and so on, but the integer part of the value jumps 6, 6, 7, 7, and at the jump an extra rib is suddenly introduced. The end position is moving smoothly, but the extra rib popping in is very intrusive. The problem is solved by adding an extra masking object at the (continuously moving) end position of the form.

The mask can be a copy of the object being used to generate the ribs of the form, or it may be an unrelated but larger object. The animation gives the impression of the masking form moving and either laying an expanding form behind it, or eating up a contracting form (Figure 6.9). Alternatively, where the required number of ribs is not a whole number we may add an extra rib at the end which is scaled according to the excess. Thus, if asked for 4.5 ribs, we have 4 full size ones, and one half size one. The animation then gives the impression of new ribs growing onto the end of the form (Figure 6.10).

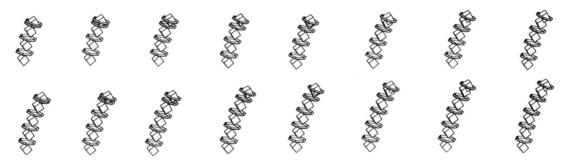

Figure 6.9. Mask laying form. The tail consists of the union of the three different elements. As the number of ribs increases the tail appears to lay out the form.

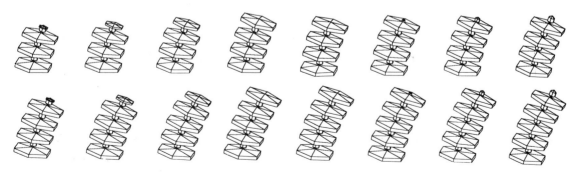

Figure 6.10. Mask growing. The tail consists of the next primitive to be added, scaled down according to how nearly complete this next primitive is. The mask appears to grow continuously at the end of the form.

The vibration problem was caused by our branch generation program. Asked to place 10 branches around a point, it produces a solution that places branch number 4 in a set position. Asked to place 10.1 branches, branch number 4 moves to a new position not very close to the old one. Thus, as the number of branches increases, we do not just get extra ones added, but the old ones move so quickly that the eye cannot follow their motion. This is rather like the strobing problem that causes wagon wheels to appear to move backwards in westerns, but in the animation *The Process of Evolution* causes a vibrating cauliflower effect.

Life cycle

The *Mutations* animation is inspired by the life cycle of simple plants and animals in the real world, depicting birth, growth and death. The forms for the actors are taken from a *Mutator* gene bank, so the film is an artistic illustration of mutation and natural selection. This involves animation software at two levels: the higher level, *Life Cycle*, described here, implements the pseudo-biological systems that drive the animation; the lower level, *Director* (see Chapter 10), takes the script output by *Life Cycle* and performs the detailed control needed to make the animation.

To set up the life cycle, we must describe how each form grows during its life, where it is, and the detailed timings.

Growth and decay of forms

During its life, each actor goes through several key forms. The artist selects up to five different forms from the gene bank, which the actor assumes at the time of conception, birth, on maturity, on starting to decay, and at final death (Figure 6.11).

The artist can leave the selection of most of the key forms for an actor to the system, but should at least specify the genes for the mature form. Here is the result if everything else is left to default. At conception the form is a bud, achieved by setting all the genes to zero so that the form is tiny and uncomplex. At birth, the genes are averaged between the parent's mature genes and the actor's mature genes. The actor does not change form between maturation and decay, and the death form is an exploded version of the form at decay time, with the individual primitives out of which the form is made disintegrated to nothing (Figure 6.12). The disintegration of the primitives requires special programming of the structure (see Chapter 8) to tie the scale of all the primitives to the first gene value, which shrinks to 0 at death time.

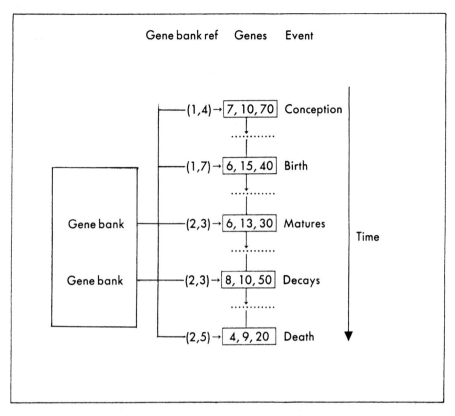

Figure 6.11. Collecting genes from the gene bank. At this stage of the process the precise timescale has not been established. Interpolated gene values will be used at the points marked . . ., the number of interpolated frames depending on the precise timescale.

At all intermediate times, the form of the actor is defined by gene interpolation as described in the previous section, though we are experimenting with more complex models based, for example, on the metamorphosis caterpillar to cocoon to butterfly, and implemented using conditional horn programming. The timings of this growth and decay are controlled by the biological clock.

Time of life   We are experimenting with defining a gene that conveys the time of life of the actor. The gene takes on a value of 0 at conception, 1 at birth, 2 at maturity, and so on, with in-between values at other times. The actor structure can then use conditional programming (see Chapter 8) to change the structure of an actor during its life cycle; for example, to open out a new fan tail on birth (Figure 8.28).

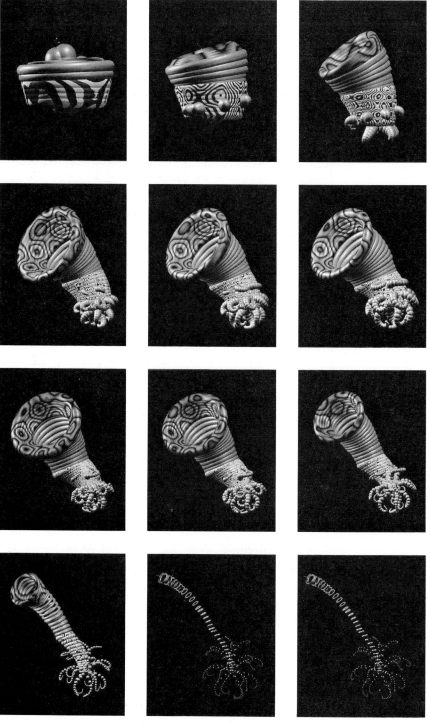

Figure 6.12. Growth and death of a form using *Life Cycle*. Growth uses gene interpolation from a bud form with all zero gene values. Death involves an increase in the scale of the overall form combined with a shrinking of the individual primitives.

Size of forms

The size of a form can vary quite considerably as its genes change. This makes it difficult to control the size of different actors. To overcome this, the computer establishes the size of all actors and scales them to a 'standard' size. The artist can then specify sizes at the key frames relative to this standard size. These key sizes are interpolated in the same way as the genes.

At first the computer scaled the forms automatically for every intermediate frame. This gave curious 'breathing' effects on the size of actors, as the automatic scaling depended on the exact orientation of the actor within a computer viewing cell (Figure 6.13). To avoid this, each actor is automatically scaled according to the size of its mature form, and this same automatic scale is used throughout its life, in conjunction with the interpolated, artist defined scale.

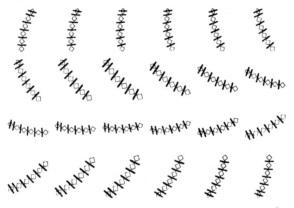

Figure 6.13. Breathing from dynamic autoscale. The camera is keeping the form as large as possible in the frame. As the form takes up a diagonal position the camera zooms in and the form appears larger.

Birth of forms

From conception to birth, an actor is inside the parent actor (Figures 6.14, 6.15). It is conceived at the head end, and moves down the parent to be born out of the tail. The motion of the head of the child follows the parent shape

Figure 6.14. Hand-drawn sketch of the movedown process prepared by Latham during the conceptual design of the film *Mutations*.

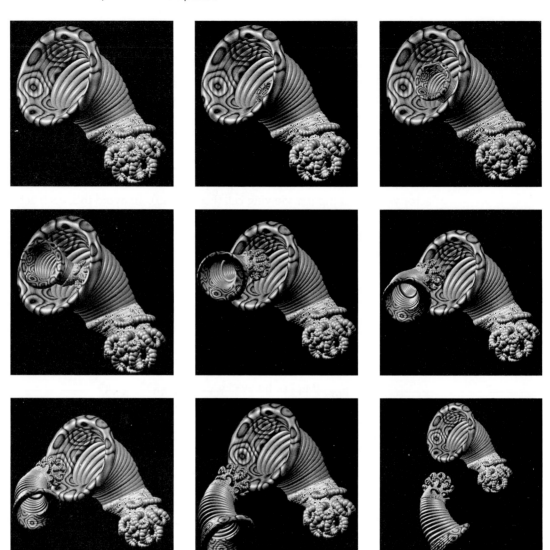

Figure 6.15. Four frames from movedown showing the frames leading up to the birth of a computer form from its parent.

in the same way that the camera follows the shape of a form for a fly-through, though with the added complication that the parent form is metamorphosing as the child moves down.

The world vortex

Once a child form is born, it is released from the parent into the world. In the world it follows a motion like that of a twig in a stream, or a leaf caught in the wind. These motions are modelled using a physical simulation techique called *field equations* (Sims, 1990; Wejchert and Haumnann, 1991). We use only physical phenomena which are useful for the artistic effect. The vortex tumbles the objects and brings out their three dimensional quality, but we do not usually model gravity (Figure 6.16).

```
whirlpool:= field
              vortex(10)
              line_sink(1)
              steady(2);
```

path of object in whirlpool

Figure 6.16. Movement of a form in a whirlpool. This shows the path taken by a computer form once it has been born from its parent and is free to move in a whirlpool vortex.

We intend to enhance the vortex rules with rules that control the distance between actors in the scene.[†] These will prevent collisions, but keep the actors sufficiently close that interesting groupings appear. They may also bring actors together to visually represent the 'mating' process of the *Mutator* program.

Interference detection   Some of the processes should ideally check two forms in detail for interference, and either move the forms as a result or even change their shapes. For example, movedown should mould the shape of the child sculpture to prevent it protruding through the body of the parent sculpture, and movement in the vortex should prevent collision of forms. To do this properly, allowing for the detailed local shaping of the forms, requires extensive processing, so we prefer to use approximations that rely only on global properties of the forms such as position and approximate size.

Biological clock

The growth and motion processes all depend on the times of key events such as birth. At first the artist specified all these times individually for each actor. This quickly became a chore, particularly when we wished to add an extra event which pushed back all the timings that followed.

[†]This is currently being implemented in a program called Dancer.

The *Life Cycle* program generates these times automatically using a simple set of rules and time intervals (Figures 6.17, 6.19, 6.20). The time at which each actor is conceived is determined by the parent actor. After that, its life is controlled by a series of time intervals set up by the biological clock:

1. Conception to birth: during this interval the actor is growing from bud to birth form, and moving along the body of the parent.
2. Birth to maturity: the actor continues to grow to its mature form, but is now released into the world vortex.
3. Maturity to first offspring: the actor continues to metamorphose. The time at which the first offspring is conceived is used to start the biological clock for that offspring.
4. Interval between each offspring: the actor continues to move towards old age as more children are conceived.
5. Birth of last offspring to old age: the actor is now free of all children, but metamorphosis to old age continues.
6. Old age to death: the fast decay and explosion sets in.

These rules have several odd effects. The more children an actor has, the longer that actor lives. This does not seem to correspond to real life, but is artistically very convenient. The children that appear in the animation are those selected by the artist from the *Mutator* session, presumbly because they are 'interesting'. An actor with many interesting children is probably interesting itself, and is therefore worth keeping in frame for a longer time.

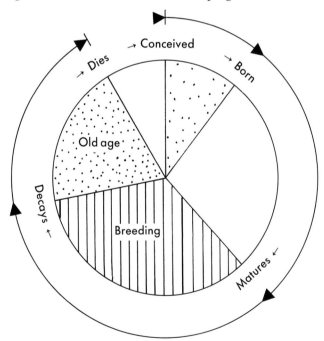

Figure 6.17. Biological clock showing the stages of life of an actor in a life cycle.

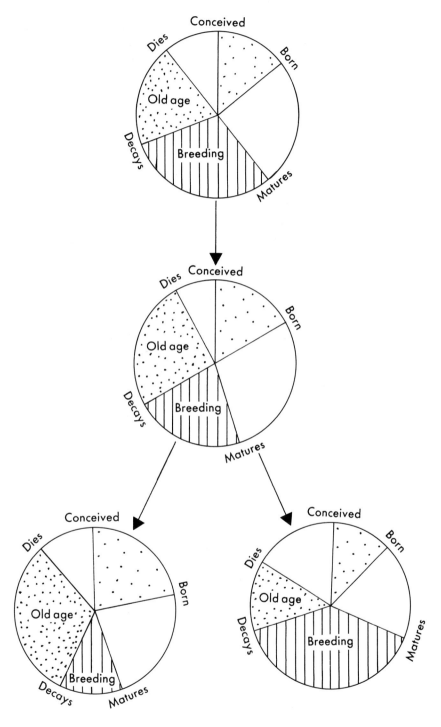

Figure 6.18. Tree of biological clocks. The clock for each child actor is derived from the clock for the parent, but with some fields overwritten.

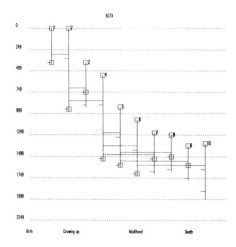

Figure 6.19. Chart describing an animation. This shows the timings for different actors. Time moves from the top of the chart, and each actor is shown as a vertical line. The full length of the line shows the span from conception to death, with each segment being one phase of the life cycle of the actor. The horizontal lines indicate parenthood, and are drawn from the parent to the child at the time of birth. The chart gives an overview of what is happening at each stage of an animation.

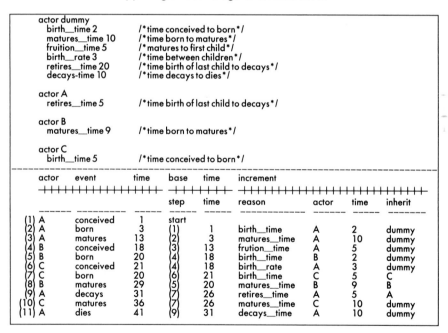

Figure 6.20. Operation of *Life Cycle* timing rules. This shows the biological clock's input to *Life Cycle*, and the times it deduces up to the death of actor A. To understand this table look, for example, at deduction 6 which finds when C was conceived. C is the second child of A, so its conception time is deduced from the conception time of its older brother B. B was conceived at time 18 (step 4), and the birth rate (time between one conception and the next) for the parent A is 3. This birth rate is inherited from the birth rate for the dummy actor. Adding increment 3 to base time 18 gives the time for the conception of C as 21. Looking at the table we see that the time for each event is computed as the sum of a base time (column 6) and increment time (column 9).

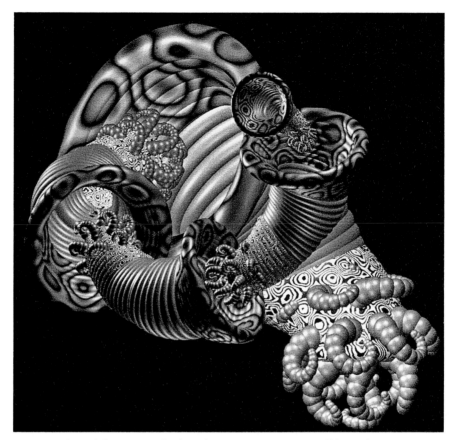

Figure 6.21. A form giving birth at the same time as it is itself being born.

Other distortions of real life are easily arranged for special effect: a child giving birth before it is born (Figure 6.21), an alarmingly fast conception rate, and so on.

The time intervals for the biological clocks may all be specified independently for each actor, but are more often derived from the time intervals of the parent so that the child inherits the parent's biological clock (Figure 6.18). These timings may in turn be specified explicitly, or derived from those of *its* parent, and so on. A 'dummy' actor that never appears is taken as the parent of actors that have no natural parent. Changing the clock for the dummy actor ripples through to change the clocks for the children, grandchildren, and so on through the entire scene. This gives us easy 'global' control of an entire scene. Changing clocks for the actors 'on scene' at a particular time ripples through to change clocks for all subsequent actors. This makes it easy to speed up a film after a particular moment in it. What seems like a small change to the dummy actor can have disporportionate effects of the complete animation, so after such a change it is necessary to make a new preview version of the complete scene.

An element of randomness and extra controls to emulate different seasons may be introduced to all derived timings to prevent the animation having too regular a rhythm. We would like to use *Mutator* to experiment with the timing rules, but it takes too long to prepare, view and animate, even in its crudest preview format, for this to be practicable.

Camera control

The camera is part of the action, and must also be animated. Cameras can be controlled in two ways: manually or automatically. With manual control we set up camera positions for key frames, and use in-betweening. Automatic control requires camera rules (Figure 6.22). One of the problems with a generative style of animation is for the camera to chase the action, automatically position itself, and smoothly frame the action.

Tracking   In *Mutations* we used a rule that set the camera frame using all forms from conception until the birth of their last child: these forms are said to be 'in frame'; 'out frame' forms remain visible if they happened to stay within the defined camera view. The effect of this is that the camera chases the main action and keeps the picture frame filled. The camera also rotates steadily around the outside of the scene, typically 2° per frame, which is about one every seven seconds.

Damping   With the tracking rule above there is a jump when an actor gives birth to the last child and is no longer in frame. This is prevented by an exponential damping factor on the camera. If the camera is at a given position and setting, and the tracking rules require these to change, only a certain proportion of the change is permitted in each frame.

```
/*Compute view required for undamped tracking*/
wanted__view: = autoview (inframe__csg);
/*If the set of inframe actors is unchanged, clamp the damping.          */
/*Otherwise, return to full damping.                                     */
/*Curdamp is the damping factor to be used on this frame.                */
/*Camerdamp is the maximum damping factor.                               */
/*Clamptime is the number of frames after a change in the set            */
/*     of current actors before the camera is fully clamped.             */
        if inframelist = last__inframelist
            curdamp: = max (0, last__curdamp – cameradamp/clamptime);
        else
            curdamp: = cameradamp;
/*Work out this view in betweening.                                      */
/*Curdamp = 1 uses last-view, curdamp = 0 uses wanted__view.             */
        view: = inter (curdamp, last__view, wanted__view);
```

Figure 6.22. Algorithm for camera control.

Clamping   If the damping factor is set too low, the camera movement is too jerky. If the factor is set too high, the camera can chase a fast moving actor, but never quite catches up. This is solved by gradually decreasing the damping factor while the set of actors being tracked remains unchanged, thus clamping the camera tracking onto the actors.

We intend to enhance the automatic camera tracking rules to allow for camera inertia, and to let the camera anticipate where the actors are going. Also, there will always be cases where explicit camera control is required to get the best views so we will integrate the manual splining with the automatic tracking rules.

"ART CREATION"   "SINTHETIC CREATION"
"SUPER CREATION".   "A NEW CREATION"

SUPER NATURE   SCULPTURAL FRUIT,
FRUIT

TRIGGERS
GROWTH.

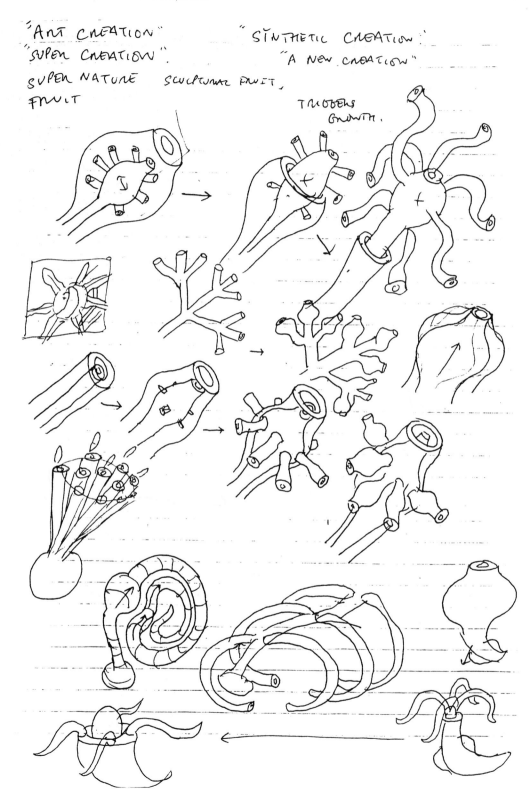

(17) Plant Centre. Latham 1989. Computer/Cibachrome. 103×103 cm.

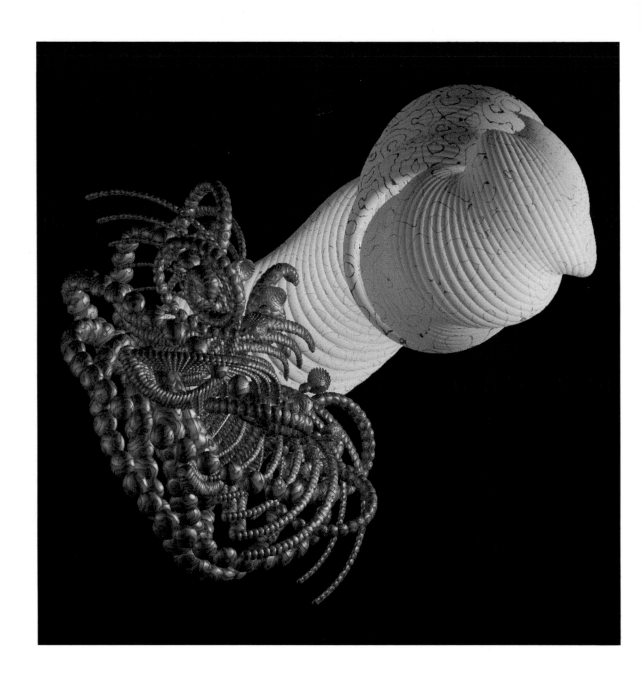

(18) White Growth. Latham 1990. Computer/Cibachrome. 125×134 cm.

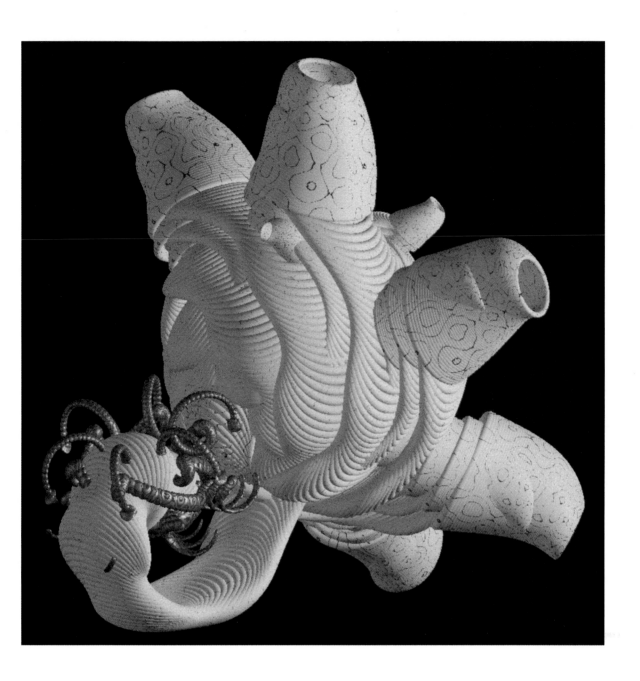

(19) Tusk 10. Latham 1990. Computer/'C' Type. 152×152 cm.

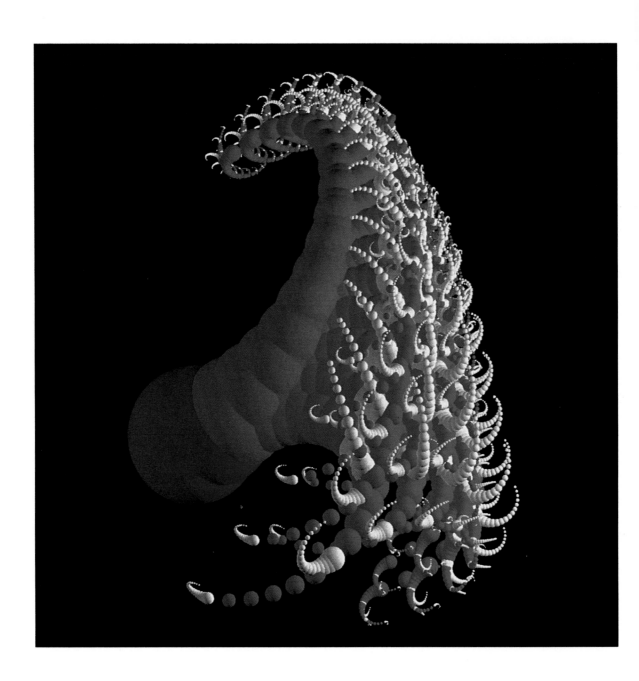

(20) Recursive Horn. Latham 1991. Computer/Cibachrome. 103 × 103 cm.

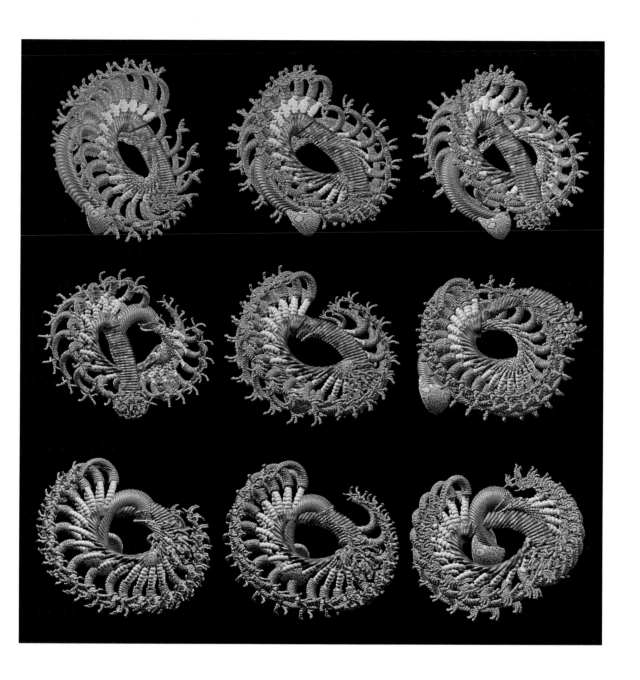

(21) Nine Mutations. (Ribbed Branched Structure). Latham 1991. Computer/Cibachrome. 4′×4′.

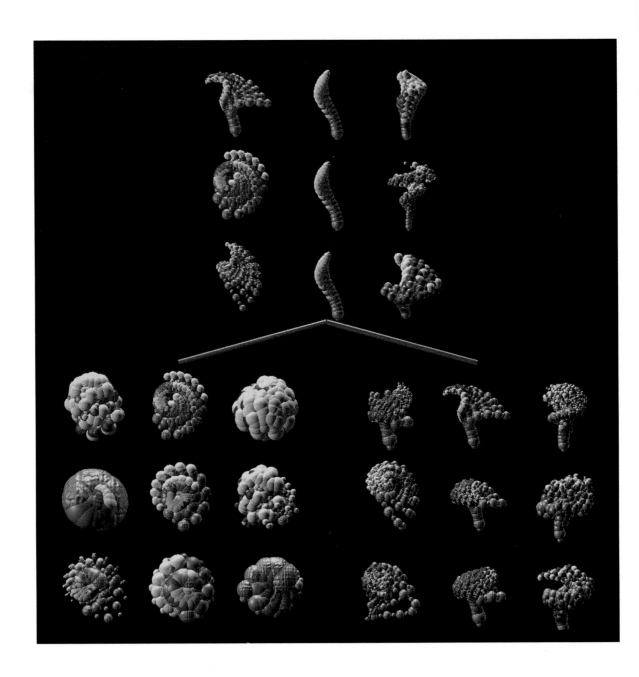

(22) Treefrac. Latham 1991. Computer Image.

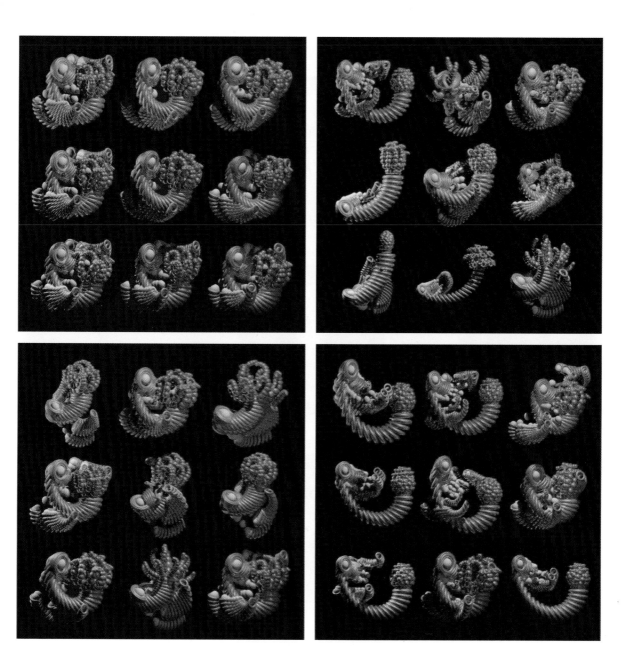

(23) Four Mutator Frames. (Bio-Form). Latham 1992. Computer Image.

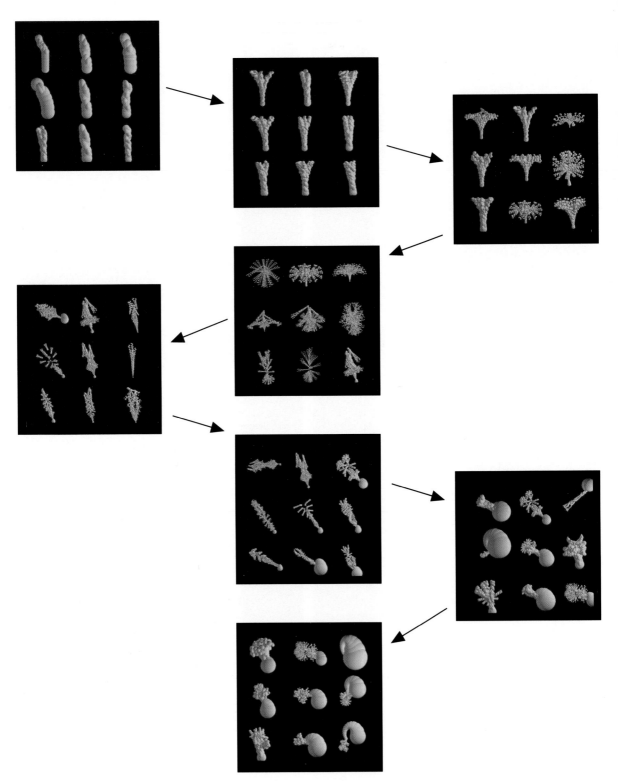

(24) Evolved Forms. 8 Generations. (Structure=RST). Computer/Cibachrome. 160×40 cm.

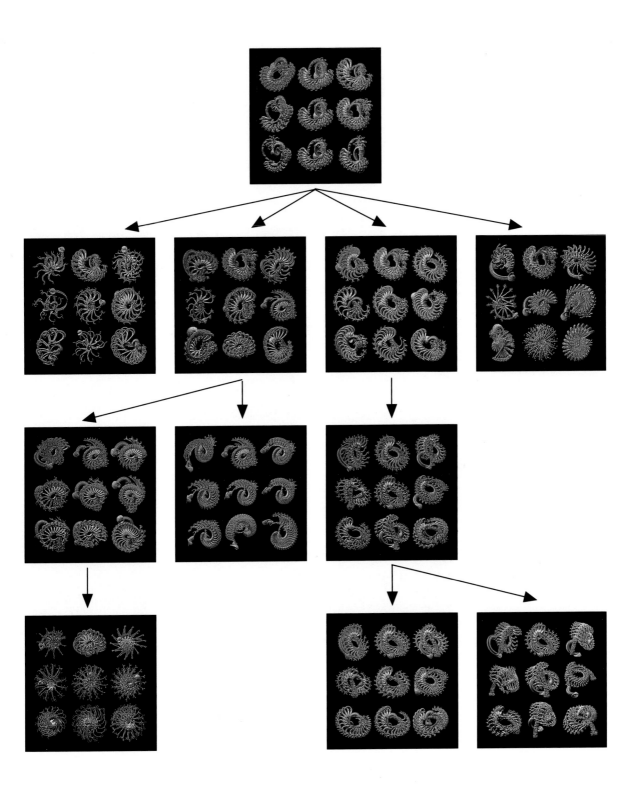

(25) Large Mutator Evolution Tree. (Ribbed Branched Structure). Latham 1991. Computer Image.

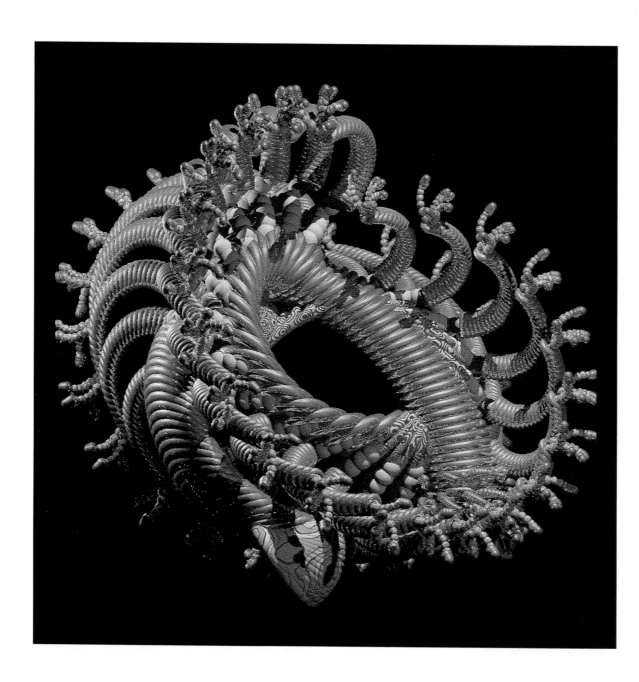

(26) Mutation Y1 Raytraced. Latham 1992. Computer Image.

(27) Mutation Y1 Raytraced on the Plane of Infinity. Latham 1992. Computer Image.

(28) Mutation X Raytraced. Latham 1992. Computer Image.

(29) Breeding Forms on the Infinite Plane. Latham 1992. Computer Image.

(30) Evolving Mutations beneath the Surface. Latham 1992. Computer Image.

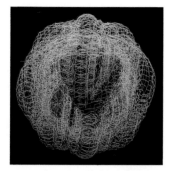

(31 a) Sculpture Wire Frame.

(31 b) Sculpture Rendered.

(31 c) Sculptured Textured.

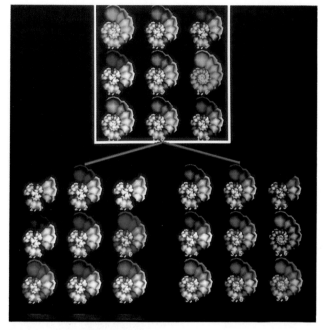

(31 d,e) Evolution of Colour.

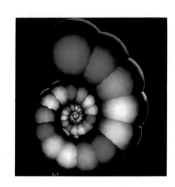

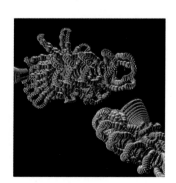

(31 f.g.h.) Sequence of Frames from the Film "Mutations". Latham 1992.

(32a) Conquest of Form Exhibition at City Centre Gallery, Dublin, Eire. 1991.

(32b) "Mutations" Exhibition at Ghislave Gallery, Paris, 1991.

(32c) "Conquest of Form" Exhibition. At The Arnolfini Gallery, Bristol, 1988.

(32d.e) "Mutations" Exhibition at The Connaught Brown Gallery, London. Video Installation 1991.

Chapter 7
Graphics programming

We have so far described some of the artistic aspects of Latham's work, and the systems built expressly to support it. The remainder of the book looks at the more technical aspects, and some computer science details. We look at those details which are specific to our environment (Figure 7.1), and which have an important influence on the work. For a reference on computer graphics the reader is referred to Foley and van Dam (1989), to Glassner (1989a) for information on rendering and ray tracing, and to Glassner (1989b) for a general survey of computer graphics and art.

Two important influences on any artist's work are the environment in which he works, and the medium with which he works. Latham's working environment over the last few years has been the IBM United Kingdom Scientific Centre in Winchester, and his medium has been the graphics tools available at the centre. This chapter describes some of the work of the centre that has surrounded Latham, and the tools that have been available.

The chapter begins with an overview of the systems available to Latham, and then describes its various parts in more detail. It describes only the general facilities available, as used both by Latham and by the scientific applications.

System overview

Latham has mainly been involved with the Visualization Applications group. Most of the tools which he uses were developed for the study of scientific data, and are therefore different from the tools often used in computer art. Most of the graphics that have been produced at the centre, though some have a beauty of their own, are produced purely for the scientific information they convey.

All the images published by Latham since 1987 have been prepared using systems written in the Extensible Solid Model Editor (ESME), a high level interactive language with graphics and geometry features. The most important of these systems is *Form Grow* (see Chapter 8).

ESME graphics are handled by the drawing system (see Chapter 9) using the technique of Constructive Solid Geometry (CSG), first exploited for computer aided design applications. This is in two distinct parts, for interactive graphics and for high quality rendered images. As the form of a sculpture is prepared, quick 'sketches' are made using interactive graphics. Graphics hardware has advanced tremendously over the last few years, and this has had a huge impact on how realistic the interactive sketches are, and how quickly they can be produced. High quality final images are produced on the Winsom renderer.

Animation (see Chapter 10), adds tremendously to the impact of computer sculptures. It allows a sculpture to be viewed from all angles, including the inside, and permits the sculpture itself to change. The distinction between interactive sketching and final form becomes even more important with animation and the need to generate as quickly as possible a preview of an animation.

An important feature of the Winsom renderer is its extensive facilities to control lighting colour and texture (see Chapter 11).

Once a still frame or series of frames has been given a fully rendered form, there is still a lot to be done to produce the final art work, be it a large colour print, three dimensional photograph, or broadcast quality video tape.

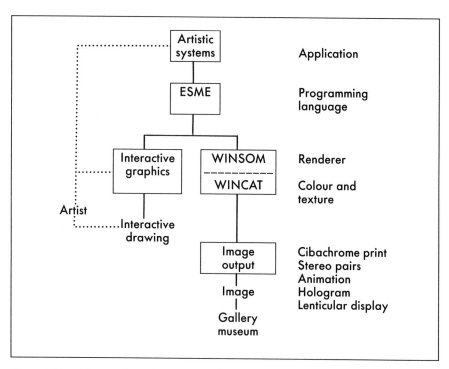

Figure 7.1. Main technical systems used to support the artistic systems described in the previous chapters.

All the artistic systems for Latham's work – *Form Grow, Mutator, Life Cycle* and *Director* – are implemented in the ESME language (Todd, 1992).

ESME history   ESME was originally intended as a language for writing CSG models (Figure 7.2), and so to provide an interactive front end to the Winsom renderer. The interactive form editor (see Chapter 3) used ESME in this way. In practice, it has been more valuable as a CSG programming and animation language, especially in data exploration and visualization applications (Figure 7.3). ESME has been applied to Latham's work to implement all the artistic systems.

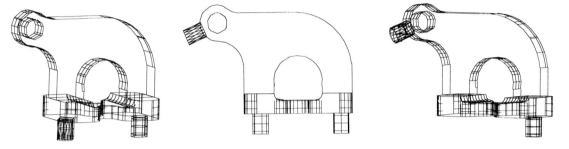

Figure 7.2.   A Constructive Solid Geometry editor built in ESME. It has not been used in our artistic applications. In the first frame the user has selected the front leg of the bracket. In the second frame he has moved it to the nose, and in the third he has committed the change and redrawn the picture.

Figure 7.3.   ESME used to display a possible structure for a proteo-glycan assembly (in collaboration with the Imperial Cancer Research Institute and the Kennedy Institute of Rheumatology).

Role of CSG   Constructive solid modelling makes constructing computer form systems very easy because of the simplicity of constructing and transforming simple and complex objects in a coherent manner (see Chapter 8). We also use these functions in animation where groups of computer forms are collected in a scene. Outside the artistic applications, we use CSG in laying out explanatory diagrams.

High level language

ESME provides an interactive programming environment, using interpretation and with the ability to change and execute programs from within a session, in a manner similar to Basic, Smalltalk or APL.

The syntax of ESME is designed to be easy to *read*. For us, the requirements for the syntax of a programming language are:

1. Ease of reading.
2. Ease of modification.
3. Ease of writing.
4. Efficiency of implementation.
5. Ability to perform formal reasoning.

Important features of the syntax are user defined infix operations and overloading, and a heavily overloaded blank operator, which are illustrated in the following example. The example shows a simple session, with user input and corresponding system response, if any, after the $\Rightarrow$:

$1 \Rightarrow 1$	– direct response to an input
$1 + 2 \Rightarrow 3$	– simple calculator mode
$x := 4$	– assignment, no response
'x is' $x \Rightarrow x$ is 4	– blank operator as string catenate
$x*8 \Rightarrow 32$	– calculation with variable

The syntax permits us both to write legible geometry programs, and also to design higher level 'artist oriented' languages such as those used by *Form Grow* and *Life Cycle*:

```
hh1: = horn
          ribs (20)     /*  Make a horn with 20 ribs */
          sphere (0.4)  /*  out of spheres, */
          stack (0.6)   /*  then stack, */
          twist (20,2)  /*  twist */
          bend (3);     /*  and bend the horn. */
```

This horn example uses the blank operator in several different (overloaded) ways: to set the number of ribs in the horn; to select the form to be used; and to set up and extend the list of twisting transforms.

Functions for geometry

ESME has a wide range of functions for handling built-in three dimensional geometry:

```
/* vector generation */
1, 2, 3        => (1, 2, 3)
1, 3+4, 5*6 => (1, 7, 30)
/* vector operations */
(1, 2, 3)+(4, 3, 2)      => (5, 5, 5)
(1, 2, 3) dot (4, 3, 2)   => 16
(1, 2, 3) cross (4, 3, 2) => −5, 10, −5)
length(3, 4, 0)=5
normal((3, 4, 0))=(0.6, 0.8, 0)
/* transform generation */
at(1, 2, 3) => at(1,2,3)   /* translation */
scale(2)    => scale(2)    /* scaling */
xrot(90)    => rotate(1,0,0, 0,0,1, 0,−1,0) /* rotation */
/* applying transforms to vectors using the blank operator */
(1, 2, 3) at(1, 2, 3) => (2, 4, 6)
(1, 2, 3) scale(3)    => (3, 6, 9)
/* composing transforms using the blank operator */
scale(3) at(1, 2, 3)     => scale(3) at(1,2,3)
at(1, 2, 3) scale(3)     => scale(3) at(3,6,9)
at(1, 2, 3) xrot(90)     => rotate(1,0,0, 0,0,1, 0,−1,0)
                            at(1,−3,2)
/* transforms do NOT commute */
(1, 2, 3) at(1, 2, 3) scale(3)  => (6, 12, 18)
(1, 2, 3) scale(3) at(1, 2, 3)  => (4, 8, 12)
/* but they do distribute */
((1, 2, 3) scale(3)) at(1, 2, 3)  => (4, 8, 12)
(1, 2, 3) (scale(3) at(1, 2, 3))  => (4, 8, 12)
/* vectors and transforms as objects */
vvec:=(1, 2, 3)
vvec            => (1, 2, 3)
tt:=scale(3)
tt              => scale(3)
vvec tt         => (3, 6, 9)
```

Notice the use of the overloaded blank operator for composing transforms, and for applying transforms to vectors.

CSG

ESME uses CSG to define solid objects in terms of simple primitives, and it uses operations to combine, transform and colour them. Constructive solid geometry was first used in Computer Aided Design applications.

Primitive solids Primitive solids are all created at the origin, and sometimes in fixed orientation. They are then moved using translations and rotatations to any required position and orientation (Figure 7.4):

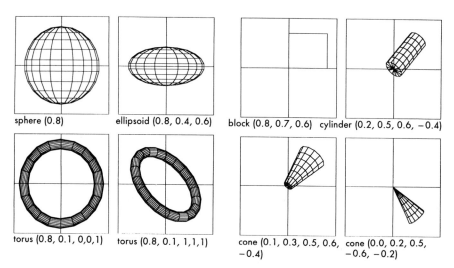

sphere (0.8)   ellipsoid (0.8, 0.4, 0.6)   block (0.8, 0.7, 0.6)   cylinder (0.2, 0.5, 0.6, −0.4)

torus (0.8, 0.1, 0,0,1)   torus (0.8, 0.1, 1,1,1)   cone (0.1, 0.3, 0.5, 0.6, −0.4)   cone (0.0, 0.2, 0.5, −0.6, −0.2)

Figure 7.4. Simple two dimensional view of some of the primitive solids used by ESME and Winsom, and their position and orientation before transformation.

sphere(r) produces a sphere with radius **r**.

blocks(s1, s2, s3) produces a rectangular block aligned with the axes, with one corner at **(0,0,0)** and the other at **(s1,s2,s3)**.

ellipsoid(r1,r2,r3) produces an ellipsoid with major radii **r1,r2,r3** aligned with the **x,y,z** axes respectively.

torus(r1,r2,d1,d2,d3) produces a torus of major radius **r1**, minor radius **r2**, and with an axis in the direction of the vector **(d1,d2,d3)**.

cylinder(r,d1,d2,d3) produces a cylinder of radius **r**, with the ends of the axis at **(0,0,0)** and **(d1,d2,d3)**.

cone(r1,r2,d1,d2,d3) produces a cone with the ends of the axis at **(0,0,0)** and **(d1,d2,d3)**, and with radii **r1** and **r2** at these ends, respectively.

plane(d1,d2,d3) produces a solid half plane through the origin with a normal pointing outwards in the direction **(d1,d2,d3)**.

There are also primitives for helices, and facilities to define solids from two and three dimensional fields and from mathematical equations. These facilities are used in scientific visualization, but we have not yet used them for computer sculptures. Most of Latham's sculptures are built from ellipsoids and tori with up to 50,000 primitives.

Transforms   Transforms can be applied to CSG solids using another overloading of the blank operator (Figure 7.5). Transforms may be applied in any order, and may be applied to single primitives or to several primitives at once.

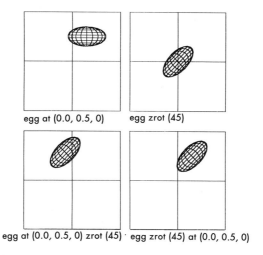

egg at (0.0, 0.5, 0)   egg zrot (45)

egg at (0.0, 0.5, 0) zrot (45) · egg zrot (45) at (0.0, 0.5, 0)

Figure 7.5. Simple egg translated and rotated.

Set operations   ESME permits objects to be combined using set operations (Figure 7.6):

Figure 7.6. Three major set operations: union (above), intersection (below left) and difference (below right).

Union adds two objects. A point that is inside either object is inside the union. Union is easily the most commonly used combination operator in the production of our sculptures.

Difference (diff) removes the second object from the first. A point is inside the difference if it is inside the first object, but not inside the second.

Intersect (int) finds the volume common to both objects.

Symmetric difference (sdiff) finds the volume that lies inside one or other object, but not both. Symmetric difference is used mainly in theoretical work.

Loops ESME permits loops to operate on solid models. For example:

$$union(i,1,10, sphere(1) \ at(0,i,0) \ colour(i))$$

makes a stack of coloured spheres.

Blending As well as using strict set operations, ESME permits more fuzzy blended operations (Figure 7.7).

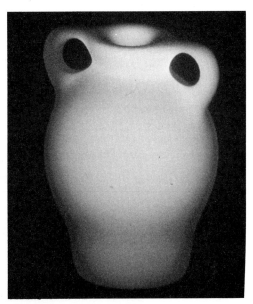

Figure 7.7. A Vase form created by using CSG on a few simple solids (sphere, torus and cylinder), and the entire object smoothed with a single global blend operation (Peter Quarendon, 1985).

Automatic scaling It is not easy to predict the size of forms generated by systems such as *Form Grow*. ESME provides various functions to automatically scale objects to fit a standard unit cube. This is like in *Alice in Wonderland* where Alice drinks the potion and increases in size to fill the room. Similarly, each sculpture is placed in a box and made to fit.

Implementation of These modelling methods are used in programs that implement Latham's
artistic systems functions. For example, the code for *Tentac* (a primitive predecessor of *Form
Grow*) which takes a single input form (*inform*) and applies a transform (*twist*) a
given number of times (*ribs*) is given here:

```
*/      ('TENTAC' function  #  /* generate stacks, horns etc */
          inform: = ?csg;         /* input form */
          ribs: = ?float;         /* number of copies of inform */
          twist: = ?trans;        /* twistup transform */

          tr: = unitt;            /* initial catenated transform is unit
                                     transform */

          union(i,1,ribs,         /* union of a set of objects */
            tr: = tr twist;       /* work out next twist**i */
            inform tr)            /* each rib is a transformed copy of
                                     inform */

        );
```

A full description of the construction of the *Form Grow* program is given in
Chapter 8.

Once ESME has prepared a computer form, it passes it to the drawing
system (see Chapter 9). The drawing system manages both interactive
drawing and high quality rendering controlled from ESME programs.

Menus ESME provides a very easy to program but rather primitive menu system.
The programmer only codes a single line for each menu item:

$$\text{menuitem('savetree',   savetree())}$$

which gives the text and action for the item, with a couple of course
placement options. We are now using OSF/Motif to produce more
sophisticated menus.

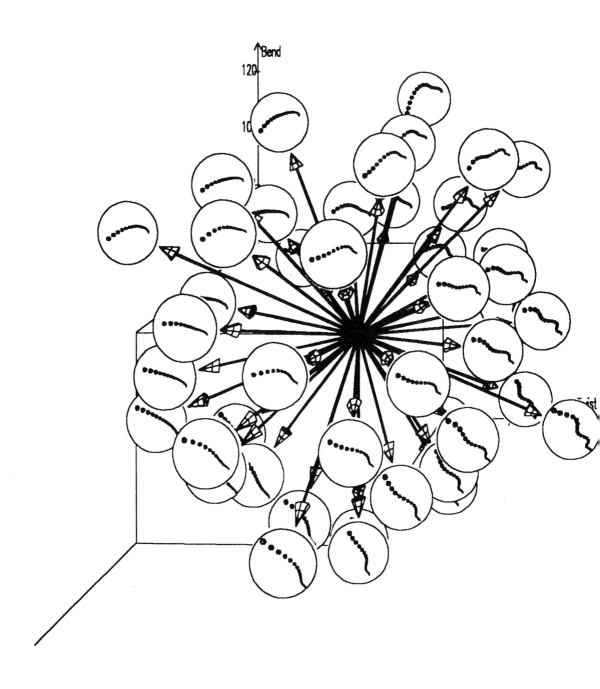

Chapter 8

Form grow

This chapter shows how artistic computer forms are derived from the mathematics of rotations and other transforms, and how they employ the ideas of iteration, recursion and conditionals, expanding on the earlier chapter on *Form Grow* (Chapter 3). It includes the methods associated with horn objects (Figure 8.1), and discusses why we found it necessary to implement each one, illustrating the many minor details that must be considered when using computers to generate artworks.

The keywords used are descriptive of the effect they were originally intended to produce. For example, the first objects looked like animal horns and the individual components that made up the horn looked like ribs, so we used the words 'horn' and 'ribs' in the language to help the artist reliably use the operations. The language often looks like a list of commands that the computer is to follow, and forms a bridge between the underlying code and the artist's perception of *Form Grow*. Most of the operations can be used to achieve many different effects. The keywords sometimes seem rather strange when operations are used outside their original purpose, but we do not generally change them once the artist is used to them. The requirements of animation have in particular shaped the details of *Form Grow*, and meant repeated extension.

Constructing horns

The basic construction of a horn takes a number (*ribs*) of input forms, an input form (*inform*) and a list (*tranrule*) of transform rules. The function *trans(tranrule, k)* works out the transform for k applications of *tranrule*. A simple horn with ribs from 1 to 4 generates the computer form:

```
              inform trans(tranrule, 0.25)   /* 1/4 total tranrule for rib */
     union inform trans(tranrule, 0.5 )   /* 1/2 total tranrule for rib 2 */
     union inform trans(tranrule, 0.75)   /* 3/4 tranrule for rib 3 */
     union inform trans(tranrule, 1)      /* last rib takes full tranrule */
```

We first explain the variations to this basic expansion, and then show how the transform rules are used in the *trans* function.

- **basic horn options**
  - *inform*   define sub-object from which horn is to be built (eg sphere, torus, other__horn)
  - *ribs*   number of the last sub-object (eg 40)
  - *start*   number of the first sub-object (eg 3)
  - *head*   object to place at head of horn
  - *tail*   object to place at tail of horn
  - *fulltail*   automatic generation of tail to hide animation popping
  - *parttail*   automatic generation of growing tail to hide animation popping
  - *texture*   define texture for a horn
  - *tranrule1*   define transforms for a horn (pre-texture)
  - *tranrule2*   define transforms for a horn (post-texture)
  - *build*   control detail of the way transforms are specified
  - *skip*   skip some sub-objects for faster display

- **fractal horn options**
  - *fracnum*   number of objects at each recursion level
  - *fraccol*   colour and texture of objects at each recursion level
  - *fracstart*   for constructing lower level details only
  - *orient*   for orientation of subhorns to main horn

- **transform construction**
  - *stack*   with numeric parameter, stack vertically
  - *stack*   with vector parameter, stack in any direction
  - *side*   stack to right
  - *back*   stack backwards
  - *twist*   with numeric parameter, twist about vertical axis
  - *twist*   with two numeric parameters, twist angle and offset
  - *twist*   with vector parameter, twist about any axis
  - *bend*   bend to left or right
  - *grow*   grow objects along horn
  - *branch*   branch objects out in all directions

- **fractal irregularity**
  - *fractal*   uses the transform rule as a fractal irregularity

- **extensions to basic horns**
  - *ribcage*   generate a symmetric 'rib cage' along horn skeleton
  - *hornweb*   generate a web shaped form

Figure 8.1. Summary of the rules of *Form Grow*.

Input form   *Inform* defines the objects out of which the horn is to be built, either primitive or compound CSG objects, or other horns (Figure 8.2). A single object can be given:

$$h1:=horn\ inform(sphere(1))\dots$$

This object may itself be a horn:

$$hx:=horn\dots$$
$$h2:=horn\ inform(hx)\dots$$
$$h2:=horn\ inform(horn\dots)\dots$$

Alternatively, a list of objects may be given. Where a list is used, elements from the list are taken in turn as ribs of the horn, giving greater visual variety:

> h3: = horn inform (sphere(1) ¢ sphere(2)) /* ¢ is list constructor */
> h4: = horn inform (sphere(1) ¢ hx)

h1: = horn	h2: = horn	h3: = horn	h4: = horn
ribs (11)	ribs (11)	ribs (11)	ribs (11)
stack (20)	stack (20)	stack (20)	stack(20)
inform (	inform (	inform (	inform (
sphere (1))	hx)	sphere (1)	sphere (1)
		¢ ellipsoid (3,1,1)	¢ hx)

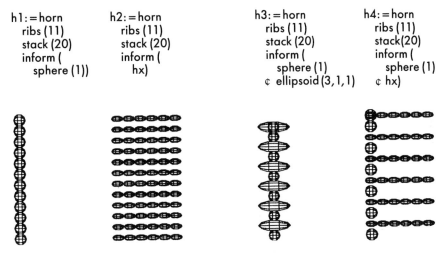

where hx: = horn inform (ellipsoid (1,0.5,1)) ribs (5) size (10)

Figure 8.2. The same transform rules used to create forms with different input forms: a simple sphere, a subhorn, alternate spheres and ellipsoids, and alternate spheres and subhorns.

Usually the blank operator between a horn and a CSG object is used to invoke *inform* implicitly; it catenates the CSG object to the *inform* list already set. Thus:

> h1: = horn sphere (1)

is equivalent to the first expression above, and creates a horn with an *inform* of a single sphere:

> h3: = horn sphere(1) sphere (2)

is equivalent to the third expression, it creates the *h1* and then modifies it to create *h3* with the catenated list of two spheres.

Where we have a 'horn of horns', *inform* must be explicitly included in the structure to prevent confusion as to whether subsequent operations such as *stack* apply to the main horn or the subhorn.

Number of input forms   *Ribs* specifies the number of the last rib to be used in iteratively constructing a horn. By default the horn starts with rib 0, so actually uses *ribs + 1* ribs. For static objects, *ribs* is usually an integer, but when gene interpolation used in an animation it generates noninteger values. The last standard rib is at the position defined by *floor* (*ribs*), the largest integer less than or equal to *ribs*. The end position of the horn, used for appending tails or further horns, is computed from the specified value of *ribs*, as this gives continuity. This means that all the transform rules such as *bend* and *twist* must be able to be applied a non-integral number of times.

Start of horn   As the number of ribs increases, the horn grows at the tip. *Start* makes it grow or shrink at the other end. The horn is still positioned based on the position of rib 0 but it is constructed with ribs for rib numbers from *start* to *ribs* (Figure 8.3). *Start* can also be used to create spirals that do not go right into the centre (Figure 8.4)

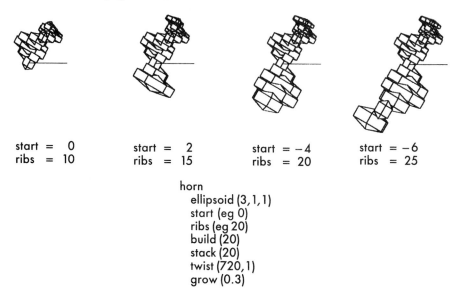

| start = 0 | start = 2 | start = −4 | start = −6 |
| ribs = 10 | ribs = 15 | ribs = 20 | ribs = 25 |

```
horn
    ellipsoid (3,1,1)
    start (eg 0)
    ribs (eg 20)
    build (20)
    stack (20)
    twist (720,1)
    grow (0.3)
```

Figure 8.3. As the animation continues the centre of the horn remains fixed, and it grows at both ends. There is more visual change at the start than at the end, even though the increase in ribs at the start (2 per frame) is smaller than at the end (5 per frame). This is because of the effect of the *grow* value.

Texture   *Texture* specifies the texture to be applied to a horn. At present, texture identifiers are used within *Form Grow* rather than full texture definitions, as they give a convenient interface between ESME and the renderer: the texture is only actually applied at the rendering stage, well after the horn is created. Texture identifiers are numbers. The renderer only accepts texture definitions for integer identifiers, but it uses non-integer identifiers to in-between two adjacent textures.

Applying   The transform rules which are applied to a horn before it is textured are set
transform rules   by *tranrule1*, and those which are applied to a horn before it is textured are set by *tranrule2*. These are usually invoked using the blank operator between

horn ribs (120)
   (sphere (1) at (0, 2.8, 0))
   grow (512)
   bend (3150);

horn ribs (120)
   start (90)
   (sphere (1) at (0, 2.8, 0))
   grow (512)
   bend (3150);

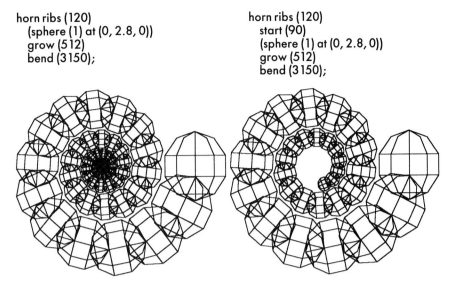

Figure 8.4. The form on the left spirals from the centre of the form. On the right the first 90 ribs are omitted, leaving a hole at the centre of the form.

horns and transform rules. For a horn with no texture set, this catenates the transform rule to *tranrule1*, and for a horn with the texture set it catenates the transform rule to tranrule2. This gives a language that looks like a string of commands, "Make this horn, stack it, apply texture and then bend it".

horn ribs(20) sphere(1)	is	horn ribs(20) sphere (1)
texture(3)	the	stack(10)
tranrule1(stack(10)	same	texture(3)
tranrule2(bend(40))	as	bend(40)

horn ribs(20) sphere(1)	is	horn ribs(20) sphere(1)
texture(3)	the	stack(10)
tranrule1(stack(10)	same	bend(40)
¢ bend(40))	as	texture(3)

Build   When constructing a single form it is easiest to describe the overall transform rules to be applied to the entire form. When the form is used in an animation this means that as the number of ribs increases, extra ribs are packed more tightly together rather than the horn growing in length (Figure 8.5). This infilling results in a dense mass of primitives.

If *build* is specified for a horn, the transform rules define the transform between one rib and the next, rather than to the transform between the first rib and the last. This permits the horn to grow as required, but makes the values needed in the transform rules difficult to specify.

To overcome this, *build* may take a parameter which says that the given transform rule applies to rib number *build*. The following is the formula used to place the *i*th rib.

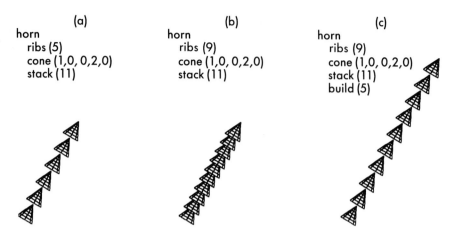

Figure 8.5. Need for build. In (a) the cones are almost touching. In (b) extra cones are added in the same space, pushing them together. The specification of build(5) in (c) restores the original spacing and increases the overall stack value.

```
if build = 0 then
    base: = ribs;                    /* NObuild, use actual
                                        number of ribs as base. */

else
    base: = build;                   /* The base number of
                                        ribs given explicitly. */
    relpos:i/base;                   /* Position of this rib
                                        relative to base. */
    trans(transrule, relpos):        /* Apply specified
                                        tranrule relpos times. */
```

Thus the forms defined below are identical:

```
horn ribs(20) stack(40)           /* NObuild implies base 20 */
horn ribs(20) build stack(2)      /* build implies base 1 */
horn ribs(20) build(10) stack(20) /* base specified as 10*/
```

The first has an overall stack value (at the 20th rib) of 40. The second is stacked two units for each rib, and thus reaches an overall stack value of 40 for the last rib (20).

The third is specified to reach a stack of 20 after 10 ribs, again two per rib and a cumulative stack of 40.

Head and tail   *Head* and *tail* permit extra objects to be stuck at the head (start) and tail (end) of a horn (Figure 8.6). They are useful for adding features at the ends of an object, or at joins in a segmented horn without altering the flow of the backbone of the horn to which the feature is attached. *Tail* was first introduced before we used horn lists to produce sequences of horns.

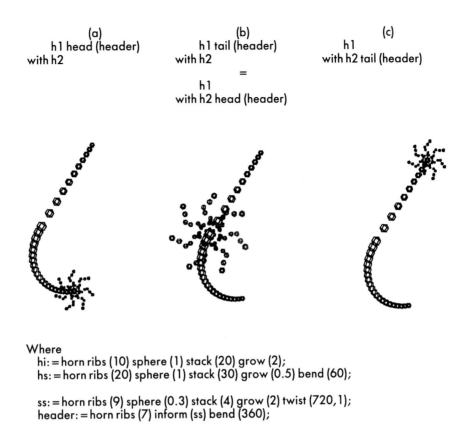

(a)
h1 head (header)
with h2

(b)
h1 tail (header)
with h2

=

h1
with h2 head (header)

(c)
h1
with h2 tail (header)

Where
hi: = horn ribs (10) sphere (1) stack (20) grow (2);
hs: = horn ribs (20) sphere (1) stack (30) grow (0.5) bend (60);

ss: = horn ribs (9) sphere (0.3) stack (4) grow (2) twist (720,1);
header: = horn ribs (7) inform (ss) bend (360);

Figure 8.6. Head and tail. The tail of h1 and the head of h2 come at the same position, so (b) may be specified in two ways. The basic header shown in (a) is larger in (b) as the transform at the end of h1 provides a scale as well as the position and orientation. It is back to its original size in (c) as there is a reduction transform over h2.

Automatic tails   Extra input forms are added as the number of ribs in a horn grows. When inbetweening is used in an animation the number of ribs is not always integral, and extra ribs pop in as the number increases. This can be hidden by automatically adding a tail (Figure 8.7), which is placed at the (possibly nonintegral) end rib position. *Fulltail* requests a tail that is the union of the elements of the *inform* list. *Parttail* requests a tail that uses the *inform* appropriate for the next full rib position, but scaled down depending on the position of *ribs* between one integral position and the next.

Horn queries   A form definition is used for more than just display. For example, animations that fly through forms use the form definition to direct the camera. This requires two query functions: *ribs* extracts the number of ribs, and *trans* computes the transform for a specified rib position. *Trans* works whether or not there is a rib at the specified position, and interpolates

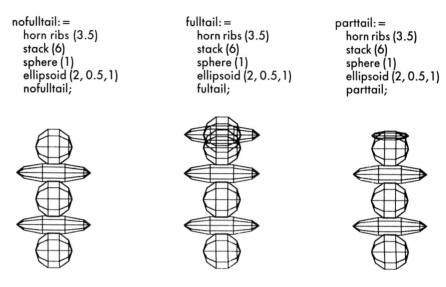

```
nofulltail: =
    horn ribs (3.5)
    stack (6)
    sphere (1)
    ellipsoid (2, 0.5, 1)
    nofulltail;
```

```
fulltail: =
    horn ribs (3.5)
    stack (6)
    sphere (1)
    ellipsoid (2, 0.5, 1)
    fultail;
```

```
parttail: =
    horn ribs (3.5)
    stack (6)
    sphere (1)
    ellipsoid (2, 0.5, 1)
    parttail;
```

Figure 8.7. Automatic tails. The right form has no tail at the position for rib 3.5. The centre form has a full tail that consists of the union of all the input forms at their fill size. The right hand form has a partial tail, which consists of the ellipsoid that would be the input form for rib 4 scaled down to half size, as 3.5 is half way from the last complete rib 3 to the next rib 4.

between two ribs or extrapolates at each end of the horn, as necessary. *Trans* with no position parameter works out the transform for the end of the horn:

$$\text{trans(horn)} = \text{trans(horn, ribs(horn))}$$

Recursive horns

The ribs of a horn can be created using another horn, as shown in Figure 8.2. Using a smaller copy of the main horn for its own ribs creates a recursive horn. The rib is itself made out of smaller copies, and so on. Applied to the limit, this would create a fractal horn, and so the term *frac* is used in the definition of recursive horns.

Complexity of fractals To simplify processing, the depth of recursion in a fractal horn is limited, and the subhorns are not constrained to be exact copies of the parent horn, but may contain fewer ribs. *Fracnum* is given a list of numbers that defines the number of ribs to be used at each level below the main level (Figure 8.8).

Fractal colouring A fractal image can be more interesting if the different levels are coloured differently, and this colouring certainly makes it easier to see the way in which the fractal horn is created. *Fraccol* takes a list of texture identifiers to be applied to each level below the main level (Plate 20).

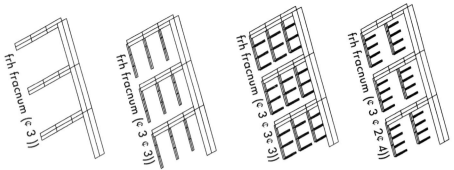

where frh: = horn sphere (1) ribs (30) stack (20)

Figure 8.8. Control of the number of fractal subhorns. The top left form uses just one level of recursion with three subhorns. The top right form uses an extra level, also with three subhorns. The bottom left form goes to a third level of three subhorns, and the bottom right form again uses three levels, but with 3, 2 and 4 subhorns in each, respectively.

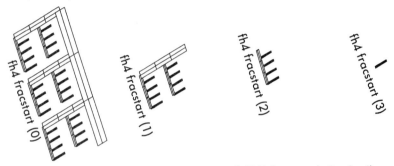

where fh4: = horn sphere (1) ribs (30) stack (20) fracnum (¢ 3 ¢ 2¢ 4)

Figure 8.9. Control of the starting level in a fractal horn. This shows a complete fractal horn, its subhorn, the subsubhorn and the subsubsubhorn. Fracstart is used internally in the implementation of fractal horns, and for debugging and rapid display.

Looking at fractal detail   Sometimes, we only want to display the simpler subribs, either to understand what is going on, or to get a much quicker image for interaction. *Fracstart* creates a fractal horn using only the level specified and below (Figure 8.9). It is also used internally in the creation of fractal horns.

Orientation and fractals   *Orient* specifies the orientation and scale of the subhorns relative to the main horn (Figure 8.10). Our fractal horns are thus generated using two transforms, the main transform specified by *tranrule1* and *tranrule2*, and this *orient* transform. These two transforms interact the same way as the generating transforms in iterated function systems (Barnsley, 1988). The main difference is that we iterate a basic input form *inform* that already has some visual interest, rather than iterating a point and relying on the fractal system to produce a filled result. Working in three dimensions this is particularly important, as it gives 'body' to the final form. Another

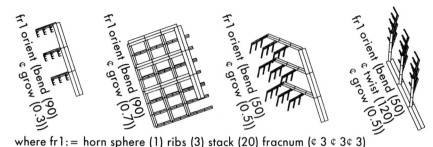

where fr1:= horn sphere (1) ribs (3) stack (20) fracnum (¢ 3 ¢ 3¢ 3)

Figure 8.10. Use of orientation on a fractal horn. This shows the use of the orientation transform which scales and positions each level of a fractal subhorn relative to the level above. The top examples both use the subhorns oriented at right angles to the horns at the parent level, with different scaling of the subhorns. The bottom left form uses a different angle, and the bottom right form is twisted into the third dimension.

difference is that we control the limits of iteration by the number of ribs and the depth of recursion. This limits the final detail of the horn, which would in any case be lost with our finite *informs*, but makes the generation of the fractal horns very much more efficient.

Transform rules

The function *trans* (Figure 8.11) is applied to transform rules to turn them into transforms. It permits a transform rule to be applied any number of times, integral or nonintegral. The original iterative application concept behind transforms only works for an integral number of applications. This had several disadvantages: it was not suitable for animation use where a consistent interpretation had to be given to 'apply this transform 3.89 times'; it required the awkward specification of transforms for a single step (effectively *build*) rather than for a complete horn; and it made it very slow to

```
trans (stack (s)      , m) =   at (0, s*m, 0)
trans (side (s)       , m) =   at (s*m, 0, −s*m)
trans (back (s)       , m) =   at (0, 0, −s*m)
trans (stack (2,vec)  , m) =   at (m*vec)

trans (twist (s)      , m) =   yrot (s*m)
trans (twist (s, off) , m =    at (off, 0, 0) yrot (s*m) at (−off, 0, 0)
trans (bend (s)       , m) =   zrot (s*m)
trans (twist (s,vec)  , m) =   rot (s*m, vec)


trans (grow (s)       , m) =   scale (s**m)
```

Figure 8.11. Implementation of transform rules. The choice of axes assumes that the horn is stacked up the y-axis, and therefore that twists are about the y-axis, and that bends are in the xy plane. The offset twist moves the object away from the axis, twists it, and moves it back.

directly find the transform for a large number of iterations. This was no problem for programs that sequentially placed the first subobject, then the second, and so on, but was awkward for more sophisticated applications such as animation fly throughs.

Iterative consistency   The iterative method guaranteed that applying a transform m times and then n more times was equivalent to applying it $m+n$ times. This is still true of most of our transform rules:

$$\text{trans(rule, m) trans(rule, n)} = \text{trans(rule, m+n), usually}$$

It is not always true, for example, that the branching rule breaches this rule.

List of rules   To compute *trans* for a list of transform rules, we compute *trans* for each element, and compose the transforms:

$$\text{trans(rule1 ¢ rule2, m)} = \text{trans(rule1, m) trans(rule2, m)}$$

Commutativity   As mentioned before (see Chapter 3), the order of the elements in a list of transform rules is very important:

$$\text{trans(rule ¢ rule 2, m) NOT EQUAL trans(rule 2 ¢ rule1, m)}$$

Even where the number of applications is an integer, we cannot work out the overall transform by working out a single application and repeating it:

$$\text{trans(rule\_list, 2) NOT EQUAL trans(rule\_list, 1) trans(rule\_list, 1)}$$

Branch   More explanation is in order for branching (Figure 8.12).[8] To give an even distribution, *branch* needs to know the total number of ribs being placed before it can decide where to place any given rib. The method draws a spiral over the surface of the sphere, and places points at regular intervals along this spiral (Figure 8.13). The distance from a point to the nearest point on the turn above is the pitch of the spiral or a little more, depending on alignment. For full regularity ($p=1$) the pitch is the same as the distance between points along the spiral, so that as more points are added the spiral makes more turns.

Changing the angle control (s) limits the surface area covered by specifying the number of degrees the branch spreads out over. Changing the regularity control (p) alters the ratio between the pitch and the distance along the spiral, and so emphasizes the spiral.

---

[8]The branch algorithm was taken from a program developed for simulation in molecular chemistry, which needed to position an awkward specified number of points as evenly as possible over the surface of a sphere. The molecular application does not require direct access to individual points, and uses an incremental implementation reliant on the relationship between sine, cosine and their derivatives to generate each point from the previous one with no calls to trigonometric functions.

```
trans (branch (s, p) , m) =
    surfprop: = 0.5 * (1-cosd (s/2));
    ncon: = ribs/surfprop;          /*number of points to fill nsurface*/
    ddd: = sqrt (pi*ncon)/p;
    y: = 1-2*m*surfprop;            /*result for this transform*/
    phi: = acosd(y);
    xrot (phi) yrot (ddd*asin(y) * 180/pi)
```

Figure 8.12. Original branch code. **Surfprop**: proportion of the surface to fill; **ncon**: number of ribs required to cover the entire surface; **ddd**: spacing between points (based on surface area 'owned'); **y**: vertical position; **phi**: rotation needed to achieve y.

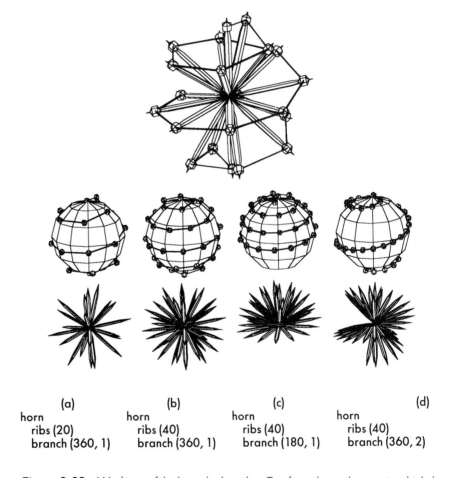

(a)	(b)	(c)	(d)
horn	horn	horn	horn
ribs (20)	ribs (40)	ribs (40)	ribs (40)
branch (360, 1)	branch (360, 1)	branch (180, 1)	branch (360, 2)

Figure 8.13. Workings of the branch algorithm. Top form shows the way in which the points on the surface of the sphere are used to generate a branching structure. In the lower group, the top row shows the construction of branching forms, and the bottom row shows the forms themselves. As the number of ribs doubles from (a) to (b), both the pitch and the spacing along the spiral decrease by sqrt(2). (c) covers only part of the surface, and (d) doubles the pitch and halves the spacing of (b).

Continuity and animation   As extra ribs are added or other small alterations are made to a branching structure, the spiral shifts a little and the existing ribs slide along it. An addition of just one rib (Figure 8.15) moves the central ribs by half a rib position. During an animation the eye cannot track the individual ribs, and as a result the branching horn appears to shimmer or vibrate. The overall visual change is small, but detailed changes are too large.

We are starting to use an alternative algorithm (Figure 8.14) that places a given rib on a fixed line on longitude, regardless of the total number of ribs. The lines of longitude are spaced at regular intervals, usually very widely spread (137.5° by default). As an extra rib is added, the existing ones merely move a very small amount down their line of longitude (Figure 8.15). This algorithm is a reinvention of Vogel's (1979) formula for the pattern of a sunflower head modified for wrapping onto a sphere, and the constant 137.5° is taken from a description of this (Prusinkiewicz and Lindenmayer). Though the algorithm is stable for animation with the second (texture) parameter, it is unstable as this texture parameter changes (Figure 5.10).

```
trans (nbranch (s, p) ,m) =
   surfprop: = 0.5 * (1−cosd(s/2));
   ncon: = ribs/surfprop; /* number of points to fill surface */
   y: = 1 − 2 * m * surfprop; /* result for this transform */
   phi: = acosd(y);
   xrot (fi) yrot (137.5 * p * m * ghornribs)
```

Figure 8.14. *n* in the relative rib position in the range 0 to 1, and so *n* * *ghornribs* is the rib number. The same vertical spacing is used as with our old algorithm to give even distribution: this does allow for the total number of ribs.

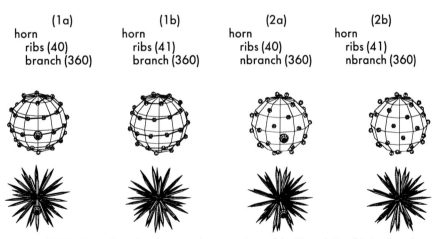

(1a)	(1b)	(2a)	(2b)
horn	horn	horn	horn
ribs (40)	ribs (41)	ribs (40)	ribs (41)
branch (360)	branch (360)	nbranch (360)	nbranch (360)

Figure 8.15. Branch and animation. Just one rib is added from (a) to (b). Look at the indicated rib in (a). Which one is it in (b)? It is easy to correlate the individual ribs in 2a and 2b which use the new branching code, but not in 1a and 1b which use the old version.

Fractal irregularity   Most of the forms that we produce are mathematically very regular. To give the forms a little overall 'wobble' we introduce fractal irregularity by adding extra transform rules with the *fractal* option (Figure 8.16). This causes the transform rule for the *i*th rib to be worked out using *trans(tranrule,fractal(i))* instead of *trans(tranrule,i)*, where *fractal* is a fractal function.

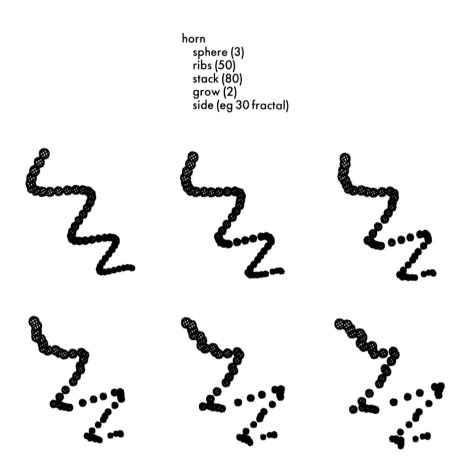

Figure 8.16. Fractal irregularity applied to a horn. The six pictures show the result of using fractal genes of 0, 10, 20, 30, 40 and 50 in the above expression.

When using fractal variation of scale or rotations it is best to apply the variation early in the transform list, but for translations it is more effective towards the end of the transform list (Figure 8.17). It is usually more effective to apply the variation in a direction not used in the transform list; for example, to use *side* fractal variation with a *stack* transform rule, and *bend* fractal variation with a *twist* transform rule. We are planning to provide more control over this fractal variation; for example, control of the fractal dimension.

```
horn                        horn                        horn
   sphere (3)                  sphere (3)                  sphere (3)
   grow (2 fractal)            ribs (50)                   ribs (50)
   ribs (50)                   stack (80)                  stack (80)
   stack (80)                  twist (1000, 15)            twist (1000, 15)
   twist (1000, 15)            grow (2)                    grow (2)
   grow (2)                    stack (20 fractal)          side (20 fractal)
```

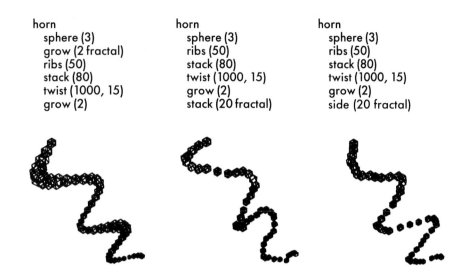

Figure 8.17. Application of different kinds of variation. In the left form the input forms have irregular scales. The centre form uses irregular stacking, and the right hand form has the objects shifted left and right by irregular amounts. Fractal irregularity in growth and orientation is usually applied early in the list of transform rules to prevent scaling and orientation also being applied to subsequent shifting transformations. Fractal irregularity for shifting is applied late in the list of transform rules to prevent the shifts being exaggerated by subsequent scaling and orientation.

Extensions to basic horns

Segmented horns   Segmented horns are defined by making a list of horns using the *with* constructor. The idea for segmented horns came from looking at skeletons where bones are connected end to end, for example in fingers. In a simple example *horn1 with horn2*, *horn1* is placed at the end of *horn1*. All the transforms that apply at the end of *horn1*; position, rotation and scaling. The following are all equivalent:

```
horn 1 with horn 2
horn1 tail(horn2) /* unless horn1 already had a tail */
horn1 union horn2 trans(horn1)
```

This fitting rule makes it easy to fit one horn precisely to the end of another, but if the first horn involves a *grow* the second horn may not be the expected size.

The query function *ribs* and *trans* are extended to horn arrays to give the total number of ribs, and the position of a specified rib. Where the specified rib number is less than zero, the first horn of the array is extrapolated backwards, and where it is greater than the total number of ribs, the last horn is extrapolated forwards (Figure 8.18). There is a problem here when the horn segments have different spacings between ribs. If the rib numbers are

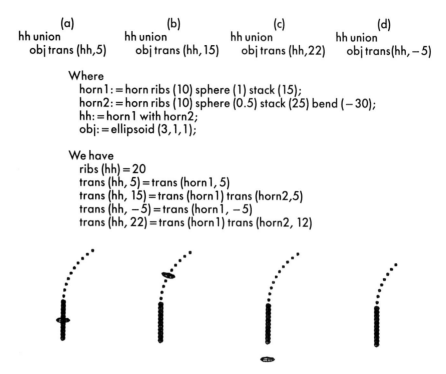

(a)   (b)   (c)   (d)
hh union   hh union   hh union   hh union
obj trans (hh,5)   obj trans (hh,15)   obj trans (hh,22)   obj trans(hh,−5)

Where
horn1: = horn ribs (10) sphere (1) stack (15);
horn2: = horn ribs (10) sphere (0.5) stack (25) bend (−30);
hh: = horn1 with horn2;
obj: = ellipsoid (3,1,1);

We have
ribs (hh) = 20
trans (hh, 5) = trans (horn1, 5)
trans (hh, 15) = trans (horn1) trans (horn2,5)
trans (hh, −5) = trans (horn1, −5)
trans (hh, 22) = trans (horn1) trans (horn2, 12)

Figure 8.18. Transforms from horn lists. The ellipsoid shows the position of the four transforms. (a) is in the first horn, (b) is in the second, (c) is extrapolated after the second, and (d) is extrapolated before the first.

used to position a camera or a child during an animation, the speed changes as the position moves from one segment onto the next.

Ribcage   *Form Grow* produces regular forms which can be made to have various symmetries, but it is not easy to produce mirror symmetry. The *ribcage* extension was designed to fit a symmetric ribcage to a 'backbone' horn. This is like a spine with a row of ribs inspired by the skeletons of snakes and animals at the Natural History Museum in London. The ribcage is described by the object to be used for each rib and the number of rib pairs. Optionally, the ribcage can be further controlled by start and end positions that prevent ribs being connected to the end parts of the backbone, and flap and sweep angles that change the orientation of the ribs on the backbone (Figure 8.19).

Hornweb   *Hornweb* produces a spider web form of horns. It is given a spoke horn and a crosspiece horn, with the number of each to use, and the optional controls for leaving a hole in the middle, for offsetting the outside crosspiece from the ends of the spokes, and for varying the relative scale of the crosspieces (Figure 8.20). Latham uses this to create gothic spiders webs made out of coiled animal horns (Plate 13).

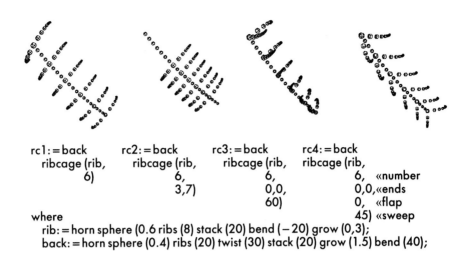

rc1: = back   rc2: = back   rc3: = back   rc4: = back
   ribcage (rib,   ribcage (rib,   ribcage (rib,   ribcage (rib,
         6)   6,   6,   6, «number
                            3,7)   0,0,   0,0,«ends
                                                   60)   0,   «flap
                                                                       45) «sweep
where
    rib: = horn sphere (0.6 ribs (8) stack (20) bend (−20) grow (0,3);
    back: = horn sphere (0.4) ribs (20) twist (30) stack (20) grow (1.5) bend (40);

Figure 8.19. Control of ribcage. rc1 is a basic ribcage. rc2 does not use the first three and last seven ribs of the backbone. rc3 flaps the wings down and rc4 sweeps the wings back.

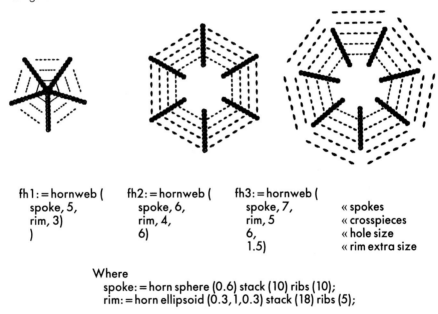

fh1: = hornweb (fh2: = hornweb (fh3: = hornweb (
   spoke, 5,   spoke, 6,   spoke, 7,   « spokes
   rim, 3)   rim, 4,   rim, 5   « crosspieces
)   6)   6,   « hole size
                                                1.5)   « rim extra size

         Where
            spoke: = horn sphere (0.6) stack (10) ribs (10);
            rim: = horn ellipsoid (0.3, 1, 0.3) stack (18) ribs (5);

Figure 8.20. Control of Hornweb. This shows three webs made from two simple straight horns *spoke* and *rim*. *fh1* uses defaults where possible; *fh2* specifies a central hole; and *fh3* also specifies that the outermost rim should come outside the end of the spokes.

Multidimension We are experimenting with multidimensional forms. All the rules of *Form*
forms *Grow* extend with no difficulty into any number of dimensions. Our main interest is the use of four dimensional forms for animation, to see whether

the visual and artistic effect of tumbling a four dimensional form is different from that of metamorphosing a three dimensional one.

Drawing horns

Form Grow turns horns into computer forms when the artist uses the *csg* function. This usually produces a full CSG model that may be displayed in either wireframe or rendered. There are various options for producing simplified output for special purposes; for example, to get a quick impression of a form which the artist can rotate for three dimensional information, or to give a fast animation preview. These simplified methods are akin to an artist drawing preparatory quick sketches, and these computer sketches often have an artistic interest of their own, much as hand-drawn sketches do. We developed the hidden line drawing options for the production of this book, though we expect to use them for other purposes. Some of the options control *Form Grow* and others the underlying ESME drawing system, but the options are all packaged into a function *drawstyle* for ease of use by the artist.

Low level drawing style The low level drawing style controls the way in which each primitive is drawn (Figure 8.21):

Wire draws in simple wireframe; best for fast interaction.
Hline draws in wireframe with hidden line removal.
Nurb draws rendered solids using the rendering power of the display device. Nurbs are only available on high powered display devices. They give quite good pictures that are properly lit and shaded, but with limited texturing capability. Each redraw takes from well under a second to several seconds, depending on complexity.
Render calls Winsom for full rendering, including texturing and raytracing if required. Each frame takes from well under a minute to several minutes depending on complexity.

Line choice Line choice controls which construction lines are to be drawn and which omitted (Figure 8.22):

Colouredge draws a mesh over a form.
Streamline draws lines along the flow of a form.
Crossline draws lines only across the flow of a form.

The terms streamline and crossline assume a typical stacked horn. For horns made in some other way (for example, pumpkin forms), the artist has to experiment with the exact effect of these options.

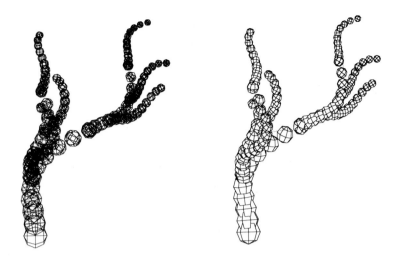

Figure 8.21. Wire frames and hidden line drawing styles. The left hand form is shown with all the wires used to construct the primitives. This style is much quicker for fast interaction. In the right hand form only the wires on the frontmost visible surface are displayed. This style more clearly shows the three dimensionsal shape of a static form.

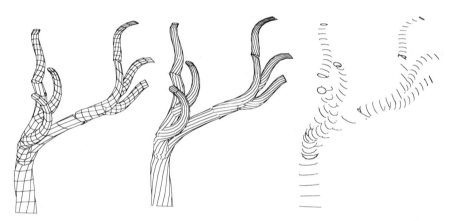

Figure 8.22. This shows colouredge, streamline and crossline styles. The streamline style is particularly effective at emphasizing the flow of a horn shape.

Horn style   Horn style controls the way in which *Form Grow* represents horns (Figure 8.23):

Full   draws in full the objects that make up the horn.

Outer   follows the outer edge of the objects that make up the horn to create an envelope of the form. This can make the structure of the horn clearer, and produces a picture with fewer lines for faster interaction and less cluttered printed pictures.

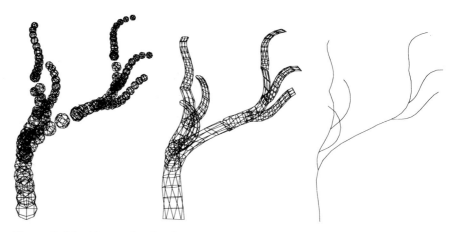

Figure 8.23. Horn style. This shows a horn drawn in full, as an outer frame and as a skeleton. The outer frame style gives a good overall impression of the form in a simpler, less cluttered picture. The skeleton style is displayed very quickly for interaction and for checking transform rules.

Skeleton draws the centre line of the horn; useful for very fast interaction or for debugging algorithms such as movedown (see Chapter 10).

Resolution All the drawing styles permit a variety of accuracy or resolution (Figure 8.24, 9.9), with low resolution being coarser but faster than high resolution. Detailed control of resolution is different for each drawing style, and some styles have several controls for different aspects. *Drawstyle* provides a simple scale of five: very low, low, average, high and very high.

All the styles above, with the exception of rendering, are capable of drawing only the union of many objects, and cannot represent the CSG capabilities of intersection and difference. This is no problem with *Form Grow*, but we sometimes also use explicit CSG operations. Another program *Fast Draw* draws wire frame or hidden line sketches of any CSG model.

Structure programming

Sometimes the artist or system developer wishes to use *Form Grow* in a way that goes outside its original purpose. This can sometimes be achieved by combining the high level power of *Form Grow*, with lower level programming.

Connected parameters There are many ideas in the artist's mind when building a complex form: for example, how the parts should fit together, and their relative sizes. Some of these such as the fitting of a horn's head to tail come naturally with the way

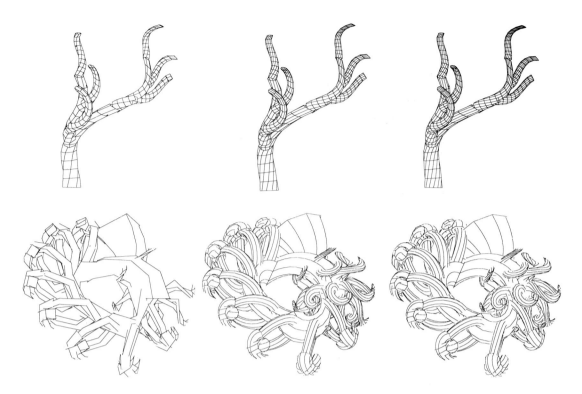

Figure 8.24. Resolution in horn sketches. As we move from left to right, increasing resolution is used. Lower resolution is quicker for interaction, and less cluttered for a complex form. Higher resolution gives a more precise picture of the form.

in which horns are defined, and others have to be programmed explicitly. The horn definition language is an extension to ESME rather than a separate language implemented in ESME, so that we can naturally mix programming at the two levels (Figure 8.25).

There are various reasons for tying parameters together in this way. One is to guarantee that parts fit, as in the above examples. One is to have variables that control the overall bendiness, twistiness, and so on of all the parts of a complex structure. The decay of objects in *Life Cycle* is programmed by using the first gene to create a scaling transform that is applied to all the primitives in the structure (Figure 8.26). As the value of the gene decreases to zero, so all the primitives shrink.

Analytic parameters   Connecting parameters by structure programming is a way of inserting extra analytic information into a structure, thus limiting the form space and simplifying the use of *Mutator*. In theory, the decorated horn shown in the example (Figure 8.25) could be created by *Mutator* without the use of connected parameters, but in practice it would take much too long.

```
br:=1;   /*big radius from the torus*/
lr:=0.3; /*little radius for the torus*/
sr:=0.1; /*radius for the decorative spheres*/

transrule:=stack (20) ¢ grow (0.6) ¢ twist(360,2); /* basic tranrule*/
tranrule2:=twist (1000) ¢ tranrule; /*extra twist for decoration*/
sp:=sphere (sr) at (br+lr+sr,0,0); /*sphere, offset touches torus*/
sps:=sp union sp yrot (120) union sp yrot (240); /*three spheres*/

main:=horn ribs (60) torus (br,lr) tranule;      /*main horn*/
deco:=horn ribs (300) sps tranrule2;             /*decoration*/
all:=main union deco;                            /*full decorated horn*/
```

Figure 8.25. Connected parameters. The various radii are saved in variables for reuse. The basic transform rule for the horn is also saved in a variable so that it can be used to create a secondary transform rule for the decoration which twists around the main horn. The decorative sphere is created with an offset calculated so that it falls outside the main torus just touching it, and three copies are made to create three decorative twists. We now make the main and decorative horns and fit them together, with an exact fit guaranteed.

```
osc:=scale (eg 1); /*osc is a scale used for all primitives*/

neck:=horn (torus (eg 1.8, eg 0.5) osc)...

tor1:=horn (torus (eg 1.7, eg 0.4) osc)...

ribs1:=horn
    (sphere (eg 0.4) osc)
    (sphere (eg 0.8) osc)
    (sphere (eg 0.7) osc)
```

Figure 8.26. Form decay by structure programming. This shows an extract from the lobster structure, with the first gene used to scale all primitives and thus to permit decay.

Fitting   Fit takes a horn and adds extra transform rules to the end of its transform rule list to force the transform for the end of the horn to match a given transform. This is used for connecting networks of horns (Figure 8.27)

Conditional programming   Another way in which to combine programming techniques with high level horn definition is to use conditional programming. The values of certain genes are used to conceal or to activate parts of a structure. The *Life Cycle* animation system is programmed to communicate via gene values to *Form Grow* how far an object is through its life cycle (Figure 8.28), or the time of day or season (if summer then flower). Care must be taken with continuity when parts of a structure are activated or concealed, so in the example the web has scale 0 when it is first activated at birth, and then grows slowly.

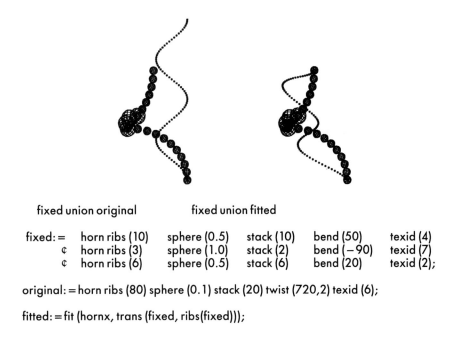

fixed union original   fixed union fitted

fixed: = horn ribs (10)   sphere (0.5)   stack (10)   bend (50)   texid (4)
      ¢   horn ribs (3)   sphere (1.0)   stack (2)   bend (−90)   texid (7)
      ¢   horn ribs (6)   sphere (0.5)   stack (6)   bend (20)   texid (2);

original: = horn ribs (80) sphere (0.1) stack (20) twist (720,2) texid (6);

fitted: = fit (hornx, trans (fixed, ribs(fixed)));

Figure 8.27. Fitting two horns. In the left hand picture the segmented horn and the simple horn start at the same position and orientation, but end at different ones. The right hand picture shows the fit operation applied to the simple horn to force it to fit the end position of the segmented horn.

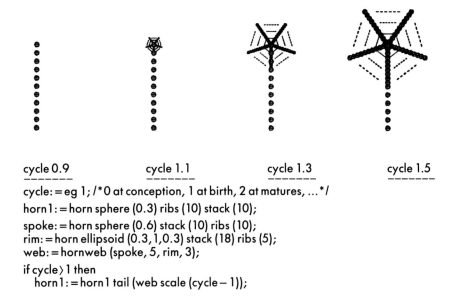

cycle 0.9   cycle 1.1   cycle 1.3   cycle 1.5

cycle: = eg 1; /*0 at conception, 1 at birth, 2 at matures, ...*/
horn1: = horn sphere (0.3) ribs (10) stack (10);
spoke: = horn sphere (0.6) stack (10) ribs (10);
rim: = horn ellipsoid (0.3,1,0.3) stack (18) ribs (5);
web: = hornweb (spoke, 5, rim, 3);
if cycle > 1 then
    horn1: = horn1 tail (web scale (cycle − 1));

Figure 8.28. Sequence of forms opening out at birth. This program generates a horn *horn1* with a conditional web that sprouts at the start of cycle 1. *Lifecycle* is set up so that the first gene is set to indicate how far through its life cycle the form is. In practice, there would be several other genes changing as well.

Conditional programming is also used to allow simple but well controlled structure mutation (see Chapter 5).

Experimentation Structures written using programming techniques such as those just outlined are difficult to write, and very difficult to read. Once we understand the implication of an application of structure programming and we can generalize it, we systematize it as an extension of *Form Grow*. *Hornweb*, *Ribcage* and fractal horns all began as experimental structure programs. However much *Form Grow* evolves there will always be new things that we want to do, so structure programming will remain an essential experimentation tool.

Chapter 9
Drawing and rendering

In the same way that there are many styles in which the artist can draw, the computer can draw the forms in different styles and with varying detail. Like a sculpture, it is important to be able to turn or move it quickly. For practical reasons, the ESME drawing system permits CSG models to be displayed in a number of ways, from immediate but very crude wireframe, which can be used for real-time manipulation, to output to an overnight (or worse) rendering run with full ray tracing. In an ideal world, a computer graphics user can move about in a complex and changing scene, seeing superbly realistic images refreshed 60 times a second, all on hardware costing very little and weighing nothing. This is not possible in our laboratory, and our research is more concerned with graphics applications than graphics techniques.

Once *Form Grow* has created a computer form, the artist interactively selects a view using primitive graphics, and then ESME sets up the Winsom rendering run using that view.

Real-time interaction with virtual sculptures

Real-time interaction is where the artist makes a continuous change to the virtual object by way of a mouse, dial or other device, and the computer redraws the changed object many times a second. Real-time interaction has a very different feel to menu style interaction, and imposes a much heavier load on the graphics software and hardware.

View interaction   It is important for artistic images or films to obtain a good view of a form. The best way to do this is using real-time interaction to spin, pan and scale the form. Controlling the virtual sculpture in real-time helps the artist to understand the three dimensional nature of the form, and to select the best view. Once the artist has chosen a view, it is automatically saved for use in rendering an artwork, or as a view for a key frame of an animation.

View clipping can be a problem with interactive view interaction. It is very obvious with a rendered image when an object is so close to the camera that it interferes with the lens (the front clipping plane), but it is easy not to notice on a simplified wireframe display. The problem is reduced by moving the front clip plane nearer to the camera for rendering than for view setup, and almost eliminated on modern hardware which gives near real-time semi-rendered display.

Manipulating form   Real-time interaction can be used to edit the objects themselves. Changes to the form of objects usually go deep into the application code, and cannot be performed in real-time except for simple changes, such as moving one part of a rigid object relative to another for layout purposes or robot programming.

Views and animations   It would be tedious to use interaction to choose the view for every frame of an animation, and probably give an irregular result. Instead, we can choose views at certain key frames, and use a splining system to compute other views. We usually obtain views for animations using animation rules such as regular rotation and fly-through that are part of the underlying systems. This does not always produce good enough results, and we combine these animation rules with interactive view selection.

To give the user the feeling that he is manipulating an object, the computer must redraw it very frequently, ideally 60 times a second, but more realistcially at least 10 times a second. This relies on special hardware. Also, movement of the object should relate easily to the user's movements. This requires effective software, and can be assisted by special interaction devices.

Real-time interaction overview

Flow of data   Figure 9.1 shows an example of the flow of data for interactive graphics using a display list architecture.

A view of the object   The user creates a form as a horn definition. *Form Grow* converts this to a computer form, held as CSG primitives such as spheres. The drawing system converts these to lines which are easy to display in real-time. The lines are written via the interface into the structure store (also called the display list), where they are saved. The display hardware reads the lines from this store, and applies the current viewing transformation to the ends of the lines so as to project them onto the viewing plane. The line drawing algorithm works out which pixels lie between the transformed end points, and sets these pixels to the appropriate colour. When all the lines have been turned into pixels in the frame buffer, the frame buffer is displayed on the screen, and the user can see the object.

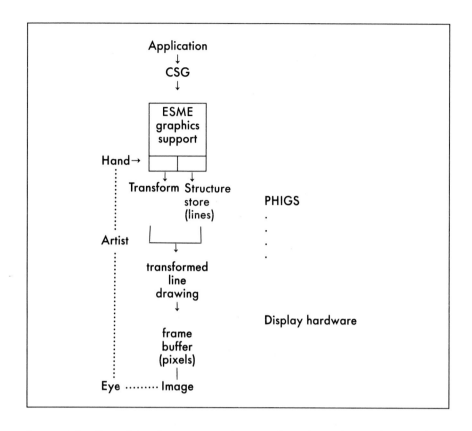

Figure 9.1. Flow of data for interactive drawing. Once the application has saved a form in the structure store the interaction loop continues without the application being involved.

A second view   If that view is not satisfactory, the user moves the mouse or one of the other interaction devices to set up a change of view. The program that interprets the action and decides how to change the view is part of the ESME graphics support. The display hardware again reads the lines from the structure store, and repeats the drawing process using the new transform. When the rescan is complete, the user sees a new view of the object.

Real-time interaction loop   This mouse interaction, transform calculation and image redraw loop continues until the user is happy with the view. If the redrawing is fast enough the user gets the feeling that he is manipulating the object, and we call the process the *real-time interaction loop*.

Double buffering   If the old lines are not cleared before the new ones are drawn, the object leaves behind a track of all its old positions, and the screen is soon full of rubbish and illegible. If the viewer sees the screen being cleared and rewritten, he gets a very flickery image. This is usually solved by having two frame stores; as one is displayed the other is cleared and written with a new computer image. When the image is ready, the second frame store is displayed and the first updated, and so on. This is called *double buffering*, and is standard for three dimensional graphics terminals, but not for simpler terminals such as X stations.

Advantage of display list The advantage of the display list architecture is that it makes it easier to optimize the interaction speed. Once the application has described the object to the display hardware it is not involved in the real-time interaction loop. A small amount of work in computing the new viewing transformation is required by the graphics support (even that is performed by the display hardware in many systems), and the rest is done by the display hardware. This must process data very fast, but the transformation and line drawing process are very simple and so easy to build into efficient hardware or microcode.

The display list is also very useful where animating the view of a fixed form. As with real-time interaction, the application stores the form just once in the display list, and the animation preview is made by sending a stream of transforms to the display hardware. The transforms for an animation are computed and sent by the application, rather than being derived directly from user interactions.

Disadvantage of display list The disadvantage of the display list is that it is inflexible. We have shown how it can be used for view interaction, and it is fairly easy to extend this to move one object relative to another, or to draw linked mechanisms such as robots. However, if we want to change in real-time a feature such as the number of ribs in a horn that lies deeper in the application, or to draw four dimensional objects where the hardware is set up for three dimensional objects, the display list becomes a barrier that slows down the interaction between the application and the screen.

In the future, as hardware costs reduce and the optimization advantages of display lists diminish, display list systems will become obsolete. For now, they provide the only efficient implementation that permits real-time view interaction.

Display hardware

Latham uses several kinds of display hardware at the Winchester Scientific Centre. They all use display list architecture, but their other features dictate the kind of image that can be used for interaction, from wireframe to fully rendered, the number of lines or primitives that can be used, and the smoothness of the interactive display. The hardware available at a particular time had a significant influence on Latham's work. With the very fast change in display adaptor hardware, features that we now describe as 'advanced' will soon be considered 'basic'.

Latham's first interactive work used a Vector General 3300 directed beam device. This could draw only white lines on black, with a maximum of about 8000 lines. The Vector General used a directed beam system that drew lines directly onto the screen without a frame buffer. If the display was too complex, the line was not revisited soon enough, and the whole image flickered. There was no possibility for hidden lines, but lines at the back of the image were less bright than lines at the front, which gave a very useful impression of depth.[9]

It was not long before we started using a raster technology device, the IBM 5080. It is not quite as fast as the Vector General, but more useful for several reasons: it draws coloured lines; as a scene becomes more complex the interaction slows down, but the image remains stable without flicker; finally, it can display the 8 bit rendered final images produced by Winsom.

We now use an IBM 6090. This is very fast as an interactive line drawing device. As well as lines, it can transform and draw polygonal patches with smooth Gouraud shading, and non-rational b-spline surfaces. It gives results nearly as good as those of Winsom for colouring and lighting (Plates 31d,e), though with only rudimentary textures. At a second or more per frame on Latham's complex sculptures, the rendered images are not produced quite fast enough for manipulation, but they are very useful for animation previews and for *Mutator* sessions, and have made it practicable for us to apply *Mutator* to colour and lighting. We also display both 8 bit and 24 bit Winsom images on the 6090.

Software

Interaction control   The view or other interaction is controlled by the user manipulating a device such as the mouse or special dials. One of the most important considerations is what Lipscomb called *kinesthetic correspondence* (Lipscomb, 1979), the movements of the interaction device should relate sensibly to the movements of the image.

Mouse or tablet   The mouse is one of the most pervasive devices, but most of our hardware uses the tablet. All our interaction software uses the tablet as a relative

---

[9]The lack of a display buffer means one fewer step between the interaction device and the screen, which in turn means a quicker response. We have still not seen the reaction speed of the Vector General approached by any other graphics hardware. With the analogue lines it drew, always staircase-free and wonderfully depth cued though not always straight, with its idiosyncratic character set, and its bulbous case, it was like a classic 1960s sports car. I swore at it every day, and I mourn its passing. SJPT.

device, and so the difference is not significant. Both are only two dimensional devices, and the movements need to be interpreted as changes to three dimensional transforms. The mouse is used in four modes, selected by a menu:

Pan	The object pans about the screen following the mouse.
xyRot	The object is rotated so that the front of the object follows the mouse. The effect is much the same as rotating a trackball.
Zoom	As the mouse moves up or right the object grows, and as the mouse moves down or left the object shrinks. A 45° motion up and left to down and right causes no change.
Zrot	As the mouse moves up or right the object rotates anticlockwise; as the mouse moves down or left the object moves clockwise.
Eye distance	Up and right motions of the mouse increase the perspective on the object; down and left motions decrease it.
Clipping	As well as an object being clipped to the edges as it covers the screen, it is also clipped at the front and the back to give a slice through the object. This slice is usually chosen to be big enough so that none of the object is sliced away. Mouse movement to the left decreases the thickness of the slice, to the right increases it. Movement up moves the slice forwards; down moves the slice backwards.

These changes only occur when a mouse or tablet button is pressed, releasing the button acts as a clutch. All the buttons on a multi-button mouse are programmed to behave the same, both for the menu and object picking and as a clutch, as this reduces confusion.

Rotation and scaling are about the centre of the screen when we are interacting with a view of a single object, and about the centre of the manipulation object when we are manipulating one object relative to another in a linked structure. There are many other ways of using a two dimensional device to interact in real-time with a three dimensional form, those outlined are especially appropriate with sculptures which have no natural axes.

Kinesthetic correspondence and linkages   Even when the mouse is being used to move one object relative to another, kinesthetic correspondence is always assured by applying the changes in *display* space. It is not easy to use a system in which a rightward movement of the mouse moves an object along the x-axis of a parent object. Changing a transform T that operates on an object O in a linkage mechanism involves three steps (Figure 9.2). (1) Work out the concatenation P of all the parent transforms in the linkage structure, including the viewing transform at the top of the linkage structure, and thus the overall transform $T\,P$ that is used to display $O\,T\,P$ on the screen. (2) Modify this transform by the appropriate change rule d to obtain a new value $d(T\,P)$, effectively making a manipulated object $O\,d(T\,P)$ in display space. (3) Back-transform the result to extract the modified value $T=d(T\,P)\,inv(P)$ which replaces T in the linkage structure.[10]

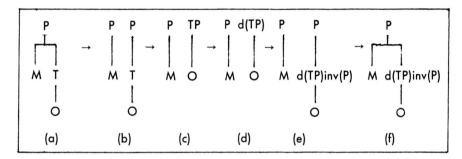

Figure 9.2. Kinesthetic correspondence and hierarchical objects. The initial network applies a transform P to the combination of base model M and object O further transformed by T. We wish to move to O by altering T. The initial network (a) is broken into a fixed and varying parts in (b). The varying part is converted by (c) into a single transform applied to O. This single transform is changed in (d) by the function that moves O with kinesthetic correspondence. The parent transform P is factored out of this new transform in (e), ready to remake in (f) the initial network with a modified value of T.

Lower level graphics support We had to write all our own low level interactive graphics support for the Vector General, but with the 5080 and 6090 we moved to industry standard PHIGS (Programmers Hierarchical Interactive Graphics System). The hierarchical structure store is very useful for horns of horns; each subhorn is transmitted just once to the device and then called many times from the main horn. This saves preparation time in our code and its interface to PHIGS, transmission time by PHIGS to the device, and storage space within the device. The graphics device still has to traverse the subhorn many times when drawing each image, and so the hierarchical definition does not assist interaction speed. Exploitation of this hierarchy enables us to work effectively on very complex sculptures.

Interaction devices

Knobs and dials are often provided to control interactions. They are usually placed all pointing in the same direction, and are extremely counter-intuitive and difficult to use. We still often use the wrong one after using the same configuration for six years.

---

[10]The expression $d(T\,P)\,inv(P)$ is a valid ESME expression for the changed transform.

Figure 9.3. Dials, ears box and mouse. This shows the main interaction devices we use. The tablet puck and dials are standard devices. We designed and built the ears box to make it easier to rotate forms. The rotation of the form corresponds in a natural manner to the movement of the various knobs on the ears box.

Ears   One solution we adopted for rotations is the *ears* box (Figure 9.3), which we constructed for the Vector General Display in 1983. A rotary knob is placed on each of the top, front, left and right faces of a cube. Turning one of the knobs turns the object in the corresponding plane; the ears take about ten seconds to learn and get used to. The left and right knobs perform duplicate functions, but are both provided to allow for use with either hand.

Three space   Another solution is the three space tracker, which uses radio signals to detect
tracker   both the position and orientation of a sensor in space, and is programmed so that the movement of the virtual object on the screen follows exactly the movement of the tracker. Experiments by Andrew Walter and Tim Rowledge[11] show that this device is much better than knobs, sliders or ears

---

[11]Private communication.

for manipulating one object exactly to fit another. When it is used as part of a larger task the advantage is less clear, as the tracker falls down when you let it go.

Virtual reality devices   Experimenters in virtual reality are inventing new interaction devices. We are planning to use these together with the associated display devices when they become easily available and not too intrusive to use. The SAFARI combination of *Mutator* with real-time animation will especially benefit.

Winsom renderer

Winsom takes a computer model as generated, for example, by *Form Grow*, and creates a rendered computer image. As ESME is the cornerstone around which all Latham's artistic systems are built, so WINSOM is the foundation. It was the impressive results produced by Winsom and the enthusiasm of its creator Peter Quarendon that first persuaded Latham to work with the Scientific Centre.

The basic flow of data in Winsom (Figure 9.4) is:

geometry	determine what object is visible at each point;
colour and texture	determine the surface characteristics of the object at that point;
lighting	determines the light given off by the object at that point in the direction of the camera;
coding	encode the red, green and blue values and save in an image file.

Geometry and algorithms for 'what can I see'

At the heart of Winsom is the code that decides which primitive object is visible at each point in the image. It uses the divide and conquer algorithm of Woodwark and Quinlan's Vole system (Woodwark and Quilan, 1982), which is very efficient for models involving large numbers of primitives. This is important for Latham, as many of his more recent sculptures involve tens of thousands of primitives.

Internally, Winsom represents a CSG definition as a tree, with primitives at the leaves and set operations at the other nodes. All the transformation operations such as rotation and scaling are pushed down the tree and applied to the primitives in a pre-pass of the tree (Figure 9.5).

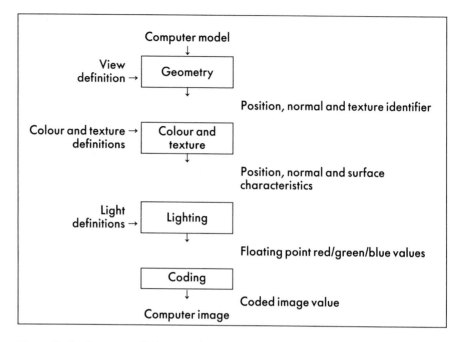

Figure 9.4. Structure of Winsom. The computer model is generated by *Form Grow*. The view definition is defined by interaction as described in the previous chapter, or by the animation system (see Chapter 6). Colour and texture are defined by the artist (see Chapter 11), and the light definitions can be defined by the artist using the lighting editor described later in the chapter.

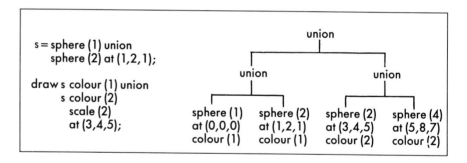

Figure 9.5. Expansion to a tree. On the left hand side we have a computer model, and on the right hand side is its expansion as a tree, with all transforms and colouring moved to the leaf nodes.

Voxels   The Winsom algorithm operates in terms of voxels, or volumes of space. The largest voxel Winsom uses is the entire volume being viewed. The smallest voxels are like three dimensional pixels, so that for a thousand pixel square image there are a million pixels, and a thousand million of these small voxels. The voxels at each level fill the viewing space, and are aligned to fall behind the screen pixels. For parallel viewing the voxels are rectangular, and for perspective viewing they are trapezoidal. The algorithm's main concerns are to make sure that it visits as few of these voxels as possible, and that when it does visit a voxel the tree is as simple as possible.

The Winsom geometry algorithm starts with the complete original tree and the complete viewing voxel (Figure 9.6). It looks at the tree and decides if there is a simpler tree which gives the same solid within the voxel. If there is, it continues operation with this simplified tree.

Classifying the primitives Much of the expression tree is irrelevant for smallish voxels, as it contains primitives that are not anywhere near that voxel. The code that decides whether a primitive is relevant in a particular voxel is called the *classifier*. The classifier understands the geometry of each primitive type, and decides for a given voxel and primitive whether the primitive lies entirely outside the voxel, entirely inside the primitive, or whether there is some interesting interaction between the two.

Simplifying the tree Every time Winsom looks at a voxel it asks the same question: is there a simpler tree that looks the same in this voxel? If the classifications for all the primitives in the voxel indicate some interesting interaction, no simplification can be made, but any primitive that has no interesting interaction with the voxel can be eliminated from the tree. If the primitive lies fully outside the voxel it can be substituted by **empty**, or if it fully encompasses the voxel it can be substituted by **full** (the solid object that fills all of space). The substituted tree is not equivalent to the original, but it produces the same object *within the voxel of interest*.

Simplification of this substituted tree uses simple set theoretic pruning rules such as:

- X union empty = X
- X difference full = empty
- X intersect empty = empty

and more complicated redundant primitive elimination (Todd and Halbert, 1991) such as:

- (X intersect Y) union (X intersect (full differenceY)) = X

Ray casting and recursive subdivision If the tree is now simple enough, Winsom uses conventional ray casting to fire a ray through each of the pixels corresponding to the voxel to find the object visible in the pixel. If the tree is still too complicated for efficient ray casting, the voxel is again subdivided. The criterion as to whether to subdivide or ray cast depends on the size of the voxel and the number and type of primitives left. At the lowest level, where the voxel size is the pixel size, it is always necessary to ray cast. At the largest voxel size it is almost always worth subdividing. Two levels from the lowest possible, where a voxel corresponds to 16 pixels, Winsom subdivides if there are five or more primitives in the tree.

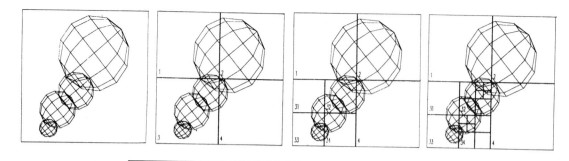

This shows the original picture (left), and four levels of subdivision (first centre left, second, third and fourth together centre right). The criterion for continued subdivision is that at least three primitives remain in the voxel.

The voxels in the first subdivision are labelled 1, 2, 3 and 4. The first two (bottom left) spheres are classified as 'outside' voxels 1, 2 and 4, so that on simplification their trees become

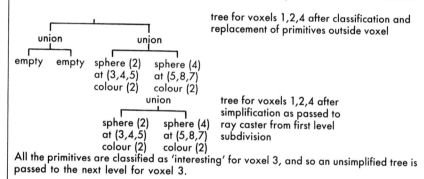

tree for voxels 1,2,4 after classification and replacement of primitives outside voxel

tree for voxels 1,2,4 after simplification as passed to ray caster from first level subdivision

All the primitives are classified as 'interesting' for voxel 3, and so an unsimplified tree is passed to the next level for voxel 3.

At the second level voxel 3 is further subdivided into 31, 32, 33 and 34. Voxels 31 and 33 are reduced to one or more primitives.

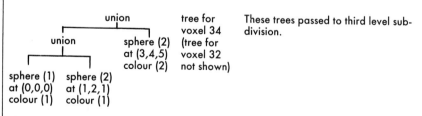

tree for voxel 31 ... tree for voxel 33 ... These trees passed to ray caster at second level subdivision.

Voxels 32 and 34 each have three remaining primitives and are passed to the third level of subdivision.

tree for voxel 34 (tree for voxel 32 not shown) ... These trees passed to third level subdivision.

The right figure shows how voxels 32 and 34c are subdivided at the third level, and voxels 322 and 341 at the fourth level.

In three dimensions, each subdivision is 8 ways.

Figure 9.6. Two dimensional recursive subdivision.

Sometimes it is not practicable for the classification algorithm to determine exactly whether there is an interesting intersection between a voxel and a primitive. For example, the code to determine whether a torus intersects a very skewed perspective voxel is extremly complicated. In this case the classifier assumes that there is an intersection, and lets further subdivision or ray casting resolve the problem. This is called *conservative* classification. It involves more processing at lower levels, but this is often more efficient than attempting precision at the high levels. In Figure 9.6 the smallish sphere at the top of voxel 34 probably does not intersect it, and so strictly the voxel contains only two primitives and need not have been subdivided.

Quadtree hiding mask   The recursive subdivision in three dimensional space always visits the front voxels before the back ones, and a quad tree is kept to reduce work looking in detail at objects that are obscured. As a visible object is found for each pixel, the geometry algorithm calls the lower level rendering algorithms, and the result is recorded in the final image, which forms the lowest level of the quad tree. In addition, the quad tree indicates groups of 4, 16, 64, and so on, pixels have *all* been set.

Once a complete quad is marked as set, recursive subdivision does not look at any further voxels that lie behind it. As an extreme example, suppose a plane sheet is placed at the front of the viewing volume. Winsom finds this sheet very quickly, and does not have to do any ray casting and only very little simplification of the objects behind it.

Colour and texture   Once the object visible at a particular pixel has been determined, the surface properties of the object at that point in space are found (see Chapter 11).

Lighting

Winsom implements a standard lighting algorithm (Glassner, 1989) which allows for the details of the lights and the surface characteristics of the object being illuminated. For each light the user specifies a light position and strength. In addition, he can specify a colour, and for a spot light a direction and concentration. Latham generally uses three to four lights based on the style of lighting painted by Rembrandt.

Lighting editor   SLED (Solid Lighting EDitor) is an interactive program associated with WINSOM that helps a user set up lights. SLED works backwards from normal lighting editors. Rather than the user placing the lights and looking at the effect, he defines the required effect by pointing at the object with the mouse and SLED places the lights accordingly.

For example, to position a light the user points at the surface of the object where a highlight is required. SLED computes where the light must be placed for the required effect. This position depends on the glossiness of the object. For a matt object the light must be placed along the normal to the surface of the object. For a very glossy object the light must be placed so that it reflects off the surface of the object into the camera. For semi-gloss surfaces the light must be placed between these extremes.

When a new light is positioned, its intensity is set to bring the total illumination at the specified highlight point to the maximum permitted value. The concentration of a spot light is set by indicating a point on the object at which the level should be 20% of the level at the centre of the beam. Other features are controlled in the conventional way by filling in values on a menu, or using increment and decrement keys.

Image coding

The lighting calculation determines how much light enters the camera from the given direction, and what its colour is. This is expressed as a triple of floating point red, green and blue values that should lie in the range 0 to 1. This value must now be stored in the computer image. It is not generally practicable to store the values in full. Winsom generally converts this triple to either 8 bits or 24 bits.

Quadratic coding   In 24 bit coding, each of the red, green and blue values is converted to an 8 bit integer in the range 0 to 255, using the formula:

$$code = 255 * sqrt(value)$$

The square root is used to compensate for the varying sensitivity of the human eye (Cowlishaw, 1984). The eye is much more sensitive to changes of intensity in dark objects than in light ones. For example, it is about ten times more sensitive to a change from 0.01 to 0.02 than it is to a change from 0.9 to 0.91, even though the intensity difference is only 1/10th as much. The exact curve for eye sensitivity depends on various factors such as ambient conditions, and the square root function we use gives good results and is convenient to compute.

8 Bit coding   8 bit coding only permits very few levels each for red, green and blue. We usually use 6, 7 and 6, respectively, though more recent experiments indicate that 6, 10 and 4 would be better. These different values allow for the different sensitivity of the eye to red, green and blue light.[12] The code value

---

[12]We are not precise enough in our use of colour to define exactly what wavelengths of red, green and blue are to be used. We performed our original experiments on a monitor which had a greenish tinge on the blue phosphor, so giving a blue light to which the eye was more sensitive than it is to pure blue. This is why we chose to use six levels of blue rather than just four.

is given by:

```
rcode: = rlevels * sqrt(red);      /* rlevels = 6 */
gcode: = glevels * sqrt(green);  /* glevel = 7*/
bcode: = blevels * sqrt (blue);   /* blevels = 6 */
code = 2 + rcode*glevels*blevels + gcode*blevels + bcode
```

The value 0 is used to indicate that no object was seen (background), and 1 to indicate an error condition such as the object intersecting the front clipping plane. The use of a square root or similar sensitivity compensation law is especially important with the limited number of levels.

Error diffusion   The small number of levels available with 8 bit coding means that the difference between levels is very marked. This produces severe thresholding bands which are compensated for by error diffusion (Floyd and Steinberg, 1975). Each time a value is coded, the error resulting from the coding approximation is carried forward to be added into the corresponding value for the next pixel. Thus a level of 3.3 is coded as a mixture of values of level 3 and level 4 to give an overall intensity of 3.3.

Several details are required to make error diffusion work well: (1) Where the required intensity is equal to an available code value the error diffusion algorithm naturally generates a smooth area. This smooth area is obtrusive when the rest of the image is roughed by the error diffusion, and so it is detected and broken up; (2) The pixels are visited following a randomized space filling curve (Figure 9.7). Raster order gives echoes of edges and worms of texture on the image, and Hilbert order gives noticeable texturing where mixing ratios of 1/4, 1/2 or 3/4 are used; (3) The diffusor includes a crude edge detector to avoid carrying errors over edges. This is important with a non-linear choice of levels as the error value from a bright pixel can be considerably greater than the intensity value of the pixel into which it is carried.

Comparison of 8   24 bit coding gives a much smoother result than 8 bit coding with a better
and 24 bit   sheen and sharper detail, and is essential for the best quality results.[13] Some people quite like the slight roughness of the 8 bit images, and we have even been asked how we managed to achieve such a pleasant result.

8 bit coding has several pragmatic advantages. The 8 bit computer images are smaller and so take up less disk space, and are quicker to move around. They do not compress as well as 24 bit images, so this advantage is not as great as it at first appears. Many display devices, for example typical X stations, cannot display 24 bit images without first converting them to 8 bits.

---

[13]It has been claimed that more than 24 bits are needed, but as long as non-linear coding is used there is no perceptual improvement from using more than 24 bits.

Figure 9.7. Randomized space filling curve. This curve is derived from a Hilbert curve but with different generators. A vertical or horizontal line is replaced either by the U or X rule, and a diagonal one with either the Z or N rules. The choices are made at random with a 50% probability.

```
                        342 452 453 463 554 563
                    222 332 342 443 443 453 553 453 564 563
                121 221 342 342 343 353 453 553 463 554 564 563
            300 200 321 332 332 442 452 453 453 453 563 564 563 564
            300 200 311 332 332 342 343 352 453 453 563 454 563 564
        300 300 300 300 321 422 332 442 442 443 453 453 453 563 553 563
        300 400 300 400 320 321 431 332 342 342 453 443 453 553 554 463
        400 400 400 400 400 311 321 332 432 343 342 453 453 453 453 453
        500 400 400 400 400 300 311 321 432 332 342 342 442 452 453 452
        500 400 400 400 400 400 400 411 321 432 442 332 343 343 443 453
        500 400 500 500 500 400 400 300 421 321 431 342 342 332 342 342
            500 500 400 400 400 400 400 300 311 322 322 332 342 332
            500 500 400 500 400 500 400 400 300 310 311 321 221 222
                500 500 500 500 400 400 400 300 300 300 200 121
                    500 500 500 400 400 400 400 400 200 200
                        400 400 500 400 400 300
```

Figure 9.8. Coded image. This shows the red, green and blue values for each point in an 8 bit image. A blank indicates a background value. the image is of a pale yellow sphere lit with a white light top right and a red light bottom left.

Intensity clipping   The lighting calculations often compute highlight intensities greater than the maximum that can be stored in the image or displayed on the screen. If all levels are lowered to compensate for this, then the overall image is too dark. The usual solution is to truncate intensity values above the maximum:

$$\text{if intensity} > \text{maximum then intensity} := \text{maximum}$$

This gives a hard edge to the saturated area. Also, if a coloured object is being shown, the red, green and blue saturate at different times, giving a white highlight with coloured bands around it. The bleaching of the highlights is similar to the colour washout on over-exposed photographs.

Winsom uses a formula[14] which avoids the hard edges and prevents the colour of highlights shifting. As an intensity exceeds a certain threshold near the maximum, it is gently attenuated to mimic the gentle saturation of photographic film, and to prevent the hard edge. The intensities for the three colours are connected so that if any of the colours exceeds the threshold they are all attenuated by the same amount. This prevents colour distortion and washed out highlights.

```
rr: = max(red, green, blue);   { rr is intensity most needing attenuation }
if rr > softt then             { softt is threshold, typically 0.975.      }
    begin                      { if attenuation required                   }
    ss: = 1 − (1 − softt)*(1 − softt)/(rr + 1 − 2*softt); { maximum is 1   }
                               { ss is intensity after rounded attenuation }
        red: = red * ss/rr;    {            All colours . . .              }
        green: = green * ss/rr; {          . . . are attenuated . . .       }
        blue: = blue * ss/rr;  {               . . . equally.              }
    end;
```

Ray tracing

Winsom includes a ray tracing algorithm. Ray tracing permits pictures that include shadows, reflections of one object in another, transparent and semi-transparent objects and refraction. The algorithms used in the Winsom ray tracer are more conventional than those used in the ray caster (Glassner, 1989). Ray tracing Latham's forms takes several hours of processor time.

Image output

Now the rendered computer image has been created it must be displayed, and if it is for gallery showing it must also be printed.

Gamma correction The major problem for both display and printing is gamma correction. On a typical display a request for 1/2 maximum intensity gives approximately 1/4 maximum intensity output, and levels of less than about 1/5 of maximum give no output at all. This is due to the physics of the screen, and is called gamma distortion. Incorrect gamma correction causes unbalanced mid-tones and a shift of colour hue and saturation.

---

[14]Patent pending.

Hard copy   The easiest way to get a hard copy of a computer image is with a screen copy device, but these do not usually give very good quality results. Using an ordinary camera to take a photograph of the screen is quite successful, but requires some experience with exposure as computer images do not have the same colour balance as natural scenes. The best results are obtained with special computer cameras, which are almost essential when preparing artworks for a gallery. Computer cameras can use computer images with resolutions of several thousand pixels in each direction, and expose either onto standard 35mm film or onto large format films such as 4×5 inch or 8×10 inch.

A computer image is just a stream of numbers which can be saved on a tape or transmitted over a network or satellite link without loss of quality (Figure 9.8). One of the best ways of getting a good photographic image is to send it on computer tape to a specialist with top quality equipment. A specialist also has the experience to use the equipment, and to develop and print the negatives properly.

Special output   We have tried several experiments in more realistic image display. Red green stereo is easiest, but the results are effectively black and white. The best result so far has been using stereo pairs projected through polaroid filters onto a polarization preserving screen and viewed through polaroid glasses. Texturing enhances the three-dimensional stereo effect as it provides depth information over the entire surface of a form. We are preparing three dimensional images for a lenticular display, and considering holograms and even the use of stereo lithography to produce real sculptures.

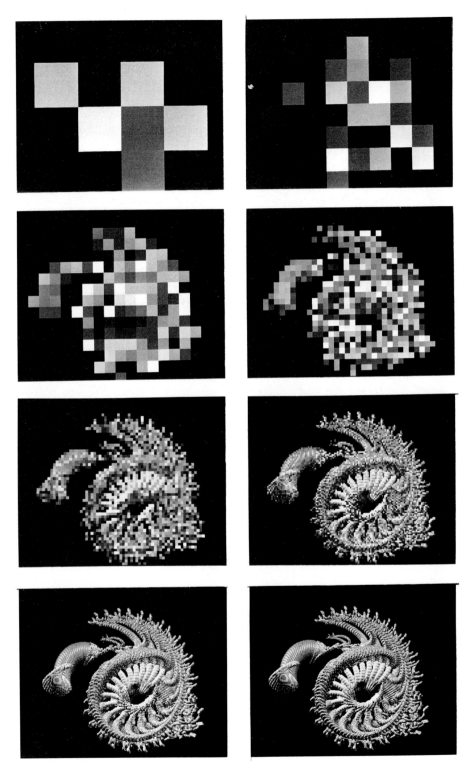

Figure 9.9. Eight rendered images with varying pixel resolution (8, 16, 32, 64, 128, 256, 512, 1024).

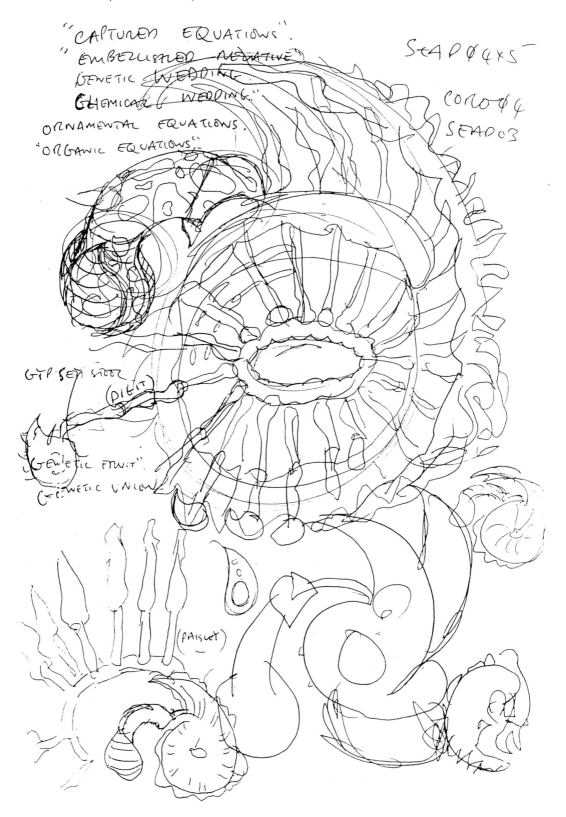

"CAPTURED EQUATIONS".
"EMBELLISHED NEGATIVE"
"GENETIC WEDDING"
"CHEMICAL WEDDING."
ORNAMENTAL EQUATIONS.
"ORGANIC EQUATIONS"

SEAP04×5
CORO04
SEAP03

GYPSEN SIZE
(DILIT)

"GENETIC FRUIT"
"GENETIC UNION"

(PAISLEY)

Chapter 10
Animation control

At one end of the spectrum of computer animation techniques, the computer is used as a tool to assist traditional hand-drawn animation of every frame; at the other, the computer performs a simulation of a physical or biological system, and the animation is a graphical representation of the simulation (Atiyah *et al.*, 1989; Reffye *et al.*, 1988; Miller, 1988; Sims, 1991). A single major problem pervades throughout the spectrum; how to specify an animation. This is a problem in human computer interaction, and where a team is working on an animation, artistic director, producer, composer, and so on, it is also a problem in human to human communication.

We use *Life Cycle* (see Chapter 6) to perform pseudo-physical and biological simulations. *Life Cycle* produces a detailed script which is then executed by *Director*, as described in this chapter.

Director is a procedural, script based program (Reynolds, 1982) with *events* such as conception triggering *processes* such as growth. The processes are provided by *Life Cycle*, and *Director* provides the control of those processes. The rules of life provide much of the detail required by an animation. The combination of *Life Cycle* and *Director* is sufficiently high level that the artist uses it directly without a technical animator to work as intermediary (Figure 10.1).

Director operates in three stages (Figure 10.2). The first (preprocess) stage collates and restructures the information in the script produced by *Life Cycle* to prepare it for use by the form and simulation rules. The second (process) stage invokes the procedures that implement these rules. These stages primarily involve organization, not graphics or computation. In the final stage, *Director* invokes the drawing system and the appropriate low-level recording mechanisms, an extremely laborious but fairly straightforward task.

Director does not itself define the processes or how they are to be used. It defines an *infrastructure* into which processes and scripts are inserted. The levels of design of an animation mirror those of a static form. The processes correspond to the building tools, the form of the scripts to the structures, and precise timings to the detailed parameters.

The remainder of this section describes how the user specifies scripts, actors, events and processes to *Director* in the first stage, starting at the script level and working down to the details of a process. An example

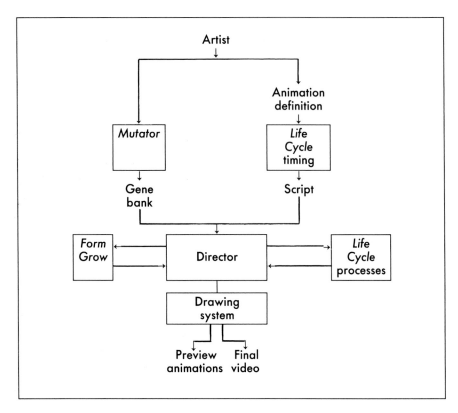

Figure 10.1. Various systems that interact with *Director* in context.

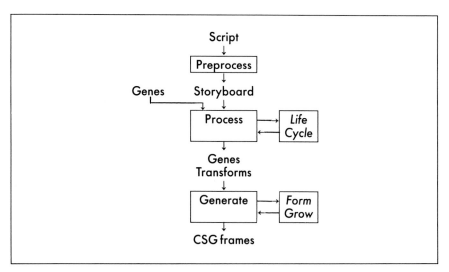

Figure 10.2. Overview of *Director* phases. The preprocess phase collects information about the events and works out a detailed storyboard collating information about process timings. The process phase uses these timings to call the *Life Cycle* processes. The generate phase uses the output of these processes to create and compose computer forms.

demonstrates the work of organization that *Director* undertakes in the second. Most of the section is a general description of *Director*, but one part describes the processes of *Life Cycle*.

The script file

The writer of a script (usually *Life Cycle*) works in terms of the *actors*, which are named forms that will appear in the script (for example, *Object1*) and the *events* in their life (for example, *conceived*). These are grouped into a series of *events*, which are 'triples' saying at what time what event happens to what actor. The events may appear in the script in any order, so that timings can easily be changed by the artist with no need to reorder the script itself.

Defining actors

Definition of an actor (Figure 10.3) gives information about it that remains true over all scripts. The information associated with an actor depends very much on the animation being provided, and would, for example, be very different in *Mutations* or in an animation of a walking human figure.

There is a fairly arbitrary distinction between information provided with the actor definition, information defined with the processes, and information provided as a parameter to an event. In an example where a sculpture is to go through a whole variety of forms, key forms are defined using genes to a 'KEY_GENES' event.

```
object1 :=  actor
                structure ('LOBSTER')
                mature__genes ( (1,3) );

object2 :=  actor
                mother (object1)
                structure ('LOBSTER')
                mature__genes ( (2,7) );
```

Figure 10.3. This shows how the forms of an actor are assumed and how the family trees are defined. Some users will prefer to give the actors and their variables more interesting names: Judith and Fred, or Art1 and Spikey, for example.

Events and processes

The script is written using events (Figure 10.4) such as *conceived*, which are implemented as switches that start and stop *processes*; for example, the event

```
myscript: = script ('Myscript')

    frame (1)    object1   at (0,0,0)
                           field

    frame (5)    object2           conceived
    frame (10)   object2           born
    frame (15)   object2           matures
                 object1   dies

    ...
```

Figure 10.4. Defining part of a script. All the times are given as absolute values, with the events that happen at that time. The frame times in the script are usually generated by *Life Cycle*, and the events are expanded into processes by *Director*.

```
conceived: = event ('CONCEIVED')
                on ('GROWTH')
                on ('MOVE_DOWN');

born: = event ('BORN')
            off ('MOVE_DOWN')
            on ('FIELD');

matures: = event ('MATURES')
               off ('GROWTH');
```

Figure 10.5. This shows how the relationship is defined between events such as 'conceived' and processes such as 'growth'.

conceived starts a *growth* process. The relationship between event and processes is defined in a process register (Figure 10.5).

Processes of Cycle

There are several major processes defined by the *Life Cycle* system (see Chapter 6). The growth process for which code is shown below (Figure 10.10), controls the genes and size of an actor. The *move_down* process moves a child form down its parent's spine, and the *field* process implements the world vortex in which sculptures float once born.

Movedown details   In the movedown process used in *Mutations*, the child form was oriented in the same direction as the ribs of the parent (Figure 10.6). This often caused the child form to stick out of the parent, a problem similar to the camera not looking where it was going in the fly-through.[15] This problem was mostly

---

[15]We assure readers that this form of life has no sense of touch, so this sticking out causes no discomfort.

solved by measuring the length of the child and scanning along the parent's backbone from the position of the child's head to find another point that length away. The child form is then rotated about its head to fit the tail to this point on the backbone (Figure 10.7).

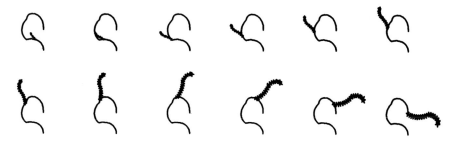

Figure 10.6. Movedown process used in the *Mutations* film. The child form is aligned with the rib of the parent at which it is positioned. The child does not always fit the parent very well, and sometimes obtrudes outside the parent form. The forms are shown in simple skeletal style to make the relative positions clear.

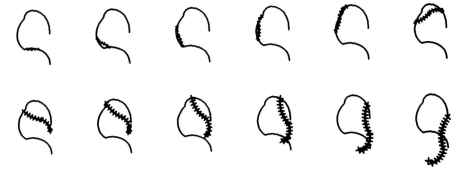

Figure 10.7. Fitting movedown. This shows an updated movedown process which scans the parent to force both the head and tail of the child to fit the parent's backbone exactly.

This fitting algorithm can fail where the child form is large and parent coiled, as the child gets too large to fit round a corner (Figure 10.8). Where the child is bent differently from the parent, the middle of the child sticks out even though both ends lie inside the parent. We prevent these problems by making sure that the child forms are not too large at birth.

Form definition and computer form   Implementation of the movedown process requires finding positions within the parent. This cannot be done from the parent computer form itself, but only by applying the *trans* function to the more abstract form definition. Our initial implementation of the form generation system merged the structure with the parameters, and generated the computer form as a single step. These steps had to be separated to permit *Director* to extract the intermediate form definition.

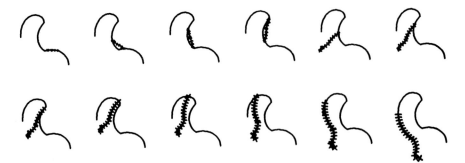

Figure 10.8. Fitting movedown error. When the child is too large and the parent too bent, the child cannot move down the parent in a natural manner. When the child reaches the tight corner on the parent the orientation of the child jumps as it finds the first possible position in which it fits.

Field vortex   A field (Figure 10.9) is defined by adding a number of primitive components such as a *vortex*, rotation about a given axis, with rotation being faster closer to the axis; a *line_sink*, a movement towards a given axis, again with faster motion closer to the axis; and a *steady flow* movement in a given direction. All of these have strengths and directions, though a default direction is provided if none is specified.

```
whirlpool: = field
            vortex (10)
            line__sink (1);
```

Figure 10.9. Sample definition of a whirlpool. **Vortex** causes a rotary motion that is stronger in the centre than at the edges. **Line__sink** causes a steady downward movement.

Types of process

While the *FIELD* process computes the *absolute* positions, *MOVE_DOWN* computes the position of one form **relative** to another, using the hierarchical parent relationship. This hierarchical relationship can go to any depth, but must not include loops, as *Director* does not currently include any equation solving constraint mechanism.

The *FIELD* process computes the positions *incrementally* based on its previous position, but *MOVE_DOWN* computes offsets *directly* without reference to the previous offset. Incremental processes prevent the user looking at the middle of a scene without *Director* doing some preparatory work on the earlier parts. *Director* tries to optimize in this case, and the optimization would be considerably simplified using lazy evaluation.

Defining processes

A process is defined as an ESME function (Figure 10.10), a lower level and more detailed matter than defining scripts and actors. All processes have the same input parameters, but some processes ignore some of the input parameters. The major input is an actor, including all its current state information such as genes and position, and the process returns this actor in processed form. The process in the example changes the genes and the size of the actor, and other processes also change its position, orientation, colour and texture.

```
/* First define BUDS, as used by growth process. */

begin 'GROWTH PROCESS' function # /* process is defined as a function */
    actor: =         ?actor;        /* actor to be processed */
    now__time: =     ?time;         /* time now */
    start__time: =   ?time;         /* start time of growth process */
    end__time: =     ?time;         /* end time of growth process */

    /* work out how far through growth, linear scale 0 to 1 */
    lt: = (now__time – start__time) / (end__time – start__time);

    /* move to cosine curve for smooth growth */
    st: = (1 – cos(pi*lt)) / 2;

    /* work out genes at this point in growth, save in actor */
    actor.genes: = actor.bud__genes* (l–lt) + actor.mature__genes * lt;

    /* record the size the actor is to have */
    actor.size: = st;

    /* return the actor */
    actor
    end;
```

Figure 10.10.   Code for the GROW process of *Life Cycle*, and the growth and decay of a simple form.

This process shows details of how the animation will work. Cosine interpolation is used to give smooth starting and stopping of the growth. *lt* gives a linear interpolation, and *st* a smooth cosine interpolation.

ESME does not support functions as first class objects, so references to the 'GROWTH_PROCESS' function are saved in the process control structure by the character string 'GROWTH'. This is used to access the function by generating and interpreting an ESME character string.

Organization by *Director*

The above sections show how information about actors, events and processes is given to *Director*. We now demonstrate the processing performed by *Director* in converting this information to computer form groups and rendered images.

Preprocess   The organization stage of *Director* begins with a preprocess step which expands the events in the script into the process switches. It locates corresponding process *on* and *off* switches, and saves them for use in the next phase.

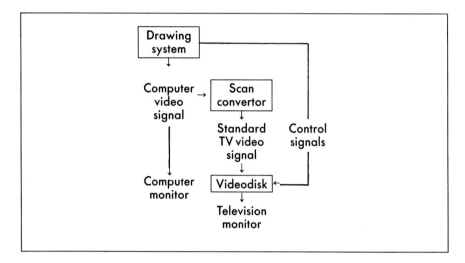

Figure 10.11. Using the videodisk. Frames are prepared by the drawing system and displayed on the computer monitor. The video signal is converted to television standard and recorded on the videodisk under the control of the drawing system. When the recording is complete the preview may be played back.

Perform processes   *Director* processes frame information in sequence for each frame. It keeps a list of active actors, that is updated whenever an actor is activated or deactivated. For each actor it keeps the state of the actor, and a list of active processes that is updated by the process switches.

At each frame it calls each active process for each active actor: thus updating the states of these actors. The order of the processes is important here. For example, the shape of a child and the shape of its parent must be established before movedown can position the child relative to the parent, and the absolute position of the parent must also be found before the absolute position of the child is finally computed.

Generate   Once the state information for all active actors is available, *Director* generates a computer form group as a constructive solid geometry model. *scsg* is the *Form Grow* entry point that takes genes and structure and generates the raw computer form. This is then scaled and positioned by *Director* using the transforms generated by *Life Cycle*.

The computer forms of all active actors are combined using the *union* operator to generate a computer form group for the given frame. This group is combined with camera, texture and lighting information that has been generated in the same way as the form information, and the complete frame definition is passed to Winsom for rendering.

Animation detail

Previewing animation

Preparation of a fully rendered animation is very expensive, so we always prepare a simplified preview version first to check that the forms and views are all as we intend. The preview is prepared with a simplified drawing style (see Chapter 8) to be as fast as possible as the creative mind is quicker than the machine.

View animation   With view animation the forms are sent once to the drawing system. We then send and display the different view definitions. This is very much like interactive manipulation (see Chapter 9), but with the views generated by the animation system rather than by direct user interaction.

Object animation   Objects that are metamorphosing must be retransmitted to the drawing system for each animation frame. If the objects are not too complex and the drawing hardware has a large structure store, then the objects for an animation sequence are saved in the structure store. Each frame is saved in a different structure, and the animation is created by hiding all the structures and then revealing them one at a time. The animation can either be displayed in the natural sequence or by interactively selecting frames.

This low level object animation software was set up for our visualization work, and we made our first real-time animation for molecular dynamics in 1983 (Todd and Gillett, 1983).

Videodisk   For complex animations the preview is still not fast enough to get a good impression of an animation. The preview is then recorded frame at a time on a videodisk and played back when the recording is complete (Figure 10.11). The signals used in the computer drawing system are different from the standard television signals used on the videodisk, and so a scan convertor is needed to connect to the videodisk. The videodisk is controlled by the drawing system to synchronize the generation of each frame with the recording.

During playback the videodisk is controlled by the user to play back the preview at different rates or to freeze selected frames.

Final generation

The creation of the final animation requires all frames to be rendered at high resolution. This requires a huge amount of computer time. Where possible, we use multiple processors with the frames shared out between them. Our code does not permit optimization to take advantage of the similarity between adjacent frames, so this sharing out of frames is fairly simple. The frames are saved on computer disk as computer images which can be transferred to exabyte tape, or transmitted over satellite links without loss of quality.

The final recording is made either on a Betacam video recorder onto broadcast quality videotape, or for high resolution (4000 by 3000) by a filmwriter onto 35mm or 70mm photographic film.[16] The Betacam recording can be made a frame at a time, in much the same way as videodisks are prepared for preview, or by saving many frames in a video frame buffer and playing them back and recording them in real-time.

---

[16]We must thank Chris Osland of the Rutherford Appleton Laboratory for the assistance they have given us with rendering and recording several of our animations.

Chapter 11
Colour and texture

Colour and texture and other surface attributes such as gloss are used to give a sculpture more realism, and to bring out the three dimensional form. This section describes how the artist defines and uses them. We have tended to define a small set of natural textures and to use them again and again. Increased graphical computer power now permits us to use *Mutator* which conveniently allows us to experiment with a much wider variety of colours and textures.

The Winchester Colour and Texture facilities (WINCAT) supplied with the Winchester Solid Modeller (WINSOM) permit a user to define a wide range of surface characteristics. The basic surface characteristics include colour, gloss, transparency, and so on. A plain surface has the same characteristics at every point on the surface. The characteristics of a textured surface vary over the surface. The texture may be defined in various ways, including fractal textures and image mapping.

WINCAT textures are defined in one of two ways. A texture field defines a scalar value at every point in three dimensional space. The range of field values is divided into bands, and surface characteristics defined for each band (Figure 11.1). Texture code operates directly, and defines surface characteristics for every point in space.

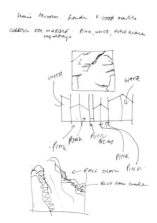

Figure 11.1. Use of colour bands for texturing. This hand-drawn sketch based on a sample of marble in the British Museum, London, shows the way in which the fields are divided into bands of colour.

WINCAT texturing supports bump mapping. With texture fields, the bumps are generated by interpreting texture field values as heights above the true surface. Each texture code implementation is responsible for its own bump mapping.

A subcolour facility permits surfaces with several layers of colour and texture. For example, a top layer may implement a cloud cover, and permit a see-through subcolour that implements a land and sea planet surface.

WINCAT surfaces are defined using *bundles*. Each object is associated with a bundle via a bundle number. In WINSOM the bundle is defined in a BDEF statement, and the bundle is associated with objects by the COLOUR operator, as shown in this example which draws a red sphere and a blue cube:

```
BDEF(1) colour(red);
BDEF(2) colour(blue);
DRAW sphere(1) colour(1) union
          cube(1) colour(2);
```

Non-integral bundle numbers may be used to interpolate the effects of two textures.

Much of the work in WINCAT is derived from previous work on textures (Voss, 1985; Perlin, 1985). The main aim has been to package texture techniques to make them available to WINSOM users in a convenient and flexible form. WINCAT is implemented as an independent set of programs written in Pascal that could easily be integrated with most rendering packages.

Colours

This section defines the basic surface colour facilities of WINCAT. These permit a definition of matt and glossy objects, and also transparent, refractive and glowing objects. A surface may be built up in several layers. An upper transparent or semi-transparent layer may permit a subsurface to be viewed.

Colours may be defined to WINSOM in one of two ways. A high level system permits surface parameters to be named using an extension of the Colour Naming System (Berk *et al.*, 1982). The lower, internal level operates on red, green and blue intensity values. It is expected that colours users will generally define colours via the high level, but that programs will code to the low level. It is also possible to mix the levels.

A common way to prepare colours is by mixing with a palette; for example, on the Quantel paintbox system. Another is to use real-time interaction methods where movements of the mouse controls colours on the image. We have used the second method with simple rendering, but as more complicated rendering methods are used the lighting and other details interact with the colouring, and it is not possible to perform real-time redisplay of the image with changed colouring. Using the colour naming system is more like choosing from a very wide range of ready mixed colours in a paint shop.

High level colour definition

The Colour Naming System (Berk *et al.*, 1982) defines uniformly coloured areas of a screen. WINCAT uses an extended Colour Naming System (CNSX). CNSX permits parameters such as gloss and polish that were outside the scope of the original system, and supports direct use of numeric values. The surface definitions for CNSX are shown here.

The description is a string of tokens separated by blanks. The tokens may take one of three forms:

- option, a word that stands on its own, such as RED;
- keyword, a word that is followed by one or more parameters, such as METAL 0.4;
- modifier, proceeds an option, such as VERY DARK;

Each parameter may either be specified as an option followed by a number (e.g. METAL 0.3) or by a keyword (e.g. PLASTIC). Where VERY is used, it may be used as a compound or separated:

VERY PALE or VERYPALE

Hue   The hue may be specified by **H value**, or:[17]

RED ORANGE YELLOW GREEN BLUE PURPLE
0   10   60   120   240   300
Default Red

Saturation   The saturation may be specified by **S value**, or:

VERYPALE	PALE	GRAYISH	MODERATE	STRONGISH	STRONG	VIVID
0.25	0.45	0.25	0.65	0.8	0.9	1

Default Vivid

---

[17]The values given here do not correspond with values often given. This is because our values assume a gamma corrected output device, whereas values are often quoted on the assumption that a 'typical' output device will be used. This affects *all* the parameters: hue, saturation, gloss, and so on.

Brightness   The brightness may be specified by **V value**, or:

VERYDARK DARK MEDIUM LIGHT VERYLIGHT
0.04   0.16   0.36   0.64   1
Default Verylight

In-between hue   Hues may be interpolated between two adjacent hues, half way by giving two names, quarter way by using -ISH names:

REDDISH ORANGISH YELLOWISH GREENISH BLUISH PURPLISH

Thus:

120 is GREEN
150 is BLUISH GREEN
180 is BLUE GREEN or GREEN BLUE
210 is GREENISH BLUE
240 is BLUE

Combined HSV   H S and V values may be specified together as:

WHITE
BLACK
HSV h-value s-value v-value
RGB r-value g-value b-value
   (The RGB values are converted to HSV.)

H and S may be specified together in:

GREY

Gloss   The proportion of light that is reflected by specular reflection controls the strength of the highlights and is specified by **GLOSS value**, by **SPEC_PROP value**, or by:

VERYMATT MATT SILK SILKY GLOSSY VERYGLOSSY
0   0.65   0.75 0.75   0.85   1
Default Verymatt

Highlight colour   The colour of the light that is given off by specular reflection may be controlled by **SPEC_COL value**. **value** is itself a CNSX definition, but only the hue and saturation values (or equivalent) of this definition are used. The amount of light is taken from SPEC_PROP, and so the intensity and any other values specified in the CNS definition of SPEC_COL are ignored.

One way of relating the specular colour to the colour of the main object is via the metallic nature of the object by **METAL value**, or:

PLASTIC METALLIC
0   1
Default Metallic

Plastic (0) gives fully desaturated white highlights, and metal (1) makes the highlights the same colour as the object. It is only valid for nonzero gloss, and may not be specified when SPEC_COL is specified.

Polish   The polish controls the spread of the specular reflections: that is the size of the highlights. Polish may be specified by **BLINN value**, or:

VERYPOLISHED POLISHED ROUGH VERYROUGH
0.1   0.2   0.3   0.5
Default Rough

Transparency   The proportion of light that is transmitted by an object is specified by **REF_PROP value.** Default is 0.

The colour of the light that is transmitted may be controlled by **REF_COL value. value** is itself a CNSX definition, but only the hue and saturation values (or equivalent) of this definition are used. The amount of light is taken from REF_PROP, and so the intensity and any other values specified in the CNS definition of value are ignored.

The default colour for transmitted light is the object diffuse colour. A completely clear object may be defined using **clear**, equivalent to **ref_col(white) ref_prop 1**.

Refraction   The refractive index of a refractive object is specified by **MU value**: default is 1. MU is not relevant for an opaque object (REF_PROP = 0).

The proportion of light that is given off by diffuse action may be specified by **DIF_PROP value**. Default is **1-SPEC_PROP-REF_PROP**. If the three proportions do not add up to 1, WINCAT will not renormalize them. A surface will then act as a light absorber or amplifier.

Glow   An object may glow by itself, in addition to any effects due to incident light. This is specified by **GLOW value**. Value is a CNSX definition that defines the colour and intensity of the glow. Any values other than HSV (or equivalents) specified in the CNSX definition of the GLOW value are ignored.

Using colour definitions

Colour definitions are used in several ways:

- In a BDEF statement for a plain object, for a flat texture band, or for top or bottom of a texture band:

      BDEF(1) COLOUR (white);

> BDEF(2) FRACTAL(0.8)
>   BAND(1) COLOUR(red)
>   BAND(2) LCOLOUR(green) HCOLOUR(blue);

- Using the CMS command CNSX, which will print the equivalent low level colour definition:
- For lookup table and background colour control in interactive picture display programs.

Subcolour

Subcolour (Todd, 1990 a) premits a layered surface effect, approximately equivalent to several almost coincident surfaces. The bundle definition for the uppermost surface is specified with the object. Part of the bundle definition for the upper surface is the SUBCOLOUR, which identifies a bundle for a lower surface. The lower surface may itself define a SUBCOLOUR, and thus any number of surfaces may be layered.

The overall diffuse, specular and glow components are computed by attenuating the respective values for the lower surface with the transmission values for the upper surface, and then adding the respective upper surface value, e.g.:

$$ambient = transmit.upper * ambient.lower + ambient.upper$$

The overall refractive index is the product of the two contributing refractive indices.

```
bdef (2) fractal (B3) /* simple fractal texture on small
                           sphere*/
   band (3)   colour (white)   /* thick white bands*/
   band (1)   colour (black);  /* and thin black ones. */
bdef (3) chess (4)             /* 4-way chess texture
                                  on big sphere*/
   stretch (0.2) spheremap     /* shrunk onto a
                                  sphere. */
/* These squares see through to texture 2. */
   band (1) colour (white ref__prop 1) subcolour (2)
/* These squares are plain grey. */
   band (1) colour (very dark grey)
/* These squares see dimly through to texture 2. */
   band (1) colour (white ref__prop 0.5) subcolour (2)

/* These squares are pure black. */
   band (1) colour (medium grey);
```

Figure 11.2. Use of subcolour. Bdef(2) defines a simple fractal texture. The first and third bands of bdef(3) use subcolour to see through to this texture. The first band sees the subtexture quite clearly, but the third band overlays it with translucent fog.

The overall Blinn value is the average of the two contributing Blinn values. This is an implementation compromise that does not give the same effect as two surfaces extremely close together. This compromise is chosen because it permits a single WINCAT bundle to be computed that describes the overall effect of multiple layers. This bundle is passed to the WINSOM: thus simplifying the interface between WINCAT and the Winsom renderer.

SUBCOLOUR is generally only useful where at least one surface is a textured surface (Figure 11.2). However, the example below shows how a simple blue surface (1) can be turned into a lacquered blue surface (2):

BDEF(1) blue;
BDEF(2) dif__prop 0.5 ref__prop 0.5 subcolour(1);

Non-integer bundle numbers

The subcolour number may be non-integral, which creates a sublayer by mixing the bundles with integer identifiers each side of the specified value (Todd, 1990 b). The mixture is performed by a linear interpolation of the low level colour parameters. This is only meaningful if bundle numbers are assigned in a sensible sequence, and again is most applicable when used in conjunction with texture (Figure 11.3). The example below shows a set of completely see-through upper layers used to mix blue and green in various proportions:

BDEF(1) blue;
BDEF(2) green;
BDEF(10) clear subcolour(1.0);
BDEF(12) clear subcolour(1.2);

```
BDEF (1) bandpass (3)/*texture for left cylinder*/
    band (1) colour (black)
    band (1) colour (white);
BDEF (2) bandpass (3)/*texture for right cylinder*/
    band (1) colour (black)/*note thinner bands here*/
    band (5) colour (white);
BDEF (3) axis ( )/*texture for joining cylinder*/
    band (1) lcolour (clear subcolour (1))
             hcolour (clear subcolour (2));
```

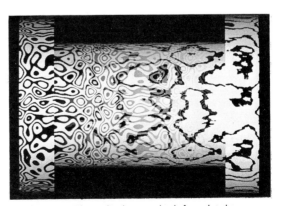

Figure 11.3. Real colour numbers used to in-between two textures. The cylinders on the left and right use the two 'pure' textures 1 and 2. The central cylinder uses texture 3. The subcolour number of texture 3 changes smoothly from 1 to 2 as we move along the axes between the two large cylinders. The in-between subcolour numbers are used to in-between the textures 1 and 2.

```
BDEF(14) clear subcolour(1.4);
BDEF(16) clear subcolour(1.6);
BDEF(18) clear subcolour(1.8);
BDEF(20) clear subcolour(2.0);
```

Texture

Texture fields are a mechanism for defining solid three dimensional textures. Every point in space is associated with a full bundle of surface characteristics in two stages. A *texture field* defines a number for each point in three dimensional space. A *band* mechanism associates these numbers with surface bundles.

Though the texture is defined everywhere in space, it is generally only sampled at visible points on an object surface. The texture field may be defined by one of a variety of methods, but the same banding mechanism is used for all of them. There is also a bump mapping facility, which applies to all texture field methods.

The rest of this section first describes the band mechanism and the bump mapping capability. It then describes the built-in texture field generators: Fourier synthesized, three dimensional chessboard, image mapping, and three dimensional fields.

Bands

Texture field values are associated with surface bundles by means of bands. The field values are divided into ranges, each range associated with a band of colour. Some bands are uniform: a single bundle is associated with every value in the range. Some ranges are non-uniform: bundles are associated with the lower and upper values of the range, and a bundle for a value within the range formed by linear interpolation of the low level bundle parameters.

A full set of bands is defined by specifying the bottom of the lowest range and the top of the highest range, (using **FIELDRANGE**) and by giving the relative size of each band (using **BAND**).

The bundles associated with each band are given immediately after the **BAND** definition. These may either be specified using high level or low level bundle definitions. Definitions are given using **COLOUR(definition)** for uniform bands, and **LCOLOUR(definition)**, **HCOLOUR(definition)** for non-uniform bands:

```
BDEF(1) FRACTAL(1) FIELDRANGE(0,1)
    BAND(1) COLOUR(red)
    BAND(2) LCOLOUR(red) HCOLOUR(green)
    BAND(1) COLOUR(black)
```

The above example defines three bands. The total range is 0 to 1, divided into proportion 1:2:1, and thus the actual range values are 0 to 0.25, 0.25 to 0.75, and 0.75 to 1. The two outer ranges are uniform, and the inner band changes continuously from red to green.

As already shown (Figures 11.2, 11.3), subcolour and non-integral bundle numbers are generally used in conjunction with non-uniform bands.

Bump mapping

Bump mapping (Figure 11.4) is a low cost method for simulating irregular surfaces. The normals used in lighting and ray casting operations are deflected from the true normal. This captures the effect of mountain slopes towards and away from a light. The surface itself is not distorted, which simplifies the basic rendering process, but means that profile and intersection edges retain their pure geometric form, and shadows are not cast. In many cases this inconsistency is not noticed.

Bump mapping treats the texture field values as height displacements of the surface from its true position, and from this computes the deviation of the normal. Bump mapping is specified by **BUMPHEIGHT(bumpheight)**. The effect on the normals is as if each point on the surface is moved up from the surface by distance **bumpheight** times the texture field value for the point. The larger the value of **bumpheight** the greater the bump mapping effect; a zero value (default) indicates no bump mapping:

BDEF(1) FRACTAL(1) FIELDRANGE(0,1)
BAND(1) COLOUR(white) BUMPHEIGHT(1);

Bump mapping is only effective on glossy objects with careful lighting.

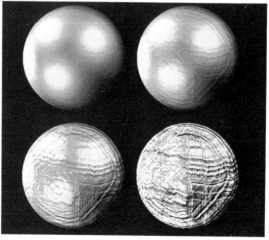

Figure 11.4. Bump mapping. The four spheres are all very glossy. They have bumpheight values of 0.0032, 0.01, 0.032 and 0.1.

Texture field generators

WINCAT provides several builtin texture field generators described in this section. Users may add their own, but we do not describe this here.

Fourier   Fourier synthesis may be used to generate a wide variety of textures (Perlin, 1985; Voss, 1985). These are all based on filtered noise. Two basic kinds of filter are supported, fractal and bandpassed: fractal noise (Figure 11.5) is given just a fractal dimension; and bandpassed noise is given a frequency and a bandwidth (Figure 11.6).

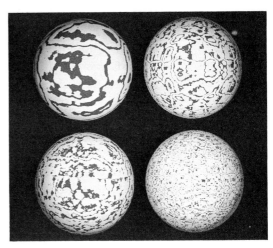

```
bdef (11) fractal (1)            bdef (12) fractal (1)
band (1) colour (white)              stretch (0.3)
     band (0.5)                 band (1) colour (white)
colour (dark grey);                  band (0.5)
                                colour (dark grey);


bdef (21) fractal (0.6)         bdef (22) fractal (0.6)
band (1) colour (white)              stretch (0.3)
     band (0.5)                 band (1) colour (white)
colour (dark grey);                  band (0.5)
                                colour (dark grey);
```

Figure 11.5. Examples of fractal texture. This shows the effect of changing fractal dimension, and of stretching the fractal textures.

```
bdef (11) bandpass (2, 0)       bdef (12) bandpass (2, 3)
band (1) colour (white)         band (1) colour (white)
     band (0.5)                      band (0.5)
colour (dark grey);             colour (dark grey);


bdef (21) bandpass (5, O)       bdef (22) bandpass (5, 7)
band (1) colour (white)         band (1) colour (white)
     band (0.5)                      band (0.5)
colour (dark grey);             colour (dark grey);
```

Figure 11.6. Examples of bandpassed texture. This shows the effect of changing bandpass frequency and bandwidth.

WINCAT supports other Fourier noise patterns, but with a more complex interface that is not described here. The three dimensional Fourier patterns are generated by lookup in several one dimensional tables (Figure 11.7).

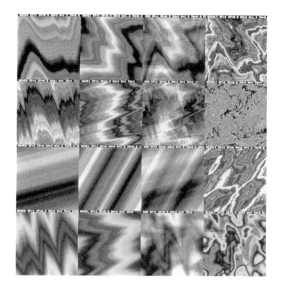

This shows the generation of two dimensional textures. For a given direction v and point in space p, a plane wave is generated from table t of size st by

w2 (t,v,p) = w (t, v dot p) = t ((v dot p) mod st))

v dot p gives the component of p in the t direction, and the mod makes the table t repeat indefinitely.

A single wave with a distorted wavefront is generated by w2 (t1, v1, p + w2 (t2, v2, p))

Single waves are shown in the first two columns. Two single waves are added to give the third column, and the result is further confused by a final lookup to give tha textures in the last column.

The full code for three dimensions with the point p expanded to its components vx, vy and vz involves lookup in ten tables.

W(t10, W(t1,   vx+W(t4,k1y*vy+k1z*vz)+W(t5,k2y*vy−k2z*vz))
      +W(t2,   vy+W(t6,k3z*vz+k1x*vx)+W(t7,k4z*vz−k2x*vx))
      +W(t3,   vz+W(t8,k3x*vx+k3y*vy)+W(t9,k4x*vx−k4y*vy)))

The tables are generated by inverse Fourier transform of the required frequency spectrum.

Figure 11.7. Generating multi-dimensional textures.

Chess   Chessboard texture produces a regular three dimensional chessboard. This is coloured with the specified number of colours. Figure 11.2 uses a chessboard that has been mapped onto a sphere using **SPHEREMAP**. The sphere in Figure 11.9 has been carved out of an unmapped chessboard. Figure 11.8 shows various mappings applied to chessboards.

Image mapping   Image mapping maps the given 2D image through 3D space by sweeping it along the z-axis. The object is then carved from this solid image. In Figure 11.9 a mapping transform has been used to make the image better fit the sphere. Figure 11.8 shows various mapping transforms applied to images.

Field mapping   Field mapping is similar to image mapping, except that the input image is three-dimensional. It can be used to colour an object according to some solid field; for example, to colour a molecule according to the surface electrostatic potential. This is a more flexible version of COLOURBY first implemented in the WINSOM field code (Quarendon, 1985).

Axis mapping Axis mapping alters the texture value linearly along a given axis. It is demonstrated in Figure 11.3, where two textures are mixed along the x-axis. It can be used to define striped textures such as carpets.

Mapping transformations

Various mappings may be applied to a texture before it is applied to a form (Figure 11.8). These include stretching, either globally or individually along each axis, and projection mappings.

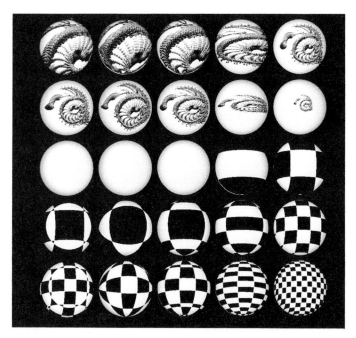

Figure 11.8. Texture mapping. The five columns show the use of five different mappings: **PLANEMAP SPHEREMAP CYLMAP POLARMAP BIPOLARMAP**. **PLANEMAP** is equivalent to no mapping. These mappings are applied to texture fields in the five rows:
>   IMAGE(PRIMS)
>   IMAGE(PRIMS) stretch(0.5)
>   CHESS(2)
>   CHESS(2)stretch(0.5)
>   CHESS(2)stretch(0.2).

```
        bdef (4)                    bdef (3) chess (3)
    image (twigtest, white)            stretch (0.2)
spheremap stretch (0.10)        band (1) colour (white
    xrange (−1,1,repeat)              ref_prop 0.5)
    yrange (−1,1,repeat)             subcolour (2)
    zrange (−1,1,repeat);        band (1) colour (orange)
                                 band (1) colour (glossy
                                         purple)
                                           ;



     bdef (2) fractal (1)         bdef (5) bandpass (8,1)
    band (1) colour (white)           stretch (5)
    band (3) colour (red)             band (1)
    band (1) colour (black)        colour (glossy white)
    band (3) lcolour (white)       bumpheight (0.1);
        hcolour (black)
    band (1) lcolour (black)
        hcolour (white)
    band (3) lcolour (white)
        hcolour (black);
```

Figure 11.9. Mixture of texture techniques.

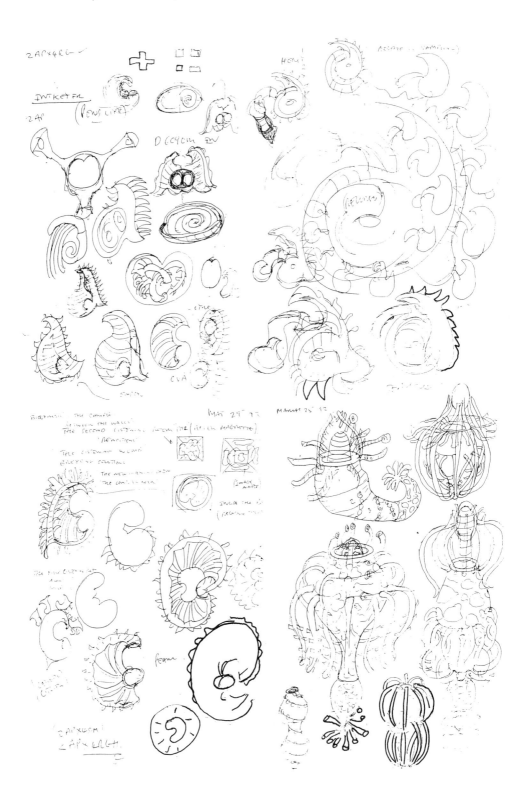

Chapter 12
Art, "Evolutionism" and computers

Relationship with other disciplines

Art

Art is sometimes described as a distorted mirror of reality. Latham's work reflects the computer age, man's genetic manipulation of nature and comments on the wanton destruction of the natural world. Art is the primary concern of the work discussed in this book. Computer graphics and other techniques are important only as means to the artistic ends. We have drawn on many of the traditional styles of art for perspective and rendering, on surrealism, and on more unusual art styles based on generative systems.

Latham has contributed novel artworks and computer systems for the generation of these artworks. More important he has created a new style of artistic working: "Evolutionism". Evolutionism divides the artistic process into two parts: in the first part, the artist creates an artificial world by defining systems and structures for form and animation generation; in the second part, he works as a gardener within this world, using aesthetic judgements to breed artworks.

Computer graphics

Latham's work relies on computer graphics, both interactive graphics used during experimentation and high quality rendered graphics for the production of final artworks. The ESME graphical programming language and Winsom renderer are major tools for his exploitation of computer graphics. Our exploitation of computer graphics has opened many people's eyes to its potential, but we do not claim that it contributes to computer graphics technology.

Computer programs and systems

Our artistic generation systems are realized as computer programs. Certain techniques recur through several systems, and we are often asked about the role of fractals and randomness in the work.

Fractals   We use fractals for the generation of complex recursive horns, and for adding slight irregularities that give forms a more natural appearance. We use fractal texturing to add variety to the surface of a form, and fractal irregularity in animation rules to liven the action. Finally, fractal analysis is an important part of the classification of forms.

One important point is that fractals are used in combination with the rules of *Form Grow* to give added visual complexity and realism. Fractal geometry is not used as an art form in its own right.

Randomness   Randomness is an essential part of the generation of fractal textures and fractal irregularity. The experimental *Form Build* form generation system permitted random selection of forms and positions, and *Mutator* relies on the combination of small random mutations with artistic selection. The lowest level of the Winsom renderer uses randomized Hilbert paths to minimize the intrusiveness of error diffusion.

Human computer interface

Our work uses many of the techniques of Human Computer Interface (HCI) such as menu systems, visual programming and direct manipulation of objects. Much of the work still relies on a simple keyword-based sculpture language.

The *Mutator* system for evolving forms defined by generative systems is a novel contribution to HCI. Where most HCI systems simplify analytic use of a computer, *Mutator* lets the user interact with the computer by making pure subjective judgements. We believe that *Mutator* will find many applications outside the computer art world. *Mutator* works at its best when combined with analytic techniques such as gene freezing to provide an accelerated and purposeful evolution.

Latham's ideas, captured in the artistic systems and embodied in the software, make the computer into a highly trained assistant. Latham thinks of the computer as a creative partner, almost a shadow of himself.

Biology

All of the artistic systems described in this book–*Form Grow, Mutator* and *Life Cycle*–are partly inspired by biology. The artworks are a form of artificial life. They use and abuse for artistic ends the current scientific theories of life, and can be viewed as a comment on later 20th century genetic engineering.

An essential aspect of evolutionism as an art style is the generation of artworks from genetic codes, and the manipulation of these codes by the artist. We create computer sculptures using a parody of genetic engineering.

Future directions

We are working on many extensions to the ideas of this book. Some of these rely on complementing our current work with the use of more traditional techniques such as the use of image processing to bring out features in system generated computer images. Most important of these are the integration of *Mutator* with analytic tools for grouping and manipulating genetic codes, and better use of interactive visual programming in the design of structures.

Other extensions move our work further into unexplored areas. Most of these are in the area of *Mutator* and form design. The mutation of structures gives much greater freedom to the artist gardener, and reduce his reliance on the technical skills of the artist creator. *Mutator* is being complemented with a system which classifies forms using various features such as the fractal dimension of the image, and the ratio of the volume to the surface area of the form. An autonomous *Mutator* will generate forms and select them based on the artist's classifications, with only limited artistic intervention during the mutation cycle.

Some of the novel extensions involve animation. The structures are modelled to change in reaction to different seasons and times of life, giving more realism and variety during animation. *SAFARI* combines *Mutator* with the realism of animation to add virtual reality to the artificial world of the artist gardener. Forms designed in four and higher dimensions literally open a new dimension in form design with great potential for animation.

The role of the artist

Evolutionism changes the role of the artist in creating an art work. The final artwork is dictated at three levels:

1. The use of evolutionism.
2. The creation of generative systems and structures (artist as creator).
3. The selection of specific forms and animations (artist as gardener).

For Latham's works there is no ambiguity. Latham is clearly the artist, he invented the evolutionism style, with Todd he created the generative systems and structures used for his artworks, and then as gardener organized breeding and selection of the artworks.

In future the role of the artist in evolutionism may become less clear. All computer art lets the computer take over some of the artist's technical skills. Evolutionism further splits the traditional role of the artist into two, the creator and the gardener, and these roles may be performed by two different people. This is somewhat like the distinction between the roles of composer and performer or playwright and actor, though the analogy does not bear detailed inspection.[18]

Who will be the creator of an evolutionary artwork? Latham will remain creator of the style in the same way that Picasso is father of Cubism and Haydn of the string quartet. An individual work within the style will be the joint creation of Latham, the artist who is creator and the artist who is gardener.

Is it art? Latham's work is art; the artistic value of future works of evolutionism depends on the creator, the gardener and the viewer.

Major results

The major visible results of our work are gallery artworks and art animations.

These visible results are underpinned by the artistic systems used to generate them: *Form Grow*, *Mutator* and *Life Cycle*. *Mutator* is the most important of these because of its potential applications outside the art world.

Behind these specific systems lies our most important artistic result: evolutionism, a new artistic style and method of working. We have crossed the divide between art and science to try to enrich both cultures.

---

[18]This question also brings up an associated question of copyright. Who owns the copyright? What is copyright? The generative system? The genetic code for a final form? The computer form? The computer image? The artwork on a gallery wall?

Glossary

animation definition The high level definition of an animation written by an artist to be processed by *Life Cycle* (Chap. 6, 10).

animation script The intermediate level of animation description, output by *Life Cycle* from the *animation definition* and input to *Director* (Chap. 10).

artistic system A set of rules defined for the construction of forms and animations (Chap. 1, 2).

bands A technique used in conjunction with *texture fields* to generate textures in WINCAT. Banding divides texture field values into ranges, and defines surface bundles for each range. To generate a *surface bundle* at a point, the texture field defines a texture field value for the point and the appropriate band is found for the texture field value. For a *uniform band*, every field value in its range is associated with the same bundle. For a *non-uniform band*, a different bundle is associated with the top and the bottom of the range, and a bundle is computed for a texture field value within the range by interpolation. The bundle for a uniform band is defined using COLOUR. The bundles for the bottom and top of a non-uniform band are defined using LCOLOUR and HCOLOUR (Chap. 11)

base colour The colour of the *diffuse reflection* of an object. Colours of highlights and transmitted light are usually derived from the base colour (Chap. 11).

bend Used to define the amount a *Form Grow* computer form is bent about the z axis (Chap. 3, 8)

branch Used to define a branching *Form Grow* computer form. Parameters control the spread and regularity of the branches (Chap. 3, 8).

bump mapping A technique by which the surface of an object is made to look bumpy by using a perturbed surface normal rather than the true surface normal. Bump mapping is specified in WINCAT using BUMPHEIGHT. *Texture field* values at a point on a surface, and at neighbouring points, are multiplied by BUMPHEIGHT, and the results interpreted as heights from the surface. The variation in these heights gives a purturbation of the surface normal (Chap. 11).

child form A computer form in an animation that is 'born' by a parent form using the *move down* process (Chap. 6).

colour number An index into the table of texture definitions (strictly texture number). When a colour number is an integer, surface characteristics are found for a point on a surface by looking up the associated texture definition and calling the appropriate code. When the number is non-integral, surface characteristics are found using the integer colour numbers just above and below the specified colour number. A linear interpolation is then applied to the surface characteristics (Chap.11).

computer form (3d) A sculptural form held inside the computer. The form is generated by *Form Grow* and held in the computer as a *constructive solid geometry* model (Chap. 3).

computer form bank The set of computer forms generated during a *Mutator* session, with one entry in the form bank for each entry in the *gene bank* (Chap. 5).

computer form group A group of computer forms composed during an animation. The group is created as a constructive solid geometry model as the union of transformed computer forms (Chap. 6).

computer image A picture stored in the computer. The computer image is normally stored as an array of codes defining the colour and intensity at each pixel. We use the term *computer image* in the way the term *image* is generally used in the computer world (Chap. 9).

constructive solid geometry A method for constructing solid objects from primitive objects such as cubes and spheres using *transformation* and the set theoretic operations union, difference, intersection and symmetric difference (Chap. 7).

continuity (animation) An animation is continuous if each frame is visually very close to the previous frame. Continuity is sometimes broken as for example when a *rib* is not present on a *horn* in one frame and 'pops' into the picture in the following frame (Chap. 10).

chessboard texture A *texture field* that divides space up into regular cuboids. The value of the texture field in each cuboid is an integer (Chap. 11).

CNSX (extended colour naming system) An extension of the *Colour Naming System* used for defining *surface characteristics* in 'natural' English (Chap. 11).

Colour Naming System (CNS) A system (originally developed at Tektronix) for defining colours in 'natural' English. We use an extended version *CNSX* (Chap. 11).

CSG see constructive solid geometry.

diffuse reflection When light that falls on a surface is re-emitted equally in every direction out from the surface. For a matt surface, which is the WINCAT default, all reflected light is diffuse (Chap. 11).

Director Low level animation control system (Chap. 10).

drawing system (3d) The drawing system takes *computer forms* and *computer form groups* and turns them into pictures. The pictures may be simple wire frame sketches, or fully rendered and textured images (Chap. 9).

ESME (Extensible Solid Model Editor) Programming language originally designed for the construction of *constructive solid geometry* model editors, and used for the design of all Latham's *artistic systems* (Chap. 7).

extended colour naming system (CNSX) An extension of the *Colour Naming System* used for defining surface characteristics in 'natural' English (Chap. 11).

family An (infinite) set of forms all derived from the same *structure* with different *genes* (Chap. 4).

form definition The definition of a form input to *Form Grow*, describing the form in terms of horns, bends, twists and so on (Chap. 3).

form generator An *artistic system* (typically *Form Grow*) that generates *computer forms* from *form definitions* (Chap. 3).

form space The mathematical space in which all forms that can be generated by a *form generator* can be considered to be laid out. Each point in space defines an input to the system and thus defines a *computer form* (Chap. 4).

fractal field A *texture field* whose spectral analysis follows a fractal pattern. It can be thought of as filtered noise. They can be used in WINCAT by TEXTURE (FRACTAL), or via the FRACTAL macro. The fractal fields of WINCAT are not true fractal fields. By suitable choice of parameters they can be made visually similar, but other parameter settings can produce bandpassed or highly directional patterns (Chap. 11).

fractal horn A horn recursively defined from subhorns that look like the main horn itself (Chap. 3, 8).

fractal irregularity Variations to *transform rules* based on fractal noise to give a form a natural rather than mathematical look.

fractal texture A texture defined by a *fractal field* (Chap. 11).

frame (animation) A single picture from an animation. An animation typically requires 25 or 30 frames for each second (Chap. 6, 10).

frame (Mutator) The set of forms displayed by *Mutator* to the user for selection and judgement (Chap. 5).

gene bank The area in which the sets of gene values generated during a *Mutator* session are saved (Chap. 5).

gene interpolation The use of interpolation on gene values to derive computer forms *inbetween* key frames of an animation (Chap. 6, 10).

gene space The mathematical space in which all gene values can be considered to be laid out. Each point in gene space defines a set of gene values, and can thus be used together with a structure to define a **computer form** (Chap. 4).

gloss Gloss defines the strength of highlights on a surface caused by *specular reflection*. It is defined in *CNSX* by a GLOSS value, or by keywords VERY MATT, MATT, SILKY, GLOSSY or VERY GLOSSY (Chap. 11).

glow Light that a surface emits even when no light is falling on it. It is specified by WINCAT by GLOW (Chap. 11).

group See *computer form group* (Chap. 6).

horn The term used to define any *computer form* generated by *Form Grow*, even if the individual form does not look like a horn. *Horn* is a keyword for the definition of a new horn in a *form definition* (Chap. 3).

hornweb A form made by an interlocking web of horns (Chap. 3, 8).

image See *computer image* (Chap. 9).

image processing A process carried out by the computer on one or more (two dimensional) computer images, generally to create a new image.

inbetweening The generation (usually by *interpolation*) of computer forms or views during an animation for frames where the artist has not given a specific *key form* or *key view* (Chap. 6, 10).

interpolation The process of generating values for a frame in an animation at which the artist has not specified key values (Chap. 6, 10).

iterate, iterative Used in computing for something which is done repeatedly. *Form Grow* makes forms by taking a simpler input form and iteratively applying transformations to it (Chap. 3).

key form A computer form explicitly chosen by the artist to take part in an animation. Other computer forms in the animation are derived by *inbetweening* (Chap. 6, 10).

key frame A frame in an animation in which some or all of the forms and views used have been explicitly defined by the artist (Chap. 6, 10).

kinesthetic correspondence A computer interaction technique where movements of objects on the screen correspond in a natural way to movements of the controlling devices (Chap. 9).

LifeCycle The high level artistic system that defines timings and motions for Latham's animations (Chap. 6).

mapping A technique used to distort textures so that they conform to particular shapes, particularly useful for *image mapping*, but may be used with any texture. Mapping is specified to WINCAT using PLANEMAP, SPHEREMAP, CYCLMAP, POLARMAP or BIPOLARMAP (Chap. 11).

metallicness Control of the whitening of highlights on a surface caused by *specular reflection.* A high value (specified by METAL) causes highlights to be the same colour as the object. A low value (specified by PLASTIC) causes white highlights. The colour of highlights whose colours are not simply related to base (*diffuse*) colour may be specified using SPEC__COL (Chap. 11).

metamorphosis The gradual change of a computer form during an animation (Chap. 6), usually achieved by defining *key forms* and using *gene interpolation* (Chap. 6).

move down The process which defines how a *child form* moves down the spine of its parent during birth. Part of the *LifeCycle* system (Chap. 6, 10).

non-uniform band A *band* of texture for which the surface characteristics vary over the band according to the *texture field* value (Chap. 11).

offspring *Child forms* derived from a parent form. In *Mutator* the offspring are produced from parents by mutation or marriage. In *Life Cycle* the offspring of a parent are the forms that *move down* the parent during birth. In a 'pure' system, the parent child relationship of *Mutator* and *Life Cycle* would be the same, but in our animations the family tree is distorted for artistic effect (Chap. 5, 6).

plain surface A surface that has the same *surface characteristics* at every point on the surface (opposite of a *textured surface*) (Chap. 11).

polish The sharpness of highlights on a surface caused by *specular reflection*. It is defined in *CNSX* by a BLINN value, or by keywords VERY POLISHED, POLISHED, ROUGH, VERY ROUGH (Chap. 11).

range The set of values that may be taken up by the x, y and z components of a point, or by a *texture field* value. They are specified by the BDEF options XRANGE, YRANGE, ZRANGE and FIELDRANGE. Where values lie outside a range, they are forced into the range either by taking the nearest point in the range (specified by TRUNCATE), or by assuming that the range repeats indefinitely (specified by REPEAT) (Chap. 11).

realtime A process that the computer performs so fast that it appears to be instantaneous.

refraction Bending of *transmitted* light as it goes through a surface. The amount of bending is specified to WINCAT by MU (the refractive index). MU is only applicable when there is transmission, that is REF__PROP is non-zero (Chap. 11).

rendering The process of turning a computer model into a realistic image.

ribs The individual forms that are used to make up a *horn* in *Form Grow*. A keyword for specifying the number of ribs in a horn.

ribcage A part of the *Form Grow* system that defines a symmetric 'ribcage' protruding from a central spine (Chap. 3, 8).

script See *animation script* (Chap. 6, 10).

sculpture (virtual) See *virtual sculpture* (Chap. 3).

spatial subdivision The process by which Winsom efficiently creates computer images from very complex *constructive solid geometry* models (Chap. 9).

specular reflection The bouncing of light from a surface to create a highlight. The proportion of light that comes of as specular reflection is defined by *gloss*. The sharpness or spread of the highlight is defined by *polish*. The colour of the highlight is defined by *metallicness* (Chap. 11).

stack Used to define the amount a *Form Grow* computer form is stacked up the y axis (Chap. 3, 8).

storyboard Low level definition of an animation, giving the genes and other information for all *key frames*. Usually generated within *Director* (Chap. 10).

stretch Used to make a texture larger, specified by STRETCH to stretch uniformly in all directions, and by XSTRETCH, YSTRETCH or ZSTRETCH to stretch in one particular (axial) direction (Chap. 11).

structure (file) The definition of a *family* of computer forms. The structure and genes combine to give a *form definition*, which is interpreted by the *form generator* to give a *computer form* (Chap. 4).

subcolour A mechanism which stimulates a multilayer surface (strictly it should be subtexturing) (Chap. 11). The top layer of the surface defines surface characteristics, and a sub*colour number*. If the top surface is transmissive and the subcolour is non-zero, surface characteristics are found using the subcolour. These are combined with the surface characteristics of the top surface to simulate a multilayered surface (Chap. 11).

surface bundle A set of values that gives the *surface characteristics* of a plain surface or a point on a textured surface (Chap.11).

surface characteristics Surface characteristics define the characteristics of a surface used by lighting and ray-tracing operations in WINSOM. They are usually collected into a structure called a *surface bundle*. Surface characteristics include the basic colour, the glossiness, polish, metallicness, glow, transparency and refractive index. Surface characteristics are defined at a high level by the *extended colour naming* (CNSX) system. They are stored and used at a low level as a set of red, green and blue components (Chap. 11).

system (artistic) A set of rules defined for the construction of forms and animations (Chap. 1, 2).

texture code A technique which associates *surface characteristics* directly with a point in space, not using an intermediate *texture field* (Chap. 11).

texture field A function that defines a scalar value for every point in space. A texture field may be defined in many ways, for example by fractals or by a three dimensional array held in a FIELD file. Texture fields are used to define many kinds of WINCAT textures. To generate a texture from a texture field requires bands. For more details, see *band* (Chap. 11).

texture table The structure that defines the texture associated with each *colour number* (Chap. 11).

textured surface A surface whose surface characteristics vary over the surface (opposite of a *plain surface*) (Chap. 11).

transformation pipe Textures undergo several transformations from the basic texture to the final pixels on the screen. A point in *basic texture coordinates* passes through the following pipeline:
- *Ranging* (optional). A cube of texture is extracted from the infinite 3-d texture (XRANGE, YRANGE, ZRANGE). This cube is made to fill space either by replication (REPEAT), or by propagating values from the cuboid face (TRUNCATE).
- *Stretching* (optional). The entire texture is stretched, either in all directions (STRETCH), or independently along the axes (XSTRETCH, YSTRETCH, ZSTRETCH).
- *Mapping* (optional). The texture is deformed by one of several deformations. (PLANEMAP (no deformation), SPHEREMAP, CYLMAP, POLARMAP, BIPOLARMAP).
- At this point the texture is applied to the object. We refer to coordinates at this time as *texture application coordinates*. Any transformations applied to the object are also applied to the texture.
- WINSOM transformations (e.g. XROT, SCALE) are applied to the texture together with the object. These place the object into *user coordinates*.
- The viewing transform is applied (VIEW). This places the object into *world coordinates*.
- The final perspective is applied, to place the object into *display coordinates*, which relate directly to pixels on the screen.

In implementation, the inverse transformation pipe is executed, and a point in display coordinates is transformed back via texture coordinates to basic texture coordinates (Chap. 11, 9).

transform rules Rules used in *Form Grow* to define the transformations to be applied to the *ribs* of a *horn*.

transmission Transmission occurs when light that falls on a surface continues through the surface, possibly being *refracted*. The proportion of light transmitted is specified to WINCAT by REF__PROP. Its colour is assumed to be the same as the base colour unless REF__COL is specified (Chap. 11).

twist Used to define the amount a *Form Grow* computer form is twisted about the y axis (Chap. 3, 8).

uniform band A *band* of texture which has the same surface characteristics for all values in the band (Chap. 11).

virtual reality A computer system in which there is sufficient realism in picture display and user interaction with the picture that the user gets the impression of reality (Chap. 5, 6).

virtual sculpture A sculpture that does not exist as a real three dimensional solid object, but only as a *computer form*, and perhaps as a **computer image** and as a photograph or on a video animation (Chap. 3, 9).

virtual world A world of *virtual sculptures* which follow *systems* of growth, breeding and motion defined by the artist (Chap. 5, 6).

voxel A three dimensional volume of space used by the *Winsom* renderer. Different voxels have different sizes, varying from the complete viewing volume of a picture to a volume that corresponds to a single pixel on the screen in all three dimensions (Chap. 9).

Winsom The renderer created by Peter Quarendon and used for all Latham's computer sculptures and animations since 1987 (Chap. 9).

Bibliography and References

Aono, M and T L Kunii 'Botanical Tree Image Generation', *Computer Graphics and Applications*, **4**(5): 10–34 (May 1984).

Atiyah, M F, N J Hitchen, J H Merlin, D E L Pottinger and M W Ricketts *Monopoles in Motion: a study of the low-energy scattering of magnetic monopoles*, Animation and IBM UKSC Report 207 (October 1989).

Barnsley, M F *Fractals Everywhere*, Academic Press, San Diego (1988).

Berk, A, L Brownston and A Kaufman 'A new colour naming system for graphics languages', *IEEE Computer Graphics and Applications*, **5**: 37–44 (May 1982).

Burridge, J M *et al.* 'The WINSOM solid modeller and its applications to data visualization', *IBM Systems Journal*, **28**(4): 548–568 (1989).

Cohen, H, Exhibition Catalogue for show at Tate Gallery, Tate Gallery Publications, London (1983).

Cowlishaw, M F 'Bit Requirements for Monochrome and Colour Pictures', *Eurodisplay '84 Proceedings*, Paris, France: 107–108 (September 1984).

D'Arcy Thomson *On Growth and Form*, Cambridge University Press, Cambridge (1961).

Dawkins, R *The Blind Watchmaker*, Longmans Scientific and Technical (1986).

Dixon, L C W and G P Szego (eds) *Towards Global Optimization 2*, North Holland, New York (1978) 1–18.

Ffoyd, R W and L Steinberg *An Adaptive Algorithm for Spacial Grey Scale*, SID, 75 Digest, Society for Information Display (1975), 36–37.

Foley, J D and A vanDam *Fundamentals of Interactive Computer Graphics*, Addison-Wesley, Reading, MA (1982).

Fujihata, M *World Graphic Design Now. Vol. 6* (M Katsui and T Kawahara, eds) Kodansa, Tokyo (1989).

Glassner, A S (ed) *An Introduction to Ray Tracing*, Academic Press, London (1989a).

Glassner, A S *3D Computer Graphics: a user's guide for artists and designers*, The Herbert Press (1989b).

Greene, N 'Voxel Space Automata: Modelling with stochastic growth processes in voxel space', *ACM Siggraph 89 Conference Proceedings*, Computer Graphics **23**(3): 175–184 (July 1989).

Haeberli, P 'ConMan: A Visual Programming Language for Interactive Graphics', *ACM Siggraph 88 Conference Proceedings*, Computer Graphics, **22**(4) (August 1988).

Industrial Light and Magic, Pseudo-pod sequence from *The Abyss*, SIGGRAPH film and video show (1989).

Kawaguchi, Y 'A Morphological Study of the Form of Nature', *Computer Graphics*, **16**(3) (July 1982).

Kirkpatrick, S, C D Gelatt Jr and M P Vecchi 'Optimization by Simulated Annealing', *Science*, **220**(4598), 671–679 (May 1983).

Kochlar, S 'A Prototype System for Design Automation via the Browsing Paradigm', *Proceedings of Graphics Interface 90*, Halifax, Canada: 156–166 (May 1990).

Lipscomb, J *Three dimensional display of molecular models using computer graphics*, PhD thesis, University of Southern California at Chapel Hill (1979).

Latham, W 'The Conquest of Form', Exhibition at Arnolfini Gallery (Bristol), The Natural History Museum (London) and UK tour (1988–1990). *The Evolution of Form*, Exhibition at Melbourne Arts Festival and Australian tour (1990). *The Empire of Form*, Exhibition at O Art Museum, Tokyo, Japan (1990).

Latham, W 'FormSynth: The Rule-based Evolution of Complex Forms from Geometric Primitives', in J Lansdown and R A Earnshaw (eds) *Computers in Art, Design and Animation*, Springer-Verlag, Berlin (1989).

Latham, W 'The Artist's View of Computer Sculpture', *Tutorial at 8th Eurographics UK Conference*, Bath, UK (April 1990).

Latham, W *Process of Evolution*, shown at Natural History Museum, London, UK (1990).

Latham, W 'A Sequence from the Evolution of Form', *SIGGRAPH Film and Video Show*, Dallas, TX (1990).

Latham, W *Mutations*, shown at SIGGRAPH Film and Video Show, Las Vegas, Nevada (1991).

Latham, W and S Todd 'Sculptures in the Void', *IBM Systems Journal*, **28**(4) (1989); *New Scientist* (1701) (27 January 1990).

Li, W 'Complex patterns generated by next nearest neighbors cellular automata', *Computers and Graphics*, **13**(3): 531–537 (1989).

Martin, K *The Late Paintings*, Catalogue for Exhibition at the Serpentine Gallery, Arts Council of Great Britain (1985).

Metropolis, N, A W Rosenbluth, A H Teller and E Teller 'Equation of State Calculations by Fast Computing Machines', *Journal of Chemical Physics*, **21**(6): 1087–1089 (June 1953).

Miller, G S P 'The Motion Dynamics of Snakes and Worms', *ACM Siggraph 88 Conference Proceedings, Computer Graphics*, **22**(4): 169–178 (August 1988).

Perlin, K 'An Image Synthesizer', *Proceedings of Siggraph Conference*, San Francisco, CA (1985); *Computer Graphics*, **19**(3): 287–296 (1985).

'Picasso', in H Osbourne, ed, *The Oxford Companion to Art*, Oxford University Press.

Pickover, C 'A Short Recipe for Seashell Synthesis', *IEEE Computer Graphics and Applications* (8–11 November 1989).

Prusinkiewicz, P and A Lindenmayer *The Algorithmic Beauty of Plants*, Springer-Verlag, Berlin (1990).

Quarendon, P *WINSOM user's guide*, IBM UK Scientific Centre Report 123 (1984).

Quarendon, P *A System for Displaying Three Dimensional Fields*, IBM UK Scientific Centre Report 71 (November 1987).

de Reffye, P, C Edelin, J Francon, M Jaeger and C Peuch *Plant Models Faithful to Botanical Structure and Development'*, *ACM Siggraph 88 Conference Proceedings, Computer Graphics*, **22**(4): 151–158 (August 1988).

Reynolds, C 'Computer animation with scripts and actors', *ACM Siggraph Conference Proceedings, Computer Graphics*, **16**(3): 289–296 (July 1982).

Sims, K 'Particle Animation and Rendering Using Data Parallel Computation', *ACM Siggraph Conference Proceedings, Computer Graphics*, **24**(4): 405–413 (August 1990).

Sims, K 'Artificial Evolution for Computer Graphics', *ACM Siggraph Conference Proceedings, Computer Graphics*, **25**(4): 319–328 (August 1991).

Steketee, S and NI Balder 'Parametric Key frame interpolation incorporating kinetic adjustments and phrasing control', *ACM Siggraph Conference Proceedings, Computer Graphics*, **19**(3): 255–262 (July 1985).

Stiny, G *Kindergarten Grammars: Designing With Froebel's Building Gifts*, Centre for Configurational Studies, The Open University, Milton Keynes, UK, Environment and Planning B 7: 409–462 ((1980).

Todd, S 'Use of Subcolour for layered textures', *IBM Technical Disclosures Bulletin*, **33**/1a 60–63 (June 1990a).

Todd, S 'Non-integer surface bundle identifiers', *IBM Technical Disclosures Bulletin*, **33**/1a 51–52 (June 1990b).

Todd, S 'Winchester Colour and Texture Facilities: WINCAT', *Tutorial at 8th Eurographics UK Conference*, Bath, UK (April 1990); and IBM UKSC report 250.

Todd, SJP *ESME, an extensible solid model editor*, IBM UKSC Report 176 (in preparation).

Todd, SJP and J Gillett 'Animation in the Winchester Graphics System', *Journal of Molecular Graphics*, **1**(2) (June 1983).

Todd, S and A Halbert *Fast redundant primitive elimination in CSG processing*, IBM UKSC Report 175 (April 1991).

Todd, SJP and W Latham 'Evolution of Programs for Defining Sculptural Forms', *Tutorial at 8th Eurographics UK Conference*, Bath, UK (April 1990).

Todd, S and W Latham *Mutator, a subjective human interface for evolution of computer sculptures*, IBM UKSC report 248 (1990).

Todd, S and W Latham 'Artificial Life or Surreal Art', *Proceedings of ECAL 91* (December 1991).

Todd, S, W Latham and P Hughes 'Computer Sculpture Design and Animation', *Journal of Visualization and Computer Animation*, **2**: 98–105 (August 1991).

Turk, G 'Generating Textures on Arbitrary Surfaces Using Reaction Diffusion', *ACM Siggraph 91 Conference Proceedings, Computer Graphics*, **25**(4): 289–298 (August 1988).

vanOverveld, CWAM 'The Generalized Display Processor as an Approach to Real-Time Interactive 3-D Computer Animation', *Journal of Visualization and Computer Animation*, **2**(1): 16–25 (January 1991).

Vogel, H 'A better way to construct the sunflower head', *Mathematical Biosciences*, **44**: 179–189 (1979).

Voss, RF 'Random Fractal Forgeries', *Proc. NATO A.S.I. 17*, in RA Earnshaw, ed, *Fundamental Algorithms in Computer Graphics*, Ilkley, UK (Springer-Verlag, New York 1985).

Wejchert, J and D Haumnann 'Animation Aerodynamics', *ACM Siggraph Conference Proceedings, Computer Graphics*, **25**(4): 19–22 (August 1988).

Woodwark, J R and K M Quinland 'Reducing the effect of complexity on volume model evaluation', *Computer-Aided Design*, **14**(2): 89–95 (1982).

Wyvill, G and P Sharp 'Commercial Animation using a Solid Modeller', *Journal of Visualization and Computer Animation*, **2**(1): 9–15 (January 1991).

Index